Natrauswen nig Efat

Stories from South Efate

Nick Thieberger

University of Melbourne, Australia
May 2011

ISBN 978-1-39-2177550-5

A pdf version of this book can be downloaded from
http://repository.unimelb.edu.au/10187/9734

Produced with assistance from the Australian Research Council and the Arts Faculty and School of Languages and Linguistics, University of Melbourne

World Oral Literature Project
voices of vanishing worlds

Produced in association with the World Oral Literature Project, University of Cambridge, Museum of Archaeology and Anthropology, Downing Street, Cambridge CB2 3DZ, United Kingdom

Cover: Apu Kalsarap Namaf and Ati Limaas Kalsarap reading stories in South Efate language at their home in Erakor village in 2000

Introduction

This book presents a selection of stories recorded mainly in Erakor village, Efate, Vanuatu since the mid-1990s.

This collection of stories is a result of my collaboration with a number of Erakor villagers. The stories presented here are not and could not claim to be a comprehensive view of Erakor tradition. Each is the result of the speaker's choice of what they would tell me and reflects their understanding of what is significant, based on my request for them to talk about any topic, but largely framed by kastom (traditional) story, history or personal story. These are the categories into which I have placed the stories. This distinction is not unproblematic as personal stories can become indistinguishable from kastom stories when magical events intervene in the narrator's life, and can also reflect historical events in which the narrator inevitably finds themself.

The collection presented here aims primarily to provide a record of aspects of Erakor life for South Efate speakers and for interested outsiders. Given that little else is published about this village the present set of stories is a first step, one that I hope will be followed up with more collaboration from Erakor villagers.

Almost all of the stories related here are transcripts of recordings. Copies of these recordings are held at the Vanuatu Cultural Centre, and a set are available on a computer at Erakor school.

Some of the stories and (interlinear) texts are available online here: http://www.eopas.org. All recordings are also held in the Pacific and Regional Archive for Digital Sources in Endangered Cultures (PARADISEC) (http://paradisec.org.au). Each text is followed by an identifying number that relates to the texts stored in item NT8-TEXT-TXT in the PARADISEC collection.

Acknowledgments

Most of these texts were recorded with the speakers in their homes. I am very grateful to the speakers who agreed to tell stories and to be recorded, especially to Kalsarap Namaf and Toukelau Takau for their patience.

Manuel Wayane transcribed many of the stories and they were then typed by Dina Thieberger. I edited the transcripts and aligned them to the original recordings so that they can be read and listened to at the same time. Endis Kalsarap, Manuel Wayane and Joel Kalpram helped with translations.

Nick Thieberger

Melbourne
May 2011

Contents

Personal life stories

Kalsarap Namaf †
Chief Samuel and Doctor
Mackenzie

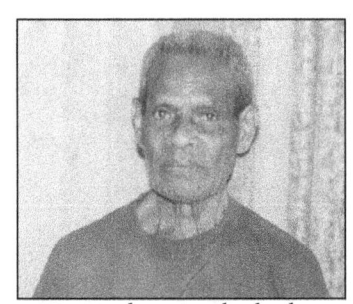

This first story is about the missionary Dr Mackenzie who had
written notes about customary knowledge, but then, as he was about
to return to Australia, had Chief Samuel take the papers and throw
them into the lagoon, as a symbolic way of destroying 'darkness' (the
traditional knowledge system of Erakor).

Natrauswen nig Samuel go Dokta
Mackenzie.
Selwan ito nag keler pak Astrelia
1912.
Mis isos Samuel.
Inag, 'Ƥafan pa raru negaag mai
sokin eslaor Elaknatu.
Go Samuel ipo pan pa raru nega
pan sak kin e-slaor Elaknatu.
Dokta Mackenzie inrik Samuel
kin nag, 'Kulek natus nen itu?
Ƥaslati pan paai luk raru negaag.'
Samuel ipo pan sol natus nen mis
inrikin kin.

Samuel ipan slati pan paai luk
raru nega panpan inom go mis
ipaoskin, 'Inom ko?' Samuel
inag, 'Or mis.' Mis, 'Ƥafa raru me

ƥafalus pak elau namos.' Samuel
ipa raru me mis iur euut pak
Elignairo pan me inrik Samuel

The story of Samuel and
Dr.Mackenzie.
When he was about to return to
Australia in 1912.
The missionary called Samuel.
He said, 'You take your canoe
and go to that place Elaknatu'
And Samuel got his canoe and
went to Elaknatu.
Dr.Mackenzie said to Samuel,
'You see these books? You take
them and fill your canoe.'
Samuel carried the papers which
the missionary had told him
about.

Samuel carried them and filled
his canoe until it was finished
and the missionary asked him, 'Is
it finished or not?' Samuel said to
him, 'Yes mis'. The missionary
said, 'Take your canoe and
you paddle out to the ocean.'
Samuel took the canoe and the
missionary ran along the shore to

kin nag,
'Selwan p̃afalus pan p̃aleka afsik naruk p̃atao nawes me natus rukmaui pak ntas pan.'

Samuel itutki natus kailer.

Selwan ipalus mai sak eslaor Elaknatu go mis ipan pak raru nega me itap lek tete natus mau go inrik Samuel kin nag, 'P̃afa raru negaag pan sak kin eslaor.' Mis ipak esum̃ nega pan go Samuel ipo pa raru imai sak Eslaorp̃ur.
This is text 025.

Elignairo and he said to Samuel, 'When you have paddled you'll see I raise my hand you put down your paddle then throw all the paper into the water.'
Samuel threw in the paper and went back.
When he paddled to shore at Elaknatu the missionary came to his canoe, but he didn't see any paper and he said to Samuel, 'You take your canoe back to land.' The missionary went to his house and Samuel went to Eslaorp̃ur.

Iokopet
The need for respect

A story addressed to children about the need to respect parents.

Teesa laap amurin nrik mus kin na nfaketanwen ipi tewi.
Kofaketanki tem mus go rait mus.

Go na kor mus go p̃al mus.

Taos teetwei, nalelewen neu, kineu apei tkos, taos aliat tap.
Nakrakpeswen itik.
Kuto, kupak sum̃ tap kumai, kutotan na kufam kumarmar panpan inom
Ale naliati m̃ol kupreg nawesien negaag, me p̃amroperkati, tepei p̃anrog nale tmam ko raitom. Go naliati gaag rukfo

Children, I want to tell you that respect is a good thing.
Respect your father and your mother.
And your sister and your brother.
As before, in my view, when I first was there, like on Sunday.
It wasn't noisy.
You went to church, came back, you sat to eat and you rested, you ate.
And for many days you will do your work, but remember, the first thing is to listen to the voice of your father and

laap.

mother. And your days will be many.

Ipi nafsan sees wan amur wan kanrik mus ki. Inom esan.

That is a little story that wanted to tell you. It is finished here.

This is text 038.

Toukelau Takau
Making thatch

A short description of making roof thatch out of sago plam (rowat).

Malen amurin na katur rowat, go apo pan slat rowat, kafan slat rowat.
Aler mai, kafo pei m̃asel rowat, am̃asel rowat inom.
Amer p̃elki, ap̃elkin itu.
Me apo mer pan tai lop. Apan tai lop, mai. Apregptaki, taiptaki

Ileg nen kin kafo tur rowat, apreg, atonkin rupitkaskei. Lop rupitkaskei.
Inrik wou kin na kafo preg namtampe neu rufitkaskei. Inom.
Amer pei takotkot lop ruto m̃it.

Kafo mer pei mas, mas pin, tenen rusoso ki 'pin'.

When I want to sew thatch, and I will get sago palm leaves (rowat), I'll get rowat.
I come back, I'll prepare the rowat, prepare it until it's done. Then I'll fold it, it is folded.
I get it ready, cut it to make it ready. Then I'll cut bamboo. I cut bamboo and come.
It is right so I can make the thatch, I measure it so that they are all equal.
He tells me that I should make my thatch all the same. That's all.
First I'll cut bamboo into short pieces.
I'll clean them, they call them 'pins'.

Amas pin ina inom.
Go apo tur rowat.
Atrus tefla inom go malfane atae na, atae tur
fifti, atae turtur ralimilim.
ko atae tur tifli iskei.
Go kafo tae na ralimilim kefo tae p̃akor nanre nasum̃
Go ralimilim kimer tae p̃akor nanre nasum̃.
This is text 102.

I clean the pins until it is done.
And then I'll sew the thatch.
I'll sew it like this, and now I can sew
fifty, I can sew fifty.
or I can sew one hundred.
And I know that fifty can cover a side of a house.
And fifty can cover a side of a house.

Kalsarap Namaf †
Tata Sailas go tuluk inru, Tata Silas and the two tuluks

This is a dense story that is difficult to understand. It starts with Kalsarap and his parents talking about getting tuluks from Tata Sailas and then goes on to describe a canoe getting broken by a small stone. The moral of the story is that 'a small stone can break a big canoe', while paying attention to what seem to be the big problems that might wreck the canoe, it is the little ones that end up doing the worst damage.

Or kafo mer nriki ki iskei. Iskei natrauswen knen
komam Limas. Kineu amai alak esan kaito esan to,

pan pan pan apiatlak nmatu go teesa. Naliati iskei,
amroki tmak go raitok. 'Kafan saofir Ertap.' Go kaipa.

Apanpan paakor go ranrik wou kin nag, 'Suker nigmam inom.'
Anrikir kin, 'Matol p̃ulp̃og kafo gamus sol suker mai'.

Okay, now I will tell this one. This is a story about
us, Limas and me. I came and got married and stay at this place,

until I had a wife and a child. One day,
I thought about my father and mother. 'I will visit them at Eratap.' And I went.

I got there and they told me, 'Our sugar is finished.'
I tell them, 'Tomorrow morning I will get you some sugar.'

Ana, 'Ato kaipa pan lek tata Sailas.' Apan alemsir raito traus atraus pan pan ...
Go kailer mai lek tmak go raitok. Kainrikir kin na, 'Kafo pan me matol p̃ulp̃og, kafo gamus sol suker mai'.

Amai na asaiki raru, sak ki Ear, raru ito. Me anrikir kin na, 'P̃afo ta mai puet raru mau Me atli nag, 'Kutap mai pa raru mau.
Raru nen kefo to. Me matol p̃ulp̃og me kafo gamus sol suker mai.'
Amai anrik mtulep neu ki, 'Apu go ati ratik ki suker.'
'Rapo gar pregptaki suker pan inom rasol tete pret.
P̃ulp̃og rik go kaitm̃alu Erakor pan sak Egis
panpan pa raru Ear apan tuer ki suker.
Kafan go iak mana rana, 'Me ag kupan lek maarik Sailas?

Me inriki ki tenamrun ko?' Ana 'Itik'.
Go ranrik wou kin na, 'Ipreg nafamwen p̃og rulau panpan ialiat.'
Go atok kaisos, Jemis. Ita sees ilakor piatlak ntau atap tae mau isees perkati.
Asoso hemia nao Jemis, 'P̃afit mai.' Imai ilauto anriki kin nag,

'P̃afak Elaknaar pa. Go p̃alek apu go ati go p̃anrikir kin nag, 'Awo ni

I say, 'I will go and visit tata Sailas.' I go to see them, they talk, I talk and talk..
And I came back and saw my father and mother. I said to them, 'I will go, but tomorrow morning I will bring sugar for you.'
I came by canoe, landed by Ear passage, the canoe there. And I said to them, 'Don't take the canoe.
The canoe should be there. And tomorrow morning then I will go and get sugar for you.'
I come and I tell my wife, 'Apu and Ati have no sugar'.
We will prepare sugar for them, we'll get some bread.
Early morning I left Erakor, and came ashore at Egis,
take the passage at Ear to give them sugar.
I'll go and my mother and the others said, 'And did you go to see Mister Sailas?
And did he say anything or not?' I said, 'Nothing'.
And they tell me, 'He had a feast last night and danced until daylight.'
And I called out for James. He is small, he is around I don't know how old, he is very small.
I called James, 'You come quickly!' He comes and stands, I tell him, I say,
'You go to Elaknaar. And you go see Apu and Ati and you tell

Erakor ipato

me kina imur tuluk iskei m̃as itap
mur inru mau.' Raktuok tuluk
keskei m̃as, Raktuok tuluk keskei.
P̃awesi mai, neu, kefo wesi pan.
P̃awesi mai. Kafami.'
Maarik go mtulep rato panpan go
tata Sailas kinriki kin mtulep
nega kin na, 'E tete tuluk itok ko?'

Mtulep ita pes mau me ipnut to.
Ito panpan go maarik neṇ ina,
maarik ito inrik mtulep kina,
'Kanrikir ki nafsan ni tiawi iskei.
Faat sees ip̃opu raru p̃ur.'

Mtulep ito ipan toto um panpan
ipam̃or tuluk inru.

Ina ito kaiwisi ina, 'Tuluk wan
rato ki.' Inrikir kin na, 'Malfanen
kafo pan lek nafit, go ipato, ni
Erakor go ifato.
Nafsan matu ni tiawi. Itok kaiwis
tuluk nen mai imai mai mai itu
esum̃ to. Esum̃ Ertap
Imai na isil, kainag nafit nen to,
'Kuto preg nafte panpan kin mer
mai to faoskin tuluk.'
'Amai apregnrogo kia nlaken
komam ratok fkaar ipi temak, me
kineu afiarkin, kat natrauswen ga
inrak laap ito neu traus.' Sup̃ ni
tiawi.

Go ito neu traus itraus iteflan kin
na.
Natrauswen ni tiawi nen inrik

them, 'Uncle from Erakor is
there
but he said he wants only one
tuluk, he doesn't want two.'
They will give you only one
tuluk. You bring it. I will eat it.'

The man and the woman
stayed on and then old Silas
said to his wife, 'Hey, is there
any tuluk left?'
The woman didn't talk, she
stayed quiet. This went on until
the husband said, 'I'll tell you a
story from the old people.
A small stone can wreck a big
canoe.'
The woman stayed and felt
around in the oven and found
two tuluks.
She wanted to get them. She
said, 'Here are the tuluks.' She
says to them, 'Now I'll go and
look at the slave at Erakor.'
A story straight from the old
people. She took the tuluk and
she came back to the house.
She went inside and said to this
slave, 'What have you been
doing until you ask for tuluk?'
'I went and tried because we
laughed because he was my
father, but I wasn't scared
because he told his story to me
many times.' That's the way of
the old people.
And he told me like this, he
told it like this.
A story from the old people

Jemis ki. Ina Jemis, imai itap inriki ki tenmatun mau? Ina, 'Itik'. Go ipo neu traus natrauswen nen kia atraus silua. 'Faat sees ip̃opu raru p̃ur'. Ser nrak natam̃ol imurin nag kefak namos. Kupan saiki raru gaag ito slaor.

Kusaiki raru. Kulek faat faat ne. Faat nen itop.
Me faat nen isees perkati. Selwan kumur na p̃afan kulek faat p̃ur ne.
Kulelua faat p̃ur nen kupan lelu teflan pan pa raru gaag kaipak namos pan. Me kusertep̃al faat ses nen. Selwan kuler mai nag p̃anros raru gaag kefak euut faat sees nen kin kefo tup̃opu raru gaag. Go p̃afo mer kano pa raru.

Raru gaag imap̃or p̃afo sm̃oli p̃afo pan. Ipi nametp̃ag natrauswen nen agaag trausi malfanen. Tangkiu.
This is text 015.

that he told, to James. He said, 'Did he say anything?' He said, 'Nothing'. And this is the story they told me which I have told. 'A small stone can break a big canoe.' Every time someone wants to go to the ocean. You push your canoe into the passage.
You push your canoe. You look at that stone. That stone is big. But that stone is really small. When you want to go you look at the big stone.
You go around the big stone to get out to sea, you don't believe the small stone (could damage the canoe). When you come back you drag your canoe ashore, the small rock breaks your canoe. And you won't be able to use your canoe anymore
Your canoe is broken, you must plug up the hole. That's the end of the story that I have told you. Thankyou.

Kalsarap Namaf †
Nmatu taar, white women. (Kalkau Kuriman's story)

This story was written by Kalsarap Namaf who read it. He used a numbered structure in his written form which is represented here. He said the story dates from sometime in the 1800s. A chief who was a 'kleva' from Efate could magically travel at night and he foresaw the arrival of Europeans. He advised his people to take advantage of all the good things that would come.

1: Amurin nag kagamus traus tete natrauswen nig tiawi negakit nig teetwei selwan Efat imalik.

Go naot nen ito Erkao go nega ipi munwei.

Tete naliati ito siwer p̃og.

Tete naliati ipak nort Efate tete naliati ipak Santo ko Amprim, Ampai.

Selwan iler mai kefo sos nam̃er nega rukfak efare me kefo nrikir ki tenag ileka. If pi Ampai ko Amprim ko tete nafanu nag ipaakor pan p̃og.

Or ikano siwer aliat me itae siwer p̃og go natam̃ol nega rumurin nag keto negar traus nafte kin ipan leka natokon nig Ampai ko Santo.

2: Or go nap̃og iskei itili nag, 'Kafo pak Etog nafanu nig nam̃er taar.' Or go ipo pan ipak etog Australia pan. Ipan sari iur taon.

Go ilek os kin ito of kat go ito kaisos os ki kori.

Ilek natam̃ol kin ruto ur taon napu itop go natam̃ol rulaap go napu negar imalmal wi.

3: Itok siwer ur taon pa kailek namatu taar rutok ur taon. Selwan rusiwer pan nalur ikof kor namter me selwan rupulki nap̃aur go nalur

I want to tell a story of our old people when Efate was in darkness.

And this chief was at Erkao and he was a 'clever'.

Some days he would walk at night.

Some days he would go to north Efate, some days he would go to Santo or Ambrym or Ambae.

When he came back he called his people to go to the nakamal after he would tell them what he had seen, if it was Ambae, or Ambrym or some island he went to at night.

Yes he can't travel in the day, but he knows to travel at night and his people wanted him to tell them what he'd seen in the village at Ambae or Santo.

Yes and one night he said 'I will go to the island of white people.' Yes, and he went to Australia. He visited the town.

And he saw a horse which had a cart on it and he called the horse a dog.

He saw people on the roads and many people, and their roads were clean.

He travelled on and saw white women walking around town. When they (the women) walked their

kimer ler pak nap̃aur pan.

Go itili nag, 'Rupi mutwam?' Or maarik nen ilek loto, raru Stimer ilek raru nlae tete natir itol go Stimer sernale nig nam̃er nig etog ilek silua.

4: Selwan kiler tok etog mai kipreg nsaiseiwen p̃ur iskei go kitili nag natam̃ol rukfo pak efare me kefo nrikir ki nafte kin ipan leka etog go kitili nag,

'Matol kofo mai pak efare.' Selwan rupan go kinegar traus tenag ipan leka etog.

5: Go inag, 'Nam̃er taar nen rulaap top, ruto ur napu negar.

Me namter iksakes taos namet pus me namatu.'
6: Negar rutaos mutwam, nalur ipram me if wel uf murin utae puetir mai nag akam kolemsir.' Go runag, 'Iwi p̃afuetir mai.'

7: Go maarik inrikir kin inag, 'Iwi matool kofo pak eslaor Emetfat me kafo preg raru nen kemai torwak eslaor Emetfat.'

8: Me maarik inrikir kin nag, 'Iwi akam tete kofo taulu namatu taar nen.
Go negar kin rukfo peiki mus kin

hair hid their eyes but when they shook their heads their hair moved back.
And he said, 'Are they devils?' He saw cars, the steam boat, a sailing boat with three masts and the steamer, he'd seen all things of the white people.
When he had come back from abroad he called a big meeting and he told them all they should go to the nakamal and he would tell them what he had seen and said,
'Tomorrow you will will come to the nakamal.' When they came and he told them what he had seen abroad.
And he said, 'There are many white people, they go around on their roads.
But their women's eyes are green like a cat's eye.'
They are like devils, their hair is long and if you want you bring them so you can visit them. And they say, 'Good, you bring them'
And he said to them, 'Good, tomorrow we will go to the passage at Emetfat, after I will get this boat to anchor at Emetfat.'
After he said to them, 'Good, some of you will marry white women.
And they will show you how

teflan ruweswes ki nasum̃, raru nlae
go kori nag ruto of kat go sernale wi
laap nag aleka. Kofo piatlaken.'

9: Me selwan rupaakor p̃ulp̃og rupak
eslaor Emetfat pan torik go rulek
natir ni raru iseesp̃al pato em̃ae to.
Rutok leka panpan go nam̃ol raru
nen kipaakor ito sef mai.

Kaitorwak Emetfat, nam̃er nig raru
rukoitao pot ipak etan me tenig euut
rutok leperkatir.

10: Selwan rutoktan nag rukfalus go
rutotoluk ki nakpei nig raru po
palus.
Itap taos raru negakit kin tulek
nakpei nig raru po palus mau.

Or selwan rutok palus raki euut mai
go rutili nag, 'Nam̃er taar nen
namter itok ntakur.'

Me rupo mos tete namatu rumaui
tok pot. Go runag nam̃er nen rutaar
taos mutwam.

Nlaken rutao nalur ipram go ipo
ipaakor namter go nagorir go negar
tete rukoisef pan kus nkas me ruto
mak leker.

11: Or nafsan nig maarik naot itili
nag, 'Iwi nag akam kofo taulu tete
namatu taar nen go negar kin rukfo
peiki mus kin teflan ruwesweski
nasum̃ go sernale wi laap.

they make houses, sailing
boats and dogs pulling carts
and many other good things
I saw. We will have them.'
And when they came in the
early morning to Emetfat
they saw the mast of a
sailing boat, small in the
distance. They watched until
they saw the ship quickly
coming in.
It anchored at Emetfat, the
people from the boat left,
and those on shore looked
after them.
When they sit to paddle they
turn their backs to the front
of the boat then row.
It is not like our canoes
where you look at the front
of the boat then row.
Yes, when they paddle close
to shore and come ashore
they say, 'White people's
eyes are in their backs.'
After they will take some
women they will all stay on
the boat. And they say these
people are white like devils.
Because they leave their hair
long and their eyes and nose
appear behind it, so some of
them ran away and hid in
the trees and stared at them.
Yes, what the chief said was,
'You will marry some white
women and they will show
you how to make houses and
many good things.'

Go rutili nag rumal.

And they say they don't want to.

12: Go maarik naot inag, 'Amroa kin nag akam uf mer taulu tete go negar kin rukfo pregwi ki nafanu negakit go akit tukfo tok wi go ntag nig teesa negakit nag rukfo inrok mai kefo wi top. Me rumal to tauluer.

And the chief said, 'I think you should try to marry some and they will make our country good and we will live well, also our children's generation in the future.' But they don't want to marry them.

Go tukfo pitkaskei tok ser ntag go ser ntag.

And so we will stay the same, generation after generation.

Nafsan nega ip̃on.
This is text 026.

His story is finished.

Kalfap̃un Mailei †
A story about the Second World War

Kalfap̃un's experience in WWII, and the way that the Americans treated everyone equally.

Go mal ni nafkal nam̃er ni America rulaap, esa rutalaap mau, me Esanr.
Nam̃er got me nam̃er taar. Navy, Army nametrau nam̃er fserser.
Rupo piatlak nmatu gar nen rumai. Nmatu gar nen rumai, rutkal faef handred.
Me nmatu nen rupi nmatu ni nafet Ofisa. Rumai,
ruwi, rusemsem lek patlas

At the time of the war, there were lots of Americans, not here, but in Santo.
Black men and white men. Army and navy, all different men.
They had their women who came too. They had 500 women with them.
They were the officers' wives.
They came
they were good, they were

natam̃ol. Me rutraif mai ko rufatlasik rumsagik.

Kuna, 'Ƥafak swa?' 'Ore'. Skotir atlag itol.

Rupi nam̃er wi. Nafisoklepwen gar itop. Kutae America, runa kopan eksesaes, pak eksesaes pa. Runa kofan ṃees baseball, upak baseball pa. Una kopan sari, upan sari.

Ko runa kopan min upa unomser of uniform upan min.

Rupanpan rutrau wi top ki wou, pan pan pan runa, 'Wik nen tu tukfak Solomon. Kuta mtak mau'. Ana, 'Kaipe saen reki nmaten, ded, ded, laif, laif.' Me kafman m̃as malen kin inrogo, go ipulu wou Suranta. Go ipiatlak natam̃ol rusot. Me ito psir me imal kin apa.

Afmer pa me afla lakor wel Jimmy Steven ko aflakor mat Solomon.

Ipi esuan nam̃olien neu. Kin mai kin itu san to. Pan pan pak mees ne, apitlak ntau 77. *This is text 041.*

happy to meet any man. They come driving or they meet you or they take you in the car. You say, 'Where are you going?', 'Okay'. With them for three months. They were good men. They were very rich. You know America, they say to do exercises, we do exercises. They say we'll play baseball, we played baseball. They say we'll go for a wander, we went for a wander. Or they say, we'll drink, we all wear uniforms and we go and drink. They were good to me, then they said, 'This week we'll go to the Solomons. Don't be scared.' I said, 'I signed up for death, if I die, I'm dead, if I live, I'm alive.' But the government heard and they pulled me out to go to Suranta. There was a shortage of men. But they were lying as they didn't want me to go (to the Solomons). If I went, I would be like Jimmy Stevens (who went to the Solomons and came back alive), or I would be dead in the Solomons. That's my life. Until today when I am 77 years old.

Kalfap̃un Mailei †
Darkness, light and Christianity

A brief description of the coming of Christianity

Teetwei esan komam upaakor mal ni namrem.

Long ago, at this place, we were born here in the time of the light.

Me mal ni nmalko komam me upo nrogo me uta leka mau. Nlaken tiawi kin ruto mal ni nmalko.

But we have heard about the time of Darkness, but we never saw it. Because it was our ancestors who lived in the time of Darkness.

Panpanpanpan malen kin nalotwen imai pa ntan sa. Go tiawi rumtak ki nmalko ruto sef sef mai. Ruto sef sef sef mai mai mai.

Until the time when prayer came to this place. And the ancestors were scared of Darkness and they ran away. They escaped and came.

Go gar rulek nmalko, me komam uta leka mau. Komam unrogo me uta leka mau.
This is text 042.

They saw Darkness, but we never saw it. We heard about it, but we didn't see it.

Kalfap̃un Mailei †
English police in Santo in the 1940s

Kalfap̃un's time in the English police in Santo in the 1940s.

Neu kin nawesien nen kin upatkos Esanr. Plisman upi ralim utiuti me apak Esanr pa Esanr ruta to sisi.
1941 me natam̃ol ruta to tmer sir. Nlaken komam utu Kanal,

The work we did in Santo. We were ten police on duty, I went to Santo. On Santo they were still shooting.
In 1941 men were shooting each other there. That's why we stayed at Luganville,

reki nam̃er ni Sak Pei, me Pot Lori, me ruto of polet mai pak hospitel.

for people from Shark Bay and Port Lory would come in to hospital with bullet wounds.

Go komam upan malen kin man pus ruta to tmer sir, me ipi mal kerkerai.
Malen kin utkos kin p̃amro ki, Totel Pei pak Sak Pei. Ipi emãe top,

me malen ana kafa. Ana kawes natus pa. Runrik wou ki, 'Malen p̃afa, p̃awalu sot ni plisman, p̃aweslu pulp̃ou, p̃aweslu polet, p̃afai nal. P̃akaro me p̃afa. 'Nlaken ipitlak man pus nmaota ni Totel Pei pak Sak Pei. Ale apa.

Rusi natamõl, rupam natamõl, pan pan pan pan pak Sak Pei pa. Malen kin apu ni Kulon nen to Kulon nen iplak Toumer to, Apu ga Kami. Kami Kulon.

Malen ito Sak Pei. Go ina, 'Boy, yu kam olsem wanem?' Nlaken ana panpan apak plantesen ga go apo of nkal.

'O me kuur naor nen to mai? Me ku, kutap piatlak trabol mau?' Ana, 'Itik'.
Malen amai asrakor sot, asrakor pulp̃ou, asrakor strap, ale amai.

Ilek wou trau mur, me ina, 'Yu laki.' Ale pan patu p̃og go amatur, p̃ulp̃og go amer ler mai pak Kanal.
Ipi emãe. Malen nafkal ito na kemai. Komam English plis uta

And we went when the bush men were still shooting each other.
It was a hard time, when we stayed there, think about Turtle Bay, to Shark Bay. It is a long way,
but back then I wanted to go. I took a letter there. They told me, 'When you go, take off your police shirt, take off your hat, take off your bullets and put them in your basket. You go without clothes.' Because there are wild men between Turtle Bay and Shark Bay.
They shoot men and eat men until you get to Shark Bay.
This time when Kulon's grandfather was there, Kulon who married Toumer, Kami is his grandfather. Kami Kulon.
Then he was at Shark Bay. And he said, ' Boy, how did you get here?' Because I put my clothes on just when I got to his plantation.
'Oh, did you follow along there to come? And didn't you have any trouble?' I said, 'No.'
When I came I hid my shirt, I hid my hat, I hid my strap, then I came.'
He looked at me and laughed, and said, 'You're lucky.' I stayed the night, slept and then came back to Kanal (Luganville).
It is a long way. Then the war was about to start. We English

matur mau.
Kanal pak Fenue, Fenue pak Kanal, p̃og go kusiwer. Me itapi napu ni natam̃ol taos napu ni loto mau.
Napu nen kupa kupu na serpal ni naniu. Nen p̃afan ke malik, p̃atpili lele kin.

police didn't sleep at all.
Kanal to Fenue, Fenue to Kanal, at night, you walked. But it wasn't a man-made road like a car road.
On this road you must carry a coconut torch (the bract of the coconut tree that can be burned to use as a torch). When it is dark, you light it and you can see.

Pan pak Fenue pa. Plis man ni English. Upi teni nam̃er, nam̃er ni Erakor. Me rutu English. Me rutatsman pak eFenue. Kunrogo rutu tm̃otum komai pak Kanal.

Go to Fenue. The English police. We were from Erakor. But they were English.
They were on attachment at Fenue. You hear they (the police) knock at the door. We came back to Kanal.

Mal ni nafkal. Ito pareki sa.

Time of the war. It came out here.

This is text 043.

John Maklen
History of villages before Erakor

A story about th history of people who live at Erakor today, startngstarting at Em̃eltafra.

Tiawi nen ruto Em̃eltafra teetwei.
Ipiatlak natam̃ol rulaap wes. Rulaap go, nawesien sa itop.

The old people who stayed at Em̃eltefra before.
There were many people there. They were many, and there were

Kin nlaken maarik naot ni
Er̃eltefra ipreglu nar̃er nen
kin ruto preg nawesien sa.
Gar kin rupan pan pak Etago

Ore, tenen nen rutu ko go rutu,
rutu nrus frafer
Rumai pak Erfat, rumai pak
Er̃elsa esan kin rusoso ki
Erakor.
Orait. Rutkos, rumer nrus mai
pak Ekasufat.
Na ruto Ekasufat. Malnen ki
nalotwen ipo mai.
Malnen nalotwen imai ol
natar̃ol runrus mram, go
rumer nrus mai.
Welkia maarik naot nen ni
Ekasufat imat, maarik naot nen
rusoso ki Nmak, Nmak.
Ina imat go ipiatlak natar̃ol
iskei ina ipo mer of natar̃ol
rumer nrus mai.
Natar̃ol nen nagien, a,
Fakalomara ga ipi natar̃ol ni
Samoa.
Iplaker runa runrus mai kin
rupo mai preg natkon elau Egis.

Me, malnen [nata-] nar̃er laap
rumai, go rumat mat.
Ipiatlak namsaki iskei, namsaki
nen ipi namsaki nen, ntafwen.
Rumatmat panpan tewarik m̃as
kin go rukfo nrookot pak naur
sees.
Rupato naur sees kin go rupo
mer stat preg natar̃ol rulaap

a lot of bad things.
So the chief of Er̃eltefra expelled
all the troublemakers.

They are the ones who went to
Etago.
Yes, those that were there, they
scattered.
They came to Erfat, they came to
Er̃elsa, to the place they call
Erakor.
Alright. They were there, they
came across to Ekasufat.
To stay at Ekasufat. When prayer
(Christianity) came.
When Christianity came the
people were in the light and then
they came.
And the Ekasufat chief died, the
chief who they called Nmak.

He died tand then there was a
man who would take the people
back.
That man was called Fakalomara,
he was from Samoa.

He came with them, they wanted
to come, they made the village by
the beach at Egis.
And, at that time, as many people
came, they were dying.
There was a sickness, the sickness
was dysentery.
They died and died until a few
went across to the small island.

They were at the small island and
their numbers started to pick up

panpan bambae itup̃ ntag ni mees ne.

and grow until this generation.

Kin go komam ufo paakor wes ki ufo mer tñalu naur ki umer mai pak esa.

And we would be born there and we would leave the island and come here.

Upo to preg esan ipi natkon

We would make this place a village.

Ore, e ma- or, Or, malnen kin utñalu natkon, naur sees kin umai, 19, e, 1959.

Yes, when we left the small island and came in 1959.

Malnen nlag kina iwat ki ga ipo pregi komam upo mai pak Efat.

As the wind began to hit it made us come over to Efate.

Go upo pregi esan ipi natkon ni Erakor.

And we would make this place Erakor village.

This is text 047.

Petro Kalman †
Villages before Erakor

There were seven villages that Erakor people lived in before settling at Erakor. The problem of starvation that occurred when Christianity took people away from their gardens and they had only poor food to eat.

Ore, taos naat mal wan ni tiawi.

Yes, about the time of the old people.

Nrak pei natkon ni Erakor Efat rupi natkon ilaru.

At that time, the village of Erakor, Efate, was seven villages.

Ipiatlak iskei rusoso ki esap Eñeltafra.

One was called Eñeltafra.

Iskei rusoso ki ena esap kia Eñelsa. Iskei rusoso ki Emlaliu.

This one is called Eñelsa. This one is called Emlaliu.

Iskei rusoso ki Ekasufat.

This one is called Ekasufat.

E, pak etan Emlasei. Emlasei.
Etmat kin ipi klates.
Esan rupiatlak natkon ilates.
Me san kin rusoso ki, ipi nр̃au
natkon ga kin Ekasufat.
Nр̃au naot itkos. Go malen kin
nalotwen imai,
ore natrauswen itili teflan
malnen nalotwen imai. Teni Efil
rumai, teni Eр̃ag rumai Ertap.

Tukfo ona ki nana, pregsaki
nafnag nen kin ruktao nalotwen
nen.
Rutrau mai. Rumai plak sernale
ni nafkal, ola me nana. Tenen
kin ruto lekor nen kin rutap pak
talm̃at gar mau.
Go nafet apu me ati gar ruto
pam namkanr.
Go kupami esan ipam nasok
nkanrom, me tiawi rupo
kerkerai pami.
Nafnag nen ita pi nafnag wi mau
me rutiki tenen rukfami.

Rupami ikat nkanror rutnoli
ipak nmarter ipo kat nmarter.
Rusuerkin ipo mer.

Me rupo kerkeraiki. Panpanpan
malen kin brown misnari rumai
pak esa.
Kin go rukir-, rutuer Ekasufat.
Go malnen kin rutm̃alu
Ekasufat,
go rumai tu elau Egis esa.
San kin skul ni teesa itkos
malfane. Me rukraksok disentri,

This one is called Emlasei. Etmat
is the sixth.
There are six villages.
But the place they call the main
village is called Ekasufat.
The head chief is there. And
when Christianity came,
that's what the story says,
Christianity came. Those from
Ifira came, from Pango, from
Eratap.
We did it, spoiled the food so
that they would leave us
Christianity.
They came with all the weapons,
spears and so on. Those who
were looking after these things
didn't go to their gardens.
And all the grandparents were
eating wild arrowroot.
When you eat wild arrowroot, it
stings your mouth, but the old
people were strong and ate it.
This is not good food at all, but
they didn't have other things to
eat.
They ate it, it stung their mouth,
they swallowed it, and it stung
their bellies. They shat it out and
it made them numb.
But they were strong for it. Until
the time when the brown
missionaries came here.
And they gave them Ekasufat.
And when they left Ekasufat,

they came to Egis, here.
The place where the school is
now. But they got dysentery and

me rutaf ki nra.
Go runa natañol rutrau mat aliat me p̃og.
Panpan kin go me tenrfaal nen ruto kin rupo nrookot.
Neu papa neu me ipi iskei. Ipi teesa nanwei me ruplaker nrookot kin rupak Erakor.
Go malnen rupak Erakor ga ipi namlas tu. Go rupan go rupo tasai naur sees nen rulaoki nasum̃
kin rupan pa tkos. Pan papa neu ga, iku kia, ipo ptour 1918 kin go komam upo paakor, naur Erakor.
This is text 056.

they shat blood.
And the people were dying day and night.
Until some that were there went across (to the island).
My father was one of them. He was a boy but they took him across to Erakor.
And when they went to Erakor it was bush. And they went and they would clear the island so that they could build houses which they went to live in. Until my father would marry in 1918 and we would be born on Erakor island.

Waia Tenene †
Mare and Erakor

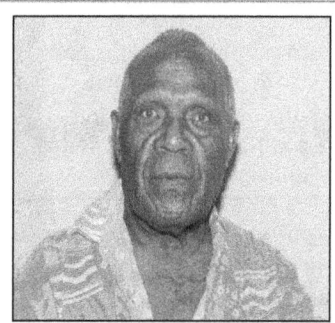

Waia Tenene tells of the Mare (New Caledonia) people who came as police to help the French suppress Malakulans. They then stayed and married into Erkor families.

A, teni Emar nen kin rumai pak san teetwei mal ni, na, kolonial kafman.

Franis kafman isent kir rumai reki na polis.
Rumai pi polis ni Efat. Nanre ni

Ah, those people from Mare (in New Caledonia) who came here long ago in the time of the Colonial Government.
The French government sent them to come as police.
They came to be police on Efate.

Franis, Franis kafman.

Go ipiatlak nafkal nen ito
Emlakul go isentkir pak
Emlakul.
Preg nafkal skot nañer nig
Emlakul.
Go, neu welkia papa neu. Papa
neu nen kin ipi tmak leg p̃alun
rusi.
Teni Emar nen kin rumai, teni
Caledoni nen rumai pak esa
nlaken Franis kafman isosor.
Nafet polis rumai rumai pak esa.

Ale rupan preg nafkal skot teni
Emlakul malnen ipiatlak na sifil
wo
Go neu taos p̃al papa neu iskei
ga ipato sanpen mai. Go rupak
Emlakul go rusi. Imat, imat
Emlakul.
Rusoso ki Nano. Me papa neu ga
ga ipi anfermie ni Nume,
hospitel p̃ur.
Ale ga imarmar, a iliv go
rusentkin ipak Franis.
Ipa na Messageries Maritimes
raru a? Raru p̃ur. Ipan raon
Franis na imai, imai pak esa.

Ale itup̃ na metotel ga. Ale
rupregi ipak euut.
Ina ipak euut imai ale, tenen kin
rupato rumai pi polis. Rutu san
to go kipe skotir.

Kin papa neu Tenene. Me ito
pan na ilak ale kipe to san to.

On the side of the French, the
French government.
There was fighting on Malakula,
and it sent them to Malakula.

Fight with the people from
Malakula.
And me, well, my father. My
straight father, his brother, they
shot him.
Those from Mare that came,
those from Caledonia came here
because the French government
called them. A group of police
came, they came here.
Okay, they went to fight with
those from Malakula when there
was a civil war.
And me, as my father's brother
came from there. And they went
to Malakula and they shot him.
He was killed in Malakula.
They called him Nano. My father
was a nurse at the big hospital in
Noumea.
He went on leave and they sent
him to France.
He went on the boat of the
Messageries Maritimes. The ship.
It went around to France and he
came back here.
Then he got his job as a maître
d'hôtel. So they sent him ashore.
He wanted to come ashore, he
came, then those that were there
became police. They were here
and he joined them.
My father, Tenene. He stayed
until he was married, then he

Itaulu iak neu go kipe to san to.

Gar rupitlak na- ntan nen naot nig Efil ituer kin Emlap̄o, san kin Kawenu itkos.

Teni Emar rutu wes teni Caledoni. Me malnen gar runa rulak, go rulak mai pak Erakor. Go ruipe muf mai.

This is text 061

stayed here.

He married my mother and he stayed here.

They had land that the chief of Ifira gave them at Emlap̄o, where Kawenu (college) is.

Those from Mare stayed there, those from Caledonia. When they married, they came to Erakor. And they moved here.

Toukelau Takau
Life today

Life today and the lack of respect shown by young people to older people. Things are much easier now, but hard work made everyone feel stronger back then.

Komam nen kin upi tiawi ulek nam̃olien pei mai paakor nam̃olien ni mees.
Me nam̃olien ni mees imsal top.
Itap taos nam̃olien ni malpei mau.
Nam̃olien ni mees teesa rumetmatu wi,
ruskul wi me rukano paketan ki tiawi.
Rukano nrog nafsan.

We old people we look at the way of life before coming through to today.
Life today is different. It isn't like life in those days.
Today, children are clever,

they go to school, but they don't respect the old people.
They can't hear the language (they can't hear what their old people tell them).

Nlaken rumro na gar rumetmatu tol tiawi.
Me tenen tiawi rutae ipi tesees.

Because they think they know more than the old people.
But what the old people know

Tiawi rutap metmatu wi mau.

Me rumroperkat, runrog perkat
nale tiawi nigmam tenen rupi
tem mom go rait mom.
Komam ukano pregsa kir,
unrog naler, rutil tenamrun,
komam upregi taosi kin gar rutli.
Me mees, naṁolien ni mees kineu
kafo to pes.
Til tenen iwi, tenen ileg, me gar
rukano rukano nrogo.

Nlaken rumrokin na gar
rumetmatu tol nametmatuan
nigmam tiawi.
Me komam ukano pregsa kir
nlaken ipi nafsan iskei nen kin
tiawi kefo tafnau teesa.
Teesa ipreg tenamrun nen
ikerkerai itakel me tenen kin ipi
rait ko tiawi ukano preg kerkerai
kir.
Go ukano pes sa kir nlaken gar
rukfo develop ki mal wi nen kefo
mai.
Kafo traus tete natrauswen taos
na naur malnen uto naur sees
Erakor.
Komam uta weswes skot loto
mau.
Komam utap weswes skot enjin
mau.
Uweswes ki narmom uweswes ki
masmes p̃ur, uweswes ki kram,
go uslasol ki np̃au mom.

Uslasol ki ntak mom,

is small.
The old people don't know
more.
But they remember the wisdom
of our old people, those who
were our fathers and mothers.
We can't criticise them,
we listen to them, they tell us
things, we do as they tell us.
But the life of today, this is
what I always say.
Say some things are good, some
things are right, but they don't
listen.
Because they think their
wisdom is better than that of
our old people.
But we can't criticise them
because its the way that the old
people teach young people.
Children follow their own
strong, crooked way, but their
mothers and old people can't
be strong with them.
We can't talk badly to them
because they are developing
their future.
I will tell the story of when we
were on the small island of
Erakor.
We didn't work with cars.

We didn't work with engines.

We worked with our hands,
with knives, with axes,
and we carried things on our
heads.
We carried things on our backs,

uslasol ki mpam mom.

Uto em̃ae uslasol mai pak elau.
Loto itik.

Komam uweswes ki nar mam,
ufarfar ki nam̃ol mam, raki
nawesien p̃afp̃of laap.
Tiawi rukfo tai raru, ruweswes ki
kram m̃as, rutap wesweski engine
mau.
Mes, nam̃olien ni mees, kafo preg
nawesien kafo sat nafnag ipatu
napu.
Me kafo preg loto kefan msagi
mai. Me malpei itik.

Nam̃olien nen kin tu pato mees
ne itik malpei.
Komam uweswes umaos umurin
na koto wi, kofo pei maos.

Nkal ni mam rumap̃rap̃or, uslat
nanrogtesan itop.
Me kofo pei inrok to wi. Kofo sur
kopra em̃ae, em̃ae.
Me kofo slati mai loto itik.
Kofo mai kofo pregi na, komer ler
nkap, komai suekro.
Pan kin gar, komer laosoki.

Me malnen rukoi pe laosok silua
rutur pek. Natam̃ol kin kefo slati.

Pan psi raru elau, kefo msagi pak
sto,
natam̃ol imaos top malpei, nlaken
kin nam̃olien ni malpei ikerkerai,
toklos teni nawesien.

we carried them on our
shoulders.
We were a long way away, we
carried things down to the sea.
No cars.
We worked with our hands, we
moved our bodies, for hard
work.
The old people cut canoes, they
worked with only an axe, they
didn't work with engines.
Today, life today, I'll do work,
I'll carry food and put it on the
road.
Then I get the truck to carry
the things. But not in those
days.
Life today is not like it was
before.
We worked and we got tired, if
we want to stay well, we would
first have to get tired.
Our clothes were ripped, we
had too many hardships.
We would then feel good. We
worked copra, a long way.
But we carried it, no car.
We would go and make it, get
firewood and smoke it.
Until it was dry, then we
pounded it.
When they finished pounding
it, they sewed up the bag. The
man would take it.
Put it in the canoe on the
beach, take it to Vila,
people got tired in those days,
because life then was hard, as
regards the work.

Me raki nanrogperkatwen
komam ukano tao nafsan ni tiawi,
tarp̃ek,
tiawi rupreg nafsan go rufla tili
na kofan gar preg talm̃at, kofo pa.

Ukano sertep̃al nafsan ni tiawi.

Na teni sup̃ ni nam̃olien ni
malpei. Go mees kin ato trausi.

Ni malpei.
Nam̃olien twei.
Paakor mees ne.
Nam̃olien kaaru ni mees ikerkerai
top.
Go itaos malpei wel kin ufla salem
ki kopra,
upiatlak taos malpei uius ki na
Australia, mane ni Australia.
Wan paon, ten slen, tefla.

Me ipi mane p̃ur, mane p̃ur.

Kofo slati pak sto, ufla sat ten slen
pak sto.
Kofo pakot tete namurien
nigmam kenom me kotfak mane
kofo sati ler mai. Nlaken prais ises
m̃as.
Ko ufla sat wan paon pak sto,
mani p̃ur, mani p̃ur.

Kofo sat tep̃ur ler, me kofo paakot
ki tesees.
Me malfanen sernale ipak elag,
pak elag, pak elag.
Go taos nanre nigmam tiawi
ukano piatlak mani nlaken

But as for remembering, we
can't ignore our old people's
talk,
the old people might tell us to
go to the garden and we have
to go.
We cannot ignore the words of
our ancestors.
That was the way of life before.
Like today that I am talking
about.
Of long ago.
Life before.
Come to today.
The other life today is too hard.

Like before when we would sell
copra,
before we used Australian
money.
One pound, ten shillings, like
that.
But it was big money, big
money.
We would take it to town, we
would take ten shillings.
We would buy what we wanted,
but we would have change to
take back. Because the price
was very low.
And if we took a pound to
town, it was big money, big
money.
I would take a lot, but I would
spend a little.
But today everything is high,
high, high.
And as for us old people we
can't have much money

nañolien ni mees ikerkerai.
Komam kofo kerkerai preg
nawesien sees go kofo tae pañor
mani.
Me ifwel kin uta kerkerai weswes
mau ukano pañor mani.
Go malpei komam kofo tae welu
tiawi.
Tiawi ifla pan sur kopra ipatu
komam natañol kerkerai kofo tae
pan gar slati mai.
Me mees itik.
Iwel kafla tp̃eki tete teesa kefa
neu preg talm̃at,
me kafo mas- kafo gar kuk, ko
tete nrak atp̃olu tete natañol
p̃tae.
Kafo paaktofir iwel kafitlak mani
kafo paaktofir.
Me wel atik ki mani kafo pan lel
nafnag talm̃at kafo gar preg.

Nañolien ni mees itefla.
This is text 064.

because life today is too hard.
We need to work hard and we
can get money.

But if we don't work hard we
can't get any money.
Before, we used to help the old
people.
The old people would cut
copra, and we strong ones
would go and get it for them.
But not today.
If I tell some kids to work in the
garden for me,
I have to cook for them, and
sometimes I send someone else.

I have to pay them if I have
money I have to pay them.
But if I have no money, I will go
to the garden and get food for
them.
Life today is like that.

Toukelau Takau
Women's life before

The way a woman's life has changed from kastom times to today.

Or ga itaos malpei nmatu komam
umtaki taos nkal ni nanwei?
Komam ukano kal ki nkal ni
nanwei.
Ikerkerai, nen kin nmatu ikal ki
nkal ni nanwei.
Go mees mees nmatu me nanwei
rukal pitkaskei.

In the olden days women
couldn't wear men's clothes.
We couldn't wear men's
clothes.
It was strong, that a woman
dress in men's clothes.
And today, today, women and
men dress the same.

Me komam malpei ukano kal ki
nkal ni nanwei.
Ko kukal ki nkal ni mam nmatu.

Me esan ni nigmam ikano paakor

Nap̃utuok ikano paakor nkal neu
kemas pram pak esa.

Nkal neu kefo pram. Me iwel ag
kuto esago.
Ag kutotan sago me kineu amurin
na kataf, o, ikerkerai top.

Kafo mtak. Kafo puetsok nakte
nkal wel atuleg me ana kataf.

Kafo siwer.
Mailum siwer nrookot wok.
Nlaken ag kuto.
Kafo pak etan kik. Nmatu itefla.

Ko natam̃ol laap rutu me nmatu
imurin na kesiwer tol nlaken
nanwei laap rutu.
Kefo nrok puetsok nkal ga ipak
etan, nen kin kemailum tol
nanwei.
Ko wel nanwei rufla pi tap̃ou tu
esa me nmatu imai, kefo pan lfek
ur em̃ae.
Nlaken ipak etan ki nanwei.
Sup̃ ni malpei itefla.
Nmatu rutefla. Ko apak esum̃ tap,
natam̃ol kin ruipe pur tu.

Kafo siwer kafo mailum nrok pan
totan.Tefla.
Go taos nmatu komam utap kal

But back then we couldn't
dress in men's clothes.
And you wore women's
clothes.
But here [indicating her knees]
couldn't show.
My knee couldn't show, my
clothes must be long down to
here.
My dress would be long. But if
you were there.
You sit there, but I want to
leave (past you), oh it is very
hard.
I would be scared. I would hold
my skirt like this, I would
stand up to leave.
I would walk.
Walk slowly in front of you.
Because you are there.
I will respect you. For women
that is the way.
Or if many men are there and a
woman wants to walk past
because many men are there.
She will bend low, and hold
her dress, show respect so that
she can slowly pass a man.
Or if there are many men here,
but a woman comes, she will
go around them a long way.
Because she respects men.
The old way is like that.
Women are like that. If I go to
church, it is already full of
people.
I will walk, I will slowly bend
and sit down. Like that.
We women didn't dress like

taos mees mau. Nmatu ukal ki nkal nen narum ipram esa.

Nawesien ni nafnag ipi nawesien ni nmatu. Nmatu kin ipreg nafnag.
Tetenrak nanwei inrom nmatu ileka nmatu imaos go nanwei ipo welua.

Me nafregnafnagwen sernrak ipi nmatu kin ipreg nafnag.
Nmatu kin ikuk, nmatu kin ipuuri, ipreg kapu.
Me nanwei ga kefo pak etalm̃at, islat nafnag ipaunamru kemai psi esum̃, me nmatu kin kefo preg nafnag.
Nanwei kefo pan lel nafnag, slat sernale mai pak esum̃, me nmatu kin kefo preg kapu esum̃.

Me mees nmatu kemur kefuuri kefreg kapu, ga kefan tmen slat nafnag.
Kefan tmen lel nrau ketmen lel nm̃arteu, nkap, mai pak esum̃ kemer preg nafnag.

Mees itefla. Sup̃ ni natam̃ol ni mees itefla. Me malpei, itik.

Nanwei kefo pan lel nafnag, slat sernale mai pak esum̃, me nmatu kin kefo preg kapu esum̃.

Me iwel rapan preg talm̃at. Ranru pan preg talm̃at.

today. Women dressed in dresses with sleeves down to here (wrists).
Food work is women's work. Women make the food.

Sometimes, if a man feels sorry for a woman he will see she is tired and the man will help her.
But getting food ready is always women's work.
Women cook, women prepare laplap, make laplap.
The man would go to the garden, get food, carry it and put it in the house, but the woman prepares the food.
Men would go and get the food, carry everything back to the house, and women would make laplap at the house.
But today it is the woman who prepares food, makes laplap, who fetches food.
She goes herself to find laplap leaves, to look for dry coconuts, firewood, and comes back to the house to prepare the food.
Today it is like that. People's ways are like that. But before, no.
The man would look for food, bring everything back to the house, but the woman would make laplap at the house.
So they both went and worked in the garden.

Me rekin kin kefan sat nafnag etalm̃at mai pak esum̃.
Nanwei kefo pan sat nafnag, me nmatu kefo preg nafnag. Kefo kuk ki, ko ipreg kapu. Tefla.

Nmatu ito esum̃ ilekor teesa, go taos malpei nmatu rutap pak hospitel mau.

Komam upiatlak tiawi, tiawi nen kin gar me ruto raki nen kin rulekor nmatu, nen kin ruslat teesa.
Esum̃ m̃as.
Ipiatlak Liaas, Limat, Ana, Sera, Pali.
Gar nen ruto lekor nmatu esum̃.

Nmatu imur na keslat teesa.
Rupan sosor rumai.

Skotir me rupo sel teesa rulekor wer esum̃. Pan pan rukerkerai.

(NT) Me teesa ipaakor ni nasum̃ nen?
(TT) Itik (NT) Malpei? (TT) Malpei, malpei nasum̃ tefla nen m̃as.
Nasum̃ kapa itik.
Rupaakor na, nasum̃ nen kin rowat, sum̃ rowat.
A.A. Naliati ilim, faef dei, nmatu imas pnut to
Go nmatu ikano taos mees. Nmatu ipan sel teesa hospitel.

Sel teesa mees, kotfan itae tuleg

But as for how they took food from the garden to the house.
The man would get food, but the woman would prepare it. She would cook it, or make laplap. That's the way.
Women stay home and look after children, and in the olden days they didn't go to hospital at all.
We have old people who helped and looked after a woman when she had a baby.

Only at home.
There was Liaas, Limat, Ana, Sera, Pali.
They looked after women at home.
When women wanted to have a baby. They went and called them to come.
With them, but they would take the child and look after it at home. Until they were strong.
(NT) Were children born at home?
(TT) No (NT) Before? (TT) Before, in the home, like that. There were no tin houses. They were born in thatch houses.
For five days the woman must stop quiet.
And a women can't do what she does today. A woman has her baby in the hospital.
Have the baby today, in the

pan was, ko ikuk.

afternoon she gets up and washes, or cooks.

Me malpei itik nmatu malen tiawi itoraki nmatu iskei islat teesa.

But not then, the old women waited for a woman to have her baby.

Kefo mas pnut to ikano farfar.

She must keep still, not move about.

Go nmatu nen kin taos Sera ifla to raki nmatu iskei.
Nmatu nen imailum pnuto. Ga kefo ga preg teesa kelos.

And the woman, like Sera, would wait with a woman.
The woman would stay there quiet. And she would bathe the child.

Kega klin ki teesa. Go iklin ki raiten.

Would clean the child for her. And she would wash the mother.

Raiten ikano tuleg pan los, kemas pnut to pan pan naliati ilim inom.

The mother couldn't stand to wash, she had to sit quiet for five days.

Go rait teesa kefo tae toleg preg tete namrun sees.

And the mother of the child would be able to stand and do small things.

Me ikano pan pai nasok, ikano pan kuk, pan kefei piatlak wik inru itol.
Ko tete nrak nmatu ilekor ptaki nmatu nen islat teesa,

But she can't clean up rubbish, she can't cook, until two or three weeks.
And sometimes the woman looking after the mother who had a baby,

itae skoti to atlag mau iskei.

she can stay with her for a whole month.

Pan nmatu ipiatlak nakerkeraian go [teesa itae nen kin-] mama ga kefo tae tmen lekor wes.

Until the woman goes into labour and [the child knows-] the mother knows how to look after herself.

Go ipo pa. Ale, nanwei kefo mer pei preg nafnag pan pan pan, welkia imer preg kastom tu doctor,
tenen ilekor nmatu ga.

Then she can go. Then her husband will make food and will make kastom to the doctor,
to the woman who looked after his wife.

Kega preg nafnag. Preg nafsawian tua. 'Kuneu lekor ptaki nmatu neu isel teesa.

He makes food ready for her. He gives thanks. 'You looked after my wife for me when she had a baby.

Malfanen rato wi. Nta kafo tuok gaag m̃iit.' Itua m̃iit, ko itua tete nafnag, ko itua tete nkal ko mane.

Now they are well. I will give you a mat.' He gives her a mat or he gives her some food, some clothes, or some money.

Ale kefo ga slati me kefo pan psi esum̃ ga, itefla.

Then he will go and take it for her, and put it in her house, like that.

Malpei komam teesa laap rupaakor. Nanre ni paptais.
Mal ni, mal ni tiawi, tiawi. Tiawi ni teetwei atap tae mau,
me tiawi nen kin taos, rupi tem mom,
go rupi rait mom rupaptais.
Go ipiatlak pasta Sope, pasta Saurei.
Gar nen kin me malpei, malpei kotkot misnari ipreg nfap̩taiswen.
Mista McKenzie kin rumai.
Rupaptais. Go rutousok natam̃ol.

In those days lots of kids were born. As for baptism.
The old people. The old people from long ago I don't know, but those who were our father,

and mother, they baptised.
There was pastor Sope and pastor Saurei.
They, long long ago, the missionaries did the baptisms.
Mister McKenzie came. They baptised. And they married people.

This is text 065.

Toukelau Takau
How girls can behave

A description of how girls used to be expected to behave.

(NT) Go sup̃ ni teesa nmatu go sup̃ ni teesa nanwei ipitkaskei?
(TT) Itik. Iwel kineu afla preg asel.
Apitlak boyfriend, kineu kafo mtak.
Taos amurin na kafestafi akano

(NT) Do girls and boys have the same fashion?
(TT) No. If I were to make a friend.
I have a boyfriend, I would be scared.
If I want to talk to him, I can't

pestafi.
Preg taktmokit lek nrae kit, itik.
Kafo preg leta, kafo mtir natus,
kamtir natus wel amurin na
kafestaf boyfriend neu akano
trau leg pan leka. Akano.
Kafo preg leta keskei. Ale atu
naat, 'Ƀafo neu tuaki.'

Ko ga ifla murin na ketao tete
nanromien sees, ikano trau leg
mai tao.
Kefo preg nanromien nen keur
tete naor ptae. Me rakin kin
komam ratrau tmom nrae ki
komam,
ipi namtakwen, a?
Tefla, nigmam malpei itefla,
ukano trau iwel kineu ato esa,
me boyfriend neu ifla paakor
tenaor ni esanpe kineu asef apan
ur eṁae.
Suƀ ni malpei itefla. Mees welkia
boyfriend, puserek naor iskei, a.
Me malpei ga, ga ikerkerai.

Iwel rakfo siwer kaaru ipa go
kaaru ipa me natus ṁas kin
rapas tmom pestaf komam ki
natus.
Ko tete nanromien sees me
iwelkin ifpi namurien ni tem go
rait na namurien ni teesa iwi.
Go malfane, tem teesa nanwei ga
kefo pak esuṁ ni tem teesa
nmatu,
kefaos ki, kefo paoski, 'Kutrok na
teesa nanwei neu kefo taulu
teesa nmatu gaag?' Iwel tem ina,

talk to him.
Face to face, no.
I would write a letter as I
wanted to talk to him, but I can't
talk directly to him. I can't.

I will write a letter. Then I give
it to someone, 'You will give it
to him for me.'
And if he wanted to give me a
little present, he can't just come
and give it to me.
He will take the present to
different places. But as for us
giving it face to face,

it's fear, ah?
Like, for us, then, it was like this,
we couldn't just, if I was here,
but my boyfriend came out here
somewhere, I would run away, I
would run a long way.
The way it was back then.
Today, as for a boyfriend,
talking in the same place. But in
those days it was strong.
If we were walking, one here,
one here, but only paper would
pass between us, talk by letter.

Or some small present, but if the
parents agree with the child, it's
okay.
And now, the father of this boy
would go to the house of the
girl's father,
to ask him, 'Do you agree that
my son will marry your
daughter?' If the father says,

'Ore, iwi.'   'Yes, it is good.'
Go malfane rakfo tmer tauluer.   Now they will marry each other.
Me welkin tem teesa nanwei ifla   But if the boy's father goes but
pan me tem teesa nmatu ifla mal   the girl's father doesn't want it,
kefo mer ler.   he will go back again.
Kefo mer ler pan kefo sos teesa   He will go and he will call his
nanwei ga.   son.
Kefo sos teesa nanwei ga me   He will go back and call his son.
kefo nrikinkin na, 'Kineu kaipe   and say to him, 'I went and
pan gaag paoski teesa nmatu.'   asked for that girl for you.'
Me raiten ifla mal ko tmen ifla   But if her mother doesn't want
mal kin ag kupiatlaken.   it, or her father doesn't want it,
    that you have her.

Go imer nom. Itap pregi nen kin,   It is over. He doesn't say, 'I will
'Kafo preg kerkeraiki nen kafo   force them so that I can have
pueti.' Tik.   her.' No.
This is text 066.

William Wayane †
Independence

Discussion of the time of Independence in Vanuatu.

Ore, ipiatlak malen kin 1980,   Okay, there was, in 1980,
malen tuksat independent.   when we got independence.
Teni esum̃ Erakor ruta sapot ki   Those from Erakor didn't support
independent mau.   independence at all.
Go rupreg tete problem p̃ur,   And they caused some big
rupreg tete nawesien nen ipi   problems, did some things in
tap leg mau taon.   town that weren't right at all.
Rupak taon rupuetlu flaik nen   They went to town and pulled
kin kafman ipsi ito taon.   down the flag which the
    government had put around the
    town.

Rupuetlua ipak etan.   They pulled it down.

Go tete krup rumpaki tanmaet
Radio Vanuatu.
Pregi tiawi laap rumtak, go rufit
pan, tete rupan los elau,

esan esto ni Fung Kuei.
Tete rupan los ntas elau sa.

Tete rufit mai pak Radio
Vanuatu,
rufit mai pak lakun.
Go polis rupuetsok tete go ru-.

Rusṁolir nasuṁ malik.
(NT) Me ni naur Erakor, ipiatlak
tete muf ni natkon ne?

(WW) Natkon ne? Naur Erakor?
Ore naur Erakor gar ruta sapot
independent malnen mau.
Gar rupan kerkerai nlaken
naṁer ni Franis ruto sursrir go
rupregi gar ruskot naṁer to
nanre ni Franis.
Go rupreg ruta sapot ki
independen mau.
Me inrok nen, malen kin tusat
independent, go rupo sapot ki
independent.
Go mees tupo leka tufri.
Namroan nen kin upiatlaken
malpei kin umalki independent,
umroki na isa me mees upo
paṁori na ipo iwi.
Nlaken ipiatlak malnen ipitlak
mal ni kolonialism go rupreg sa
ki namroan ni nataṁol.
Ruto sursur nataṁol, rupregi
nataṁol rusapot kir.

And some groups threw
dynamite at Radio Vanuatu.
It made many old people scared
and they ran away, some jumped
into the sea,
where Fung Kuei's store is.
Some went for a swim in the sea
there.
Some ran to Radio Vanuatu.

some ran to the lagoon.
And the police held some and
they-.
They stuck them in gaol.
(NT) But on Erakor island, were
there moves (against
independence)?
(WW) This village? Erakor? Yes,
Erakor island didn't support
independence.
They were strong because some
French people had tricked them
and made them go together on
the French side.
And they made it so they didn't
support independence.
But later, when we got
independence, they supported
independence.
And today we can see we are free.
Before independence we thought
it would be no good, but today
we find that it is okay.

Because then it was a colonial
attitude that was no good for the
people's minds.
They tricked people and made
people support them.

Me inrok knen go upo paṁori na isa.
Go mees uipe free.
Utae preg tenmatun nen kin umurin, nlaken uipe slat independent nigmam.
This is text 068.

But later we found that it was wrong.
And today we are free.
We can do what we want because we got our independence.

Kalfap̃un Mailei †
On stories about land

Arguments about land titles and the way that land was aken from the traditional owners. The old man talks and talks and talks, his story is like the wind. He tells it and it is gone.

Nlaken umrokin tetemal kefo mai,
taos mees kin tupo tkos. Mees ne ruple, ruple ki ntan. Malen alel histri asup̃neki,

Because we think about sometime in the future, like today when we would be here. Today they argue, they argue about ground. When I look at history I don't know,

kineu afla leles, asup̃neki, me ag nen p̃ato ṁeltig ki tiawi, kufla psir ko kufla tilṁori, me kufnrog natrauswen.

I might have seen it but I don't know, but you who are close to the old people, you may lie or you may tell the truth but you may have heard the story.

Gawankia, me telaap ruta murin rufi ṁeltig ki tiawi mau. Mees kin rutu, rulel natrauswen ni ntan.

But many people don't want to be close to the old people. Today they see the story of the ground.

P̃aleles paṁori sua? Tiawi kipe mat. Mees nen koipe tu wel, utu tefla, tefla tefla, wel p̃aror.
Teflan pa, kaipe tu wel p̃aror, naat itrau, iṁit- ipaoski ki kwestin iskei akano tli.
(NT) Me nlaken iku tiawi rutap mtiri mau?
(KM) Tiawi ni teetwei gar

You look for it but where is it? The old people have died. Today we are here like, like idiots.
Like that, I was there like an idiot, someone might ask a question but I can't say.
(NT) But why didn't the old people write it down?
(KM) The old people before

rusuꝑnekin mtir, tiawi rukano mtir. Me igaag traus, ag kupitlak ntaewen, ag ꝑafo tmom mtiri.

Me, selwan ag kupi eꞥae, tiawi itraus traus traus traus, natrauswen ga itaos nlag. Itrausi pan kaipa.
Me iwel runi teesa iskei traus nen kin, ipitlak nꝑaun, kefo wes pen, natus, ale, 'Ꝑatraus me neu kamtir.'
Me selwan kuna ꝑato nrogo, ꝑato nrogo isil sa itaf sa ipa. Taos nlag.

(NT) In one ear and out the other
(KM) Gawan kia, me komam uta laap kin uto mau, a? Malen umat, inom.
Tenen rumer nrkos mom me rukuipe suꝑneki serale. Rufo tu psir ꞥas. Kupaoski kwestin iskei, rupsir.
Ifla nrogo ki naat ꝑet, ifla sati sanpe, ifla nrogo ki radio.

Me malen kupaoski kwestin, iansa pelpel, without knowing.

Ita tae mau me iansa. Gawankia iansa without, iansa, me naꝑeten itik.
Gawankia. Tete naat rutraus, rutraus, rutraus. Me rusati ki

didn't know how to write, the old people couldn't write. But they tell it for you, you have the knowledge, you will write it yourself.
But when you are far away the old man talks and talks and talks, his story is like the wind. He tells it and it is gone.
But if they tell it to a smart child, he will take a pen and paper and say, 'OK, You talk and I'll write.'
But when you want to sit and listen to him, you sit and listen to it go in and it comes out (of your ears) and goes. Like the wind.
(NT) In one ear and out the other
(KM) That's it, but there aren't many of us left. When we die, it will be finished.
Those who follow after us will have forgotten everything. They will only lie. You ask a question, they lie.
Maybe they heard it from another man, maybe they got it from somewhere, maybe they heard it on the radio.
But when you ask a question, he answers quickly, without knowing.
He doesn't know at all but he answers. So he answers, but there is no meaning to it.
That's it. Some men will talk and talk and talk. But they got it

tete naat p̃et,
rusati ki tete naat p̃et rumai
gaag trausi. Me itap tenen, gar
rutkos, gar rupakes, gar rupregi,
go ipi nafsirwen.

from some other people,
they got it from some other
person and they come to tell
you the story. But it is bad, they
are there, they go there, they
get it and it is lies.

Wel kutil natilm̃orian, kutotan
round table, ale kutil
natilm̃orian, kumur, kupaos ki
kwestin agaag trausi.
Kupaos ki nfaoswen, 'Amur
teflan tefla.' Kafo gaag tli tenen
aleka, ko tenen apregi. Me rekin
tenen kin, kanrogo kaitli, ifla
tilm̃ori ko ifla psir.
This is text 072.

So you tell the truth, you sit
around the table, you tell the
truth, you ask questions and I
talk to you.
You ask questions, 'I want this
or this.' I will tell you what I see,
what I have done. But as for
what I have heard it might be
true or it might be lies.

John Kaltap̃au †
Roi Mata

A story about Roi Mata, the chief who came to Efate and
broughbrought the naflak or clan system

Naot ne, ito esan rusoso ki, esap,
me, atae ipi naot ata aelan,

This chief was at this place
called, but, ... I know he was a
chief of another island.

Ito, ito me ipitlak na, tete sup̃
ipaakorkin, go
rupestafi- natam̃ol runrogtesa
wes go rupes top. Rupes top
panpanpan go inrikir kin na,
'Iwi.'

Then something came to him
and
people felt bad about it and they
grumbled. They grumbled until
he said to them, 'Okay.'

Mees nen kin tuto, tuto tmokit
pregsa kit, preg saki kit.
Natkon nen ipato, ko Emlalen
ipato, imaet imai wat nen isa.

Today as we are, we are hurting
each other.
The village is there, Emlalen is
there, he is angry, he comes and
hits whoever is bad.

Tenen ito esan imaet ipan watgi
natkon kaaru.

Teni natkon kaaru imaet. ipan
watgi natkon kaaru.

Go ipregi panpan Efat negakit
nen natam̃ol rumat panpan
natam̃ol ruitik.
'Go amurin na, naliati keskei
kafo preg nafnag p̃ur keskei me
kofo mai.
Naliati ne kofo preg nafnag p̃ur
iskei.'
Ipreg nafnag p̃ur me isos natkon
nen kin kaipe puetlu nagien rupa

rumaui mai pak naor iskei me itli
na,
'Ag p̃amai, p̃aslat namrun taos
kufla slat nap̃rai,

ko kufla sat nawi, ko kufla slat na
naik, ko kufla slat tete nmatun
teflan ne, me koslati mai.'

Me kafo kafo kafo preg nafnag
keskei ne malnen tuna tuto fam,
tuto fam me kafo sos iskei. 'Ag
kupi naflak nafte. Kutap pi
naflak mau, me p̃aslat nafte kin
kuslati mai.'
Me imai ifla sat nap̃rai iskei. Go
nap̃rai ne, nap̃rai wan kin nen
rusosoki kram p̃og,
kram p̃og ne, ga kin ipo laotu
Erakor tu mees. Iskei imai sat
nap̃rai mai.
Malnen ileka go itua nagi, 'Gaag

The one from here got angry,
and went and hit the other
village.
The one from the other village
got angry. He went and hit the
other village.
And he made it so that people in
our Efate were dying until there
were no more people.
'And I want that, one day I will
make a big feast and you will
come.
That day you will make a big
feast.'
He made a feast and he called
the villages that I told you about
to all go
to one place and he said,

'You come here, you take
something, like if you take
sugarcane,
or if you take a yam, or if you
take fish, or if you take
something like that, you take it
and come.'
I would get some food, we
would eat, but I would call out,
'You are which naflak? You
aren't any naflak, but you take
whichever food you have
chosen, that is your naflak.'
Then he came, he might take
sugarcane. The sugarcane they
call 'night clam',
that 'night clam', the one that
still grows at Erakor today. One
took sugarcane and came.
So he looked and he gave him a

ki, gaag ki kupi naflak na kram p̃og, pan pato sanpe.'

Isos kaaru imai, isos kaaru imai ina, 'Kusat nafte mai?' Imer sat nap̃rai iskei mai.

Sukaken ia. Nap̃rai iskei mau, malnen ileka, ina, 'O? Me naflak gaag kin kaipe mtalua ipato. Ag p̃afo pi naflak ga.'

Ale isos kaaru imai.

'Go ag kupi naflak natop p̃afan totan sanpe.' Ipan totan.

Isos kaaru imai, ileka, isat nawi iskei, 'O me natop ne, gaag kin pato kaipe gaag mtalua, ag p̃afo pi naflak ga.'

Ale tep̃tae imai, ina, isat, ina, 'P̃amer mai'. Imer sat ga mai, islat nawi isat nawi, nawi neu mleomiel.

Ale imai na ileka, ina, 'O, me ag kupi mleomiel. Me p̃afan pato sanpe'. Kaaru imai, ileka ipi mleomiel, ia, naflak gaag kin pato.

P̃afo pan leka sanpe. Akam rapi naflak iskei. Ipreg iur ser nagi, naflak paakor, naflak tefserser tefserser ruto tan. Pak teni ntas.

Ipam̃or naflak ina inom, kineu ipo tli na, 'Malfane akam nen kin tenen pato nmaten pato nen rapi naflak ne, itap nen rakmer komam utmo mus wat mus.

name, 'You are naflak 'night clam', go over there.'

He called another to come, and said, 'What did you bring?' He brought sugarcane too.

When he saw the sugarcane he said, 'Oh, but I've chosen your naflak already over there. You can be that naflak.'

So he called out to the next to come.

'You are naflak [natop] yam, go and sit over there.' He went and sat down.

He called the other to come, he looked, he took this yam [natop], 'O, this yam, I have chosen yours for you, you will be his naflak.'

So a different one came, he took it, and said, ' You come again.' He took his again, he took a yam, my yam, red mleo.

So he came and looked, 'Oh you are red mleo. You go over there.' The other one came, he saw it was red mleo, his naflak was there.

You go and look there. You are all one naflak. He went through every name, the naflaks were created, all different naflaks were there. Down to those from the sea.

He found all the naflaks and he said, 'Now all who are at the funeral they are this naflak, they musn't hit each other.

Ramer kano ple. Me rakmaomao. Rapi teskei mau.

They can't argue anymore. They will talk about their troubles. They will all be one.

Tenpato itefla, ten pato itefla go malfanen ipo pregi pan watu imer sak.

The one there is like this, the one there is like this, and now it will grow (i.e., things will get better)

Amur kafa me amtak nlaken naflak neu pato kefo watgi itap leg mau. Kaaru ipregi itefla

I want to go but I am scared because my naflak was going to get into trouble, it wasn't right. The others would do that.

Ipi nlaken Vanuatu ipo mer sak panpan kin go natam̃ol rupo ftom. Natam̃ol nen rusosoki, kalo, RoiMata.
RoiMata. Maarik ne. RoiMata kin ipreg itmat
This is text 093.

That is why Vanuatu was able to get ahead and its people were able to grow. That man was called, Roi Mata.
Roi Mata, this man. It was Roi Mata who brought peace.

Kalsarap Namaf †
Wak nmatu, the pig wife

The story of the pig who seemed like a good wife (it did a good job of digging the garden), but maybe lacked in other aspects of wifely duty.

Amurin na katrausi te natrauswen ni maarik Wili Santo ineu trausi teetwei.
Itil natam̃ol ni Ermag inru.

I want to tell the story by this man Wili Santo, he told it to me long ago.
It tells of two Erromangan people.

Kaaru ipiatlak nmatu. Selwan ralak ratap mer tao mau.

One has a wife. When they were married they did not leave each other.

Rato panpan go naliati iskei tenen ipitlak nmatu ipitlak nmatu nega rapan sari.
Rapan rasoki asler.

They stayed until one day this one with a wife went walking with her.
They went to see a friend of

Rakaito puserek aslen Ipiatlak wak iskei.

Wak nen ipi wak nmatu.

Tenen ipiatlak nmatu itok lek wak nen ito su entan.

Go kinrik kaaru kin na, 'Alek nmatu gaag, itae weswes wi.

Me neu nmatu nigneu itap weswes mau.

Tete nrak apestafi itap nrog wou mau. Amurin na kefreg tenen. Anrikin kin me ita pregi mau me nmatu gaag nen itae weswes wi. Ifwel ag kuf murin go katuok nmatu neu me ag p̃atao nmatu gaag.

Go tekaaru nen ipiatlak wak nmatu nen inag, 'O iwi top. Ifwel kin taftigpielkin ilakor wi. Kineu katuok nmatu neu me ag p̃atao nmatu gaag.'

Natam̃ol ne ina, 'O iwi.'

Selwan iplak nmatu ni tekaaru itrapelpel plake pak em̃ae, ipak esum̃ ga.

Me kaaru iplak nmatu ga, nmatu ni wak ne, kaipak esum̃ ga pa.

Malnen ratigpiel inom. Selwan iplak nmatu nen pan ipan pa teesa ga go inrikin kin na, 'E kuipe preg tete nafnag sees takfami me takfo to.'

Wak nen ipan su panpan ipreg saki sernale ni em̃rom.

theirs.

They talked with his friend. He had a pig.

The pig was a female pig.

The man who had a wife looked at the pig which was digging the ground.

And he said to the other, 'I see your wife knows how to work well.

But my wife doesn't work well.

Sometimes I ask her to do this, I tell her but she doesn't do it, but your wife works well.

If you want, I'll give you my woman but you give me your woman.'

And the other who owned the female pig said, 'Oh very good. If you exchange it could be good. I will give you my woman, but you will give me your woman.'

The man said, 'Oh it's good.'

When he was with the other's woman he hurried with the woman and they went a long way to his house.

But the other one took his woman, the woman pig, and they went to his house.

Then the exchange was finished. When he went with his wife, his child said, 'Eh, you've made some food we can eat, and we will stay.'

The pig dug and made a mess of everything inside the house.

Maarik nen itok, ito leka panpan. Go kinrus nrogtesakin me ina, 'E p̃afreg nafnag takfam, ag kutap nrog nalek, p̃ata freg nafnag mau.'
P̃aleperkati kafo watgik.'

Kutae sup̃ ni teem̃ol itap tae nafte kin marik nen inrikin kin mau.
Ipreg namurien ga ipregsaki sernale ni em̃rom go maarik nen kinrogtesaki inrikin kin ina,

'Ifwel kufto preg teflan pan kafo watgik tete nrak.'
Go naliati iskei ito panpan go kinrikin kin na kefreg tenmatun kefreg ptaki em̃rom.
Esan eswei. Kefreg ptaki em̃rom, kefreg tete nafnag rakfami. Imal.

Nlaken wak ikano tae nafsan nen kin akit natam̃ol tuto tli.

Inrogtesaki wak nmatu nen go kiwatgi ikrakpuni.
Go ipi nametp̃ag na natrauswen nen atrausi.
This is text 013.

The man looked for a long time. And he felt bad and said, 'Eh, get some food for us to eat, but you don't listen to me, you don't prepare the food.
You look out, I am going to hit you.'
You know how animals are, it didn't understand what the man said to it.
It did what it wanted to and spoiled everything inside and the man felt bad about it and said,
'If you keep doing this then I am going to hit you sometime.'
And one day he said she should make something, she should make the place ready.
In the kitchen. She should make ready inside the house, she should cook food for them to eat. She doesn't want to.
Because the pig can't know language that we, people, would speak.
He felt bad about the pig and he hit it and killed it.
And that is the end of the story I have told.

Kalsarap Namaf †
Kalsarap on coconuts

A well-known story building on the notion that a coconut looks like a human face. In this story, the coconut tree grows from the father's head after he is buried.

Itili nag tiawi iskei itok kaipiatlak teesa nanwei iskei nega go nmatu nega.

Me nmatu nega imat, me tmen go teesa nen ranru to

Panpan go tiawi nen itok pi tiawi go kisos teesa nega

Tmen inag, 'Ƥamai na kafo pestafik.' Teesa nen ito kaipan lek tmen.

Go tmen kinrikin ki nag, 'Akit tanru tok me selwan kineu afla mat.

Tete naliati ag kin ƥafo tanki wou.

Me ƥafo to mai leperkat emat nigneu.

Ifwel kuf lek tete nkas iftom emat nigneu, ƥatap m̃okus mau. Me ƥaleperkati panpan ketau.'

Selwan ratorik go temen kimat go teesa nen ipo pan ofakin temen.

Me itap metƥakor nafsan nig apap nega mau.

Itok rik go kipak emat temen pan. Me itap lek tete nakas iftom emat temen mau.

Itok panpan mer pak emat nig temen pan, kailek nkas sees nen iftom tok eƥau temen. Go kitok leperkati panpan go nkas nen kitau ipi nuan go ipi naniu.

This is text 014.

He told that there was this ancestor who had a son, he and his wife.

But his wife died, and the father and son were left.

Until this old man became old and he called his son.

His father said, 'Come here, I want to talk to you.' The boy went to see his father.

And his father said to him, 'We are both here but when I may die.

Some day you will bury me.

And you will come to look after my grave.

If you see a tree growing from my grave.

don't pull it out. But look after it until it bears fruit.'

They waited and the father died, and the child went to bury his father.

But he didn't forget his father's story.

He waited a while then he went to his father's grave. But he didn't see any tree growing out of his father's grave.

He stayed until he went back to the grave and saw a small tree growing from his father's head. And he looked after it until that tree bore fruit, and it was a coconut.

Silas Alban
Wak ntwam - the devil pig

The story of a devil pig who wants to eat a man but, after a discussion with the man, realises that he may end up being eaten instead.

Nrak iskei ipiatlak apu go ati iskei ratok.

Once there was a grandfather and grandmother

Rapreg nasum̃ gar, itok em̃ae ki talm̃at.

They made their house a long way from the garden

Ratok panpanpan nrak iskei rana rakfak talm̃at gar.

They were there until one time they wanted to go to their garden one day.

Raslat sernale ni talm̃at gar kaipa.

They carried everything for their garden and they went.

Raslat masmes, raslat kram, raslat naal nen rakfo paai sernale wes, rapa.

They got their knife, their axe, and their basket which they would fill with everything, then they went.

Rapan panpanpanpan, rapato m̃eltig ki talm̃at, go wak p̃ur iskei imai.

They went close to their garden and a big pig came near.

Wak p̃ur nen imai, kaip̃asir.

The big pig came and chased them (the two old people).

Wak nen ip̃asir.

The pig chased them

Rafit fitfitfitfit panpan rana ratkal esum̃.

They ran and ran until they reached the house

Me maarik nen ina itok go kipregptaki sernale.

Then the man began to get everything ready.

Kipregptaki ola, nas, plak timen nega.

He got his spear, bow and arrow ready.

Go isol kram go masmes kailer.

And he got his axe and knife,

Kinrik mtulep kin nag, 'Ag p̃atok me kineu kamer pak talm̃at pan, kafan lel wak p̃ur na kia ip̃as kit.'

Selwan ipanpanpan na itkal talm̃at kius nalof wak.

Kius nalfen panpanpan kipe tok malik, nmalko sa kipe tok mai.

Selwan ipanpanpan isiwer panpanpan ina itkal natik erfale. Go nmalko kipe tok mai go maarik wan kimurin nen kin kefan sil pak erfale, me kefo matur p̃og paakor p̃ulp̃og kefo mer us nalof wak p̃ur nen.

Me selwan kin itok panpanpan. Kitok toto nfal faat nen kin kesil wes. Selwan kitok toto panpan, kito nrog namrun.
Ito nrog namrun, Go, Kitok mrokin na, 'Nafte kin?' Selwan kin itok panpan na itok tkali go kitok takinrog kin pan kinrogo na ipi natam̃ol.
Ale kipestafi, 'E me ag kutfale mai pak nfal faat nen?' Maarik nen itok em̃rom nfal faat nen kipestafi, 'Me ag kutfale mai?' Go maarik nen kiga trausi. Kitli na, 'Komam mtulep ramai pak talm̃at me wak p̃ur iskei ip̃as komam.
Ale raler pak esum̃ pa me ato kia akraksoksok me aparekin mai.

Me kutae wak p̃ur nen ita pi wak

and went back. He told his wife, 'You stay, but I will go back to the garden, to look for the big pig that chased after us.'
When he got to the garden he began following the pig's tracks.
He followed its tracks until it was dark, deep darkness was coming in.
He went on until he got to the edge of a cave.
It was getting darker and the man wanted to go inside the cave, and then he would sleep the night until the morning when he would follow the tracks again.
But as he stayed and stayed.
He felt around the cave that he got into. As he felt around he heard something.
He heard something, 'Oh'. He thought, 'What's that?' He felt around until he touched something and he listened and heard that it was a man.
He said, 'Hey, but how did you get into this cave?' The man who was inside the cave said, 'But you, how did you come here?' And the man spoke, he said, 'We, my wife and me, we went to our garden, but a big pig chased us.
So we returned to the house, and I prepared and I came here for it.
But you know that that big pig

mau.
Me wak p̃ur nen ipi ntwam.
Me malen kin ipan ipan kaiwaalu
namlun kaiof nasok natam̃ol.'

Malnen kin inrik ntwam nen kin
ntwam nen ina, 'A me kineu ana
kafo pam akam kia me akam
rasef.
Me ipi malfanen takto
panpanpan na p̃amatur go kafo
pamik.'
Me ntwam ita nrikin kin mau.
Ntwam ito mrokin teflan na kefo
wat maarik nen p̃og.

Me selwan kin itok panpanpan
ratok panpanpan kitok malik sa
kitok tarup̃ ntan mai
kipe tok pareki maloput p̃og go
ntwam nen itok kainrikin kin na,
'Me ag kuipe fam ko itik?'
Go maarik nen ina, 'Kineu ata ta
fam mau.'
Me selwan kin maarik nen ito us
napu kin ito us nalof wak pan
malen ita pi aliat to, ipan ilek
nlak nafil iskei ito.
Ale itai nafil.
Itok itai nafil panpanpanpan
kaipaai nafil rupak em̃rom naal
ga.
Selwan rapa ntwam ina, 'Rakfan
fam p̃og.'

Itok p̃as maloput p̃og. Selwan
rato na rakfareki namlas pan rato
na rakfarekin nen rakfan fam.
Maarik nen imrokin nen rakfo

is not a pig.
But that big pig is a devil.
But it took off its skin and
changed to wear the skin of a
man.'
When he said this to the devil,
the devil said, 'Ah but I wanted
to eat you, but you ran away.

But now we'll wait until you are
asleep and then I will eat you.'

But the devil didn't tell the
man. The devil was thinking
about how to kill the man at
night.
They stayed until it grew dark,
then the darkness fell on the
ground.
until the middle of the night,
and the devil said, 'Have you
eaten already?'.
And the man said, 'I still have
not eaten.'
When the man followed the
tracks of the pig while it was
still daylight, he saw a navele
tree.
He cut a navele nut.
He cut the navele and he filled
up his basket with them.

When the two went, the devil
said, 'They've gone to eat at
night.'
It was the middle of the night.
When they ran away to the
bush they ran to get food.
The man thought they would go

pan pam ntal ko nawi ko nanr ko tete nafnag nen kin ito mrokin nen rakfo pan pami.

Selwan rapa, ntwam ito kainrikin kin na 'Ƥafag sago?' Rato rakelkelki nlak nait iskei pak elag pa.

Ntwam ina ito islatlu nua nait iskei kaipami.

Itok inrik apu kin na, 'Ƥaslat nafnag me ᵽafam.'

Selwan apu inrogo, apu ina 'E, me kineu akano pam nua nait.'

Malnen ntwam ipam nua nait iskei, apu islatlu nafil iskei em̃rom naal ga kaipami.

Me apu kinrus fam pelpel.

Selwan ranrus torik ntwam kipaoski, 'Ag kuipe pam natam̃ol ipi?' Go maarik nen itok kinrikin kin na, 'Me ag?' Go ntwam kina, 'Kineu apam natam̃ol itol su.'

'Me ag?' Go maarik nen kina, 'Kineu kaipe pam natam̃ol ilatol ki.'

Ntwam ina ito kaimrokin na, 'Kaipe en mrokin pan kaipe tok nrus mroput.'

Ina, 'Me kineu ga ana kafo pam maarik nen tok, me malfanen ga kipe pam natam̃ol ilatol.

Me malfanen kineu apam natam̃ol itol m̃as.

Go malfanen kefo lakor wat kineu kin to.'

Ntwam ien mromromro pankisa. Ipato elag nait iof nra nait mai

and eat taro and yam and banana and some food which he thought they would go and eat. The devil said, 'You climb here?' They climbed up the fig tree.

The devil carried some figs and ate them.

He told his grandfather, 'You take the food and eat.'

When his grandfather heard, he said, 'Hey, but I can't eat Nait figs.'

As the devil ate the fig, grandfather took out the navele from his basket and ate it. Grandfather ate quickly. When they were there for a while the devil asked, 'How many men have you eaten?' And the man said, 'What about you?' The devil said, 'I have eaten three men.'

'And you?' And the man said, 'I have eaten eight men.'

The devil stopped and thought, 'I thought about this and I am a little worried.

He said, 'I want to eat this man here, but now he has eaten eight men.

But I have only eaten three men.

And now he might hit me.'

The devil thought and thought and thought. He was up on the

pak etan nra nait imakot wes.

Nait tree, he fell and he broke
the branches and wore them
like clothes as he fell down.

Selwan iofa nra nait mai tik ntan
teflan namlas imakot kot wes pan
kin imtaki maarik nen ki.

When he broke the fig branch
he fell down and the bush was
broken and he was scared of
this man.

Kisef pan me maarik nen me
kitok mroput.

He ran away and then the man
sat and worried.

Selwan ntwam isef maarik me
isu, ga me namlas imakot kot wes
reki esum̃.

When the devil escaped the
man came down and broke the
bush up to the house.

Go ipi esuan natrauswen kinom
wes.

And that's where the story
finishes.

This is text 019.

Kalsarap Namaf †
Map̃er, the fish that hides (Apu Ntan's story)

A parable about a fish that lives in darkness to hide all its misdeeds.

Natrauswen nig Apu Ntan
maarik Kalpog Ertap.

The story of Apu Ntan, mister
Kalpong of Eratap [he died in
1922].

Itil, nega naik, itili nag, 'Akit
tupitlak naik laap me naik iskei
ipi map̃er naik sees me itap
murin nag kelek ko keur naor
mram kaiures mau.

The fish said, 'We have many
fish, but this fish, the map̃er, is a
small one and it doesn't want to
see light or be in a bright place.

Me selwan iur nmalnawen
itrapelpel sef nag kekus naor
nag ipi faat.

But when he follows the beach
he hurries to escape and hide in
a place among stones.

Or selwan map̃er iur nmalnawen
kuleka itrapelpel sef nam̃len.
Ifarfar top me selwan ipaakorki
faat imer tap malier mau. Go
natrauswen nig Apu Ntan
np̃eten itop.

So, when the fish follows the
beach, you see it hurry to escape
to its place. It moves its tail
quickly, after when it appeared
at the stone, it was not ashamed.
The meaning of Apu Ntan's
story is very good.

Itili nag, 'Nega itaos naik nag rusoso ki map̃er nawesien sa laap nega nag ito wesweskin itok enali.'

He said, 'He is like the fish they call map̃er, his many bad works are out in the open.'

Nalotwen 1: Iwat nap̃au. 2: Iplak namatu p̃tae. 3. Ipnak. 4: Itauso. Me selwan nalotwen imai nawesien sa laap nega rumaui tok enali.

Prayer 1: He kills, 2: He steals other women, 3: He steals, 4: He commits adultery. But when Christianity comes all his bad work is out in the open.

Nmalnawen ipi namrem faat ipi namaliko go nega ipi map̃er.
This is text 020.

The beach is in light, the stone is in darkness and it is the map̃er.

Kalsarap Namaf †
Kalsarap and a story of a whale

A parable that tells a story within a story about a whale that waits until too late to eat and gets stuck on the reef

Selwan tupaakor nametp̃ag ntau, rato tu teesa tete nanromien ruto nig Apu go Ati negar wes nanromien sees pan tuer kin Ertap.

When we got to the end of the year we would give the children a present for them to take to their Apu and Ati, a small present they could give to them at Eratap.

Ntau 1956, komam ramer tuer tete nanromien sees rumer negar wesi pan tuer kin.

The year 1956, we gave them the small present again for them to give to them.

Apu ni Elaknar, go Apu nig Elaau rupan tuer kin kailer mai utu.

Apu from Elaknar and Apu from Elaau they went to give it, then came back.

Me utol Janweri go komam Limas ramer nag rakfan saofir.

After January, Limas and I wanted to go and visited them.

Pastor Kalagis, imurin na komam komau pak Ertap.

Pastor Kalagis wanted us to go to Eratap.

Upan paakor Elaknar go Tata Sailas ito esum̃ nega to. Selwan ilek mam

We went to Elaknar and Tata Sailas was at his house. When he saw us

go ina, 'Webe naik seserik rumai

and he said, 'Webe, small fish

kaifam lu nafnag wi pan.'

Me tafra rupo inrok mai.
Tafra rukfam faat nen ruto me
rukmer ler pan.
Selwan Paster Kalagis inrog
nafsan ni Sailas inrogteesa wes.
Me kineu atap nrogteesa wes
mau.
Atae nag kefo nrik mam ki naρ̃et
nafsan nag itili. Go ipo nrik mam
kin.

Itili nag naliati iskei naik seserik
ruto fam,
me tafra ito wat ur elau.

Me naik seserik runag malfanen
elau imu,
tete rukfan tili nag kemai,
'Tukmaui en nasusu fam.'

Selwan elau kemat go kefo mer
ler
go tafra inag, 'Iwi akam koen
nasusu fam.
Me kineu ka= fo mailum net.'
Naik seserik ruen fam panpan go
elau kimat rukoiler.
Tafra ipato elau to pulki nam̃elen

me isok ipturki ntas panpan
kaiptol. Go kimro kin nag kefo
mer mai fam.
Selwan imai me elau kipe mat
ikon kailer.

Or selwan kulefeki Efat negakit,
ρ̃afo lek nasi tafra iuserek ki

they come and eat all the good
food.
But the whales will come later.
The whales eat stones then they
return.'
When Pastor Kalagis heard
Sailas' talk he felt bad. But I
didn't feel bad.

I already knew that he would
tell us the meaning of this story
that Sailas told us. And then he
told us.
He said one day small fish came
would come out to eat
but the whale was hitting the
water (with its tail).
But the small fish said now the
tide is high
some would go and say he
should come.' 'We will all come
and eat at the turn of the tide.
When the tide was out and he
returned
and the whale said, 'Okay, you
eat on the incoming tide.
I will come later.' The small fish
lay down and ate and the tide
went out and they went back.
The whale stayed at sea
thrashing its tail
and spurted water until it
became hungry. And he
thought he would go and eat.
When he came and the tide had
gone out, he got stuck and went
back.
Okay, when you look around
our Efate, you will see whale

nagis negakit nig Efat.

shit rings the points around Efate.

Go akit tusoso ki nasi tafra. Natrauswen nig tiawi negakit nig teetwei.
This is text 023.

And we call it whale shit. A story from the old people.

Kalsarap Namaf †
Maal go sokfal, the hawk and the owl

The hawk has special magic herbs it uses to fly high, and the owl wanted to drink the same herbs to be as powerful as the hawk. However, a different bird (mlpauas) stole the herbs so it can now fly as high as the hawk.

Naliati iskei maal ruto ruto puserek.

One day the hawks were telling stories.

Maal itli na, 'Neu apitlak nalkis iskei amingi go atae nrir pak elag.'

The hawk said, 'I have a herb, I drink it and I know how to fly up high.'

Go sokfal inrik maal kin nag, 'Ᵽafo neu preg nalkis.' Go ruinpa ki natut. Maal teflan p̃afo mai.

And the owl said to the hawk, 'You go and get the herbs.' And they promised to meet back again. 'That is the time you will come.'

Kafo tuok nalkis p̃afo mingi.' Ruto panpanpan mal natut ipaakor, go maal kiwes nalkis mai.

I will give you herbs, you drink it.' They stayed until the time to meet back again, and the hawk brought the herbs.

Sokfal me kimai, me inrik maal kina, mlapuas kina, 'Ag kin p̃afo na- p̃afo ga wis nalkis tua kin kemingi.'

The owl came, then he told the hawk and mlapuas, 'You will get the herbs for him and give it to him to drink it.'

Me mlapuas ina ito kaimin nalkis ni sokfal, me kini sokfal uut nai.

Then mlapuas drank the owl's herbs, and he poured water for the owl.

Ipan min nalkis, nen kin runi sokfal pregi pan. Imin silua me kiga uut nai pan tua kin imingi.

He went and drank the herbs that they got for the owl. He drank it all, but he poured water

Selwan imin silua go, rupan saisei go rutli, 'Malfanen mal natut kemai go tukfo pregnrogo nrir.' Panpan mal natut imai go ruipan saisei. 'Malfanen tufo nrir.'

Malnen runrir, sokfal kin inrir ur etan. Ito ur etan m̃as, me maal go mlapuas ranrik, panpanpan maal mlapuas itol maal pak elag. Ipi stori m̃it m̃as. Sokfal ikano nrir nlaken itap min nalkis mau, me mlapuas kin imin nalkis ni sokfal. Nlaken sokfal ikano nrir pak elag, nlaken itap min nalkis, ga iur etan me mlapuas itol maal pak elag. Ipi stori m̃it m̃as.
This is text 024.

for the owl and took it to give him to drink. When he drank it all they met together again, and they said, 'Now is the time for us to meet again and we will try to fly.' Until it was the time of the meeting and they met. 'Now we will fly.' Then they flew, the owl flew below. He only flew below, but the hawk and mlapuas, mlapuas beat the hawk up high. It is just a short story. The owl can't fly high because it did not drink the herbs but mlapuas drank the owl's herbs. Because the owl can't fly high, because it didn't drink the herbs, he flies below, but mlapuas beats the hawk up high. It is just a short story.

Iokopeth
The story of Katapel

A well-known story about Katapel who would get seafood by magically turning a stone by the seashore. Langtatalof sees her and tries to copy what she does, only to cause a flood that ends up killing Katapel and creating places around Erakor village.

Ipiatlak malnen kin tiawi ni Erakor teetwei ruto Ep̃uf to me ipiatlak naot gar ipi nagien Langtatalof, me ipiatlak nmatu inru, iskei nagien Katapel. Naliati ilaap maarik naot ito

At that time the old people stayed at Ep̃uf, and they had a chief whose name was Langtatalof, he had two wives, one was Katapel. On many days the chief called

preg nsaiseiwen.

Preg nsaiseiwen nrikirkin rukfo
til usus natowen gar go teflan
kin ruto preg sernale.

Me mal nsaiseiwen go inrik
nmatu laap kin na, rukfo preg
nafnag wesi pak efare.

Reki nen kin rukfo tuaal me
rukfo fam.

Me ser naliati nen kin mtulep
Katapel go tekaaru kefreg
nafnag kefo preg nafnag me
tekatpi kefo pi teni elau ntas.

Kepiatlak kai, go kefo piatlak
wit, go kefo piatlak naik, go kefo
piatlak tefserser ilaap nen ito
slati elau, ntas.

Me nmatu laap p̃afo pam̃ori na
tekatpi gar ipi teni euut.

Ser naliati nen rukfreg
nsaiseiwen, mtulep Katapel
ipreg nafnag. 'P̃afo pam̃ori nag.'

Tekatpi ipi teni elau ntas, pregi
pregi pan me maarik naot ito
leka pan me ina, 'Mtulep Katapel
ga ito pam̃or tekatpi elau itfale?'

Ser p̃ulp̃og Katapel isu mai pak
etan, ipiatlak nai sees iskei.

Nen kin ito mai pai kai ni elau
wes.

Pregi pan pan me maarik naot
ina, imurin na ketae itfale, teflan
ito mai slat tekatpi ni elau.

Trau p̃ulp̃og nen kin kefo
pam̃ori teflan mtulep Katapel ito
mai pak elau wis tekatpi elau.

Me selwan imai p̃ulmatlen imai,
kuskor mtulep Katapel.

Malnen mtulep Katapel imai

meetings.

Have meetings to tell them, to
talk about their life and how to
do things.

After the meeting he said to all
the women, they should make
food and take it to the nakamal.
They should stay all day and
they should eat.

Then, every day Katapel and the
other wife made food, but the
meat was from the sea.

There was shellfish, and
octopus, and fish, and many
other things from the sea.

But the women, you'll see they
find the meat along the shore.
Every day they had a meeting,
Katapel got the food. You'll find
out about it now.

The meat was from the sea, but
the chief watched but he said,
'How does Katapel find meat
from the sea?' Each morning,
Katapel went down to a small
water hole.

This one from which she filled
up with cockles from the sea.
She kept on doing this until the
chief wanted to know how she
got the meat from the sea.

This morning he went to find
how Katapel came from the sea
with meat.

After he came early, he came
and hid from Katapel.

Katapel came near, to her small

itermau pak eluk sees ga nen,
malnen kin ipa kefo mailum nre
faat nen itkos.

Ipai kai ni elau islati em̃rom pan
na inom mailum pus faat. Me
maarik Langtatalof ina ipam̃ori
selwan mtulep Katapel ina iler
pa go maarik Langtatalof ina
kefo pregnrogo taos mtulep
Katapel teflan ito mai slat kai.
Ina ipak eluk sees, nen inre faat.
Ipam̃ori na ipiatlak kai, go
tefserser laap ni ntas.

Islati pan na inom, nen kin
kemer mailum pus faat keler me
itermau tik ki faat nen iler pan.

Go eluk sees ina ito nai itrau
pespur, ipur pur pur pan pan go
imalig.

Imalig trau ser.

Iser ser me mtulep Katapel ito
elag ntaf nrogo ki nai iser ifit
mai tu leg ki Ewenesu. Isel
nawen nen kin ketfag kor nai
me, nai ikerkrai top, itrau ser lu
ki nawen go imer fit mai to leg
ki narfat.

Imer tfagkro itfagkro pan pan
inom nai imai imer serlu faat
ipa.

Mtulep imer fit ifit mai ito
Efatposfiu itfagkro panpanpan
naor sees ito selwan kin nai
imai.

Iser top ina imai kai serlu
mtulep.

well, as she went, she slowly
turned the stone that was there.

She filled up with cockles until it
was finished, slowly put the
stone back. Then Langtatalof
wanted to find it when Katapel
went back and Langtatalof
wanted to try like Katapel to get
cockles.

He went to the well and turn the
stone. He found shellfish and
other things from the sea.

He took it until he was finished,
he put the stone back slowly but
the stone wasn't put back
properly.

And the small well just started
to get big, until it overflowed.

It overflowed and started to run.
It ran and ran, but Katapel was
up on the hill and heard the
water run right to Ewenesu. She
got sand and built a wall against
the water but the water was too
strong, it flowed over it and the
sand, and it flowed down to the
bridge.

She went to build a wall until it
was finished, the water came
near and flowed over the rocks,
and kept going.

Katapel ran until she got to
Efatposfiu she built a small place
was left when the water came.

It flowed quickly, it wanted to
keep coming, and it flowed over

Iserlua panpanpan ipato elau, kin go nao ipo mer pak euut slati mai pak euut, me kipe mat. Kimat go nao ina ito mer slati ler mai slati ler mai kaitasak nagis ni Elakatapel, go rutua nagi nen Elakatapel nlaken mtulep nen ipi Katapel.

Go iwelkin kufmer us lakun p̃afo pam̃ori na Ewenesu ipiatlak nawen itop nlaken kin ipregnrogo nen ketfagkor nai me nai islatlua.

Kumai pak brij, ipiatlak naur sees go faat ilaap nlaken kin ina ketfagkro me nai imer slatlua ipa.

Kumai pak Efatposfiu kupam̃ori na ipiatlak naor sees imaag nlaken kin. Ipregnrogo na ketfagkro me nai imai kerkrai, go islatlua plak faat. Mees p̃apam̃ori na ipiatlak pasis isees m̃as, go natrauswen ni lakun itefla.

Ipi tesees nen kin atae.
This is text 029

It flowed on until it got to the sea, and a wave came back to shore but she was dead. She died and the wave carried her back and threw her ashore at Elakatapel, and they gave that point the name Elakatapel because of the woman called Katapel. And that's why if you go along the lagoon you will find that Ewenesu has lots of sand because she tried to build a wall to block the water but the water carried her away. You come to the bridge, it's a small place with lots of rocks because she wanted to build it, but the water came and took it away. You go to Efatposfiu, you see that there is a small open place because of it. She tried to build a dam but the water was too strong, and it carried her away with the stones. Today you see the passage there is only small, and that's how the story of the lagoon goes. It is the little that I know.

Frank Alfos †
Taligter and Tagiter
The seaslug (Tagiter) cries out a warning when someone is going to

---

die, but Taligter is a fish that chases you.

Tagiter, ga iwelkia ipi namrun nen kin itag nen kin itag tunrogo itag ter naat, itag ter tete naat.

Tagiter (seaslug) is something that cries out for us, when it cries you know it cries out a warning that someone will die.

Malran kunrog tagiter itag p̃og, itag ter tete naat.
Tete nat kefo tm̃alu, kefo mat.
Me taos tutli plak taligter.
Taligter ga ga ipi naik.
Ga ipi naik, me malran kin akit tulek taligter.
Tulek taligter, go iwelkia tupi teesa me tulek taligter, tukfo mtaki, nlaken kin tumroki tagiter.
Nlaken tagiter, ga welkia ipi namrun p̃al, me taligter, ga ipi naik.
Ga ga ipi naik.
Ipi nametrau nig mra iskei.
Me ntalgen san igot, ga ipitlak ntalgen.
Go taos sup̃ ni taligter, ga me ito kop natam̃ol, kukano meski.

When you hear it cry at night, it is crying for a man.
Someone will leave, will die.
But as for Taligter.
Taligter is a fish.
It is a fish, when we see Taligter,
When we were children and we see Taligter we are scared because we think it is Tagiter.
Because Tagiter is a devil, it is nothing, but Taligter is a fish.

He is a fish.
He is the same family as eels.
Its ears are black, it has ears.

The way with Taligter, it follows people, you can't play with Taligter.

Malran kumeski, ifwel kin kuf mroki na p̃aska ki ola kefo kop ag.

When you play with it, if you think you will spear it, it will chase you.

Kefo kop ag, kefo kop ag.
Itae kop ag em̃ae.
Kutae sef teflan, sef teflan me, itae kop teflan kin itae nlaken kefo taos nalo gaag, ga ipi naik.
This is text 031.

And chase you and chase you.
It can chase you a long way.
You can run away, but it will follow you, it will follow your dust trail, but it is a fish.

Kalsarap Namaf
A story of Rentapau and Erromango

Rentapau is a major powerful place on Efate, with links across to Erromango. It is a tabu place that was built on by a resort in the late 1990s.

Kafo gaag traus naor sees a?	I'll tell you about a small place eh?
Ermag. Ag kutae Erontp̃au?	Erromango. Do you know Rentapau?
Erontp̃au ipiatlak natiel iskei itok. Aleka ki namtak.	Rentapau has a vine there. I have seen it with my own eyes.
Natiel wan rop mifala i talem natiel	A vine ([Bislama] a vine that we call 'natiel').
Me natiel nen ito, esan kin na fei kia, Thanh	This vine is there, at the place where, who now, Thanh,
Kutae ana katraus natiel nen kin, me	You know, I want to talk about this vine, but
kafo psa ki etog, me akam kin kofo ona, konrog soksoki teplan ato traus me go kofo welu wou wes.	I will talk about a foreign place, and you will listen carefully as I talk, and you will help me with it.
Rupaoski, rupaoski Ermag, Ermag ituer sernale.	They ask Erromango, Erromango will give them everything.
Kumur tenamrun Ermag kefo.	If you want something, Erromango will.
Ipiatlak natiel iskei ito san kin aa,	There is a vine at the place which,
Thanh ipreg nasum̃ wes mees ne.	Thanh has made his hotel there today [Blue water resort].
Ipiatlak natiel iskei, natiel p̃ur aleka ki namtak.	There is a vine, a big vine, I've seen it with my own eyes.
Ito pau pag, e-, ito pau elag nana, natog.	It climbs up the mangrove.
Me natiel ne hem i no gat stampa blong hem.	And this vine (Bislama) hasn't got a trunk.
Be yu ko yu luk we hem i stap antap long, long ol natogtog.	You go and look at it where it climbs up the mangroves.
(Iokopeth) hem i wan rop.	(Iokopeth) It is a vine.

(KN) Long ples ia. Yu luk we i
defren, yu luk we yu no save
faenem stampa blong hem.
Kutap lek na nlaken mau.
Ipi nmaagwen, me ipiatlak afsak
iskei itok, naik, afsak. Rusoso ki
afsak.
Ito na eluk sees nen kin Thanh
ipo preg ptaki. Naik rupo tu wes
to.

Itototo panpanpan malnen
rustat klinki Erontp̃au.
Go namrun nen rusef ler pan
pak Ermag pa.
Ruto Ermag panpan tuk mees
ne.
Natiel ipuel. Afsak ipuel.

Tep̃ur knen nen amurin kanriki
ki kin mees ne, natam̃ol kin ruto
pan puel Erontp̃au.
Ipiatlak natlaken, ito watgir.

Akit tuf laap pa, akit iskei kefo
puel.
Go Erontp̃au ipiatlak nlaken.

Nam̃er ni Ermag rutae, teflan
sernale gar ruto mai pak,
Erakor.
Erontp̃au. Erontp̃au itp̃au ser
naor naor ilfeki Efat,

Ipi naor nen kin itap top.
This is text 032.

(KN) At this place. It is different,
you can't find its trunk.

You don't see its trunk.
It is unbelievable, but there was
a turtle there, fish, a turtle. They
call it a turtle.
It lived in the small pool which
Thanh would make (into the
Blue Hole resort). Fish would be
in it.
It stayed and stayed until they
started to clean Rentapau.
And these things ran away back
to Erromango.
They are at Erromango until
today.
The vine has gone. The turtle has
gone.
The most important of this that I
want to tell you about today,
people go missing at Rentapau.
There is the owner of it who
hurts them.
If many of us go there, one will
go missing.
And Rentapau has the trunk (of
the vine).
Erromangans know, this is how
all their things come to Erakor

[corrected to] Rentapau.
Rentapau is the head place of all
places around Efate.
It is the most taboo place.

Harris Takau
Ririel and Ririal

Ririal is a story about two brothers who go to gather fruit. Ririel climbs a nakavika (Syzygium malaccense) tree and Ririal catches the fruit. Ririel falls and dies. Ririal sings a song asking first a pig, then a horse then a flying fox to take a message back to this parents. The first two ignore the request, but the flying fox takes the message and the parents come to take their son and bury him.

Ipiatlak nmatu iskei, nmatu tiawi iskei ipiatlak teesa inru rana rato panpan.

There was this old woman, she had two children.

Go, teesa nra nen nagier kaaru nen ipi Ririel go kaaru ipi Ririal.

And these two children, one was called Ririel and the other was called Ririal.

Go rato panpan go teesa nen rana rakfan lel gkafik, mal ni gkafik.

And they stayed until the children wanted to look for nakavika fruit (Syzygium malaccense), it was the nakavika season.

Gkafik imam, rana rapa.

The nakavika were ripe, they wanted to go.

Ale, kaaru ina,

One said,

Ririel inrik Ririal kina, 'Ag p̃afei. Ag p̃afag.'

Ririel said to Ririal, 'You go first. You climb!'

Go Ririal imer nrik Ririel kina, 'Tik, ag p̃afag.'

And Ririal said back to Ririel, 'No, you climb!'

Rana rapregi pan pan go Ririel kin ipo pag.

They kept on until Ririel climbed the tree.

Ipagki gkafik pak elag, me Ririal ito etan.

He climbed up the nakavika but Ririal stayed down below.

Ririel ipanpan pagki gkafik pan na ilel gkafik.

Ririel climbed the nakavika until he saw the fruit.

Ina israf trau m̃el, itarp̃ek.

He missed it and fell, he fell.

Itarp̃ek mai pak etan.

He fell back down to the ground.

Ina itarp̃ek mai pak etan trau

He fell down to the ground quite

mat.
Ale Ririal ina isatsok, ina islati kaipe to tag.
Ito tagsi panpan go
wak iskei imai, wak ina imai go
Ririel inrik Ririal, e, Inrik wak ki na, 'Ᵽafa neu ona.
Ᵽafa neu nrik mama neu go papa neu ki na,
Ririel ina itarᵽek me imat.'
Ale ga ipo laga ipi nalag

Wak e ᵽaginau rorogo ki tete go mame.
Ririel o kitiroa matetoko.
Ririal eselatia toko tagisi ae.
Ririelo ririelo rielo. i.
Ale ina- wak ina ipak me ita ler mau.
Itapa nrik, itapa nrik mama ga go papa kin mau,
Ale ina ito panpan go, hos imai hos ina imai ale imer nrik hos ki na,
hos kefan nrik papa ga go mama ki, ale itli ipi nalag ina:

Hos e ᵽaginau rorogo ki tete go mame.
Ririel o kitiroa mate toko.
Ririal Eselatia toko tagisi ae
Ririelo Ririelo Rielo i.
Ale, hos ina ipa ita pan nrik tmen go raiten kin mau. Me ina ipan kaipe pa.

Ale islati to pan pan go mantu imai,
Mantu ina imai go imer nrik

dead.
So Ririal took him, he carried him and he cried.
He cried for him until
a pig came by, the pig came and Ririel said to Ririal, no, he said to the pig, 'You do it for me.
You go and tell my mother and father this for me,
'Ririel fell and he died.'
Then he began to sing it as a song,
Wak e ᵽaginau rorogo ki tete go mame.
Ririel o kitiroa matetoko.
Ririal eselatia toko tagisi ae.
Ririelo ririelo rielo. i.
So the pig was going, but he didn't go back.
He didn't go and tell the mother and father about it.
Then a horse came by so he told the horse,

the horse should go and tell his mother and father about it, and he sang this song.
Hos e ᵽaginau rorogo ki tete go mame.
Ririel o kitiroa mate toko
Ririal Eselatia toko tagisi ae
Ririelo Ririelo Rielo i.
So the horse went but didn't go and tell his father and mother about it. He went and didn't come back.
He was there holding (his brother) and the flying fox came.
The flying fox came and he said

mantu ki:
Mantue p̃aginau rogorogo ki tete go mame.
Ririel o kitiroa mate toko.
Ririal eselatia toko tagisa e.
Ririelo ririelo rielo. i.
Ale Mantu ina ipan pan ki, po nrik tmen go raiten ki. Ale, tmen go raiten rana rato me rapo mai,
mai na ruslati kin po pan tan ki.

Go natrauswen nen inom esa.
This is text 034.

to the flying fox.
Mantue p̃aginau rogorogo ki tete go mame.
Ririel o kitiroa mate toko.
Ririal eselatia toko tagisa e.
Ririelo ririelo rielo. i.
Then the flying fox went and told his (Ririel's) father and mother about it. Then his father and mother came,
came to get him and to bury him.
And this story is finished here.

Harris Takau
The story of the group of children

A group of children get trade goods from a ship, and one buys a mouth organ. He plays it and a devil who hears it steals the moth organ. The children dig up the banyan tree the devil is hiding in, but the imported tools don't work. A cabbage digging stick is used and it topples the banyan.

Natrauswen ne rusosoki naferkal.
Naferkal ralim iskei.

Naferkal ga taos ipi teesa, teesa laap rutu naor iskei kin rusosor kir Naferkal.
Naferkal ralim iskei.
Naferkal ralim iskei ruto pan pan go ruto preg talm̃at rulao sernale, rulao nafnag, altuk, ntal, nawi.

Ale runa ruto panpan go rupam̃or, rule pak elau go rupam̃or raru p̃ur iskei imai.
Raru p̃ur iskei imai. Ina imai na

This story is called 'The group of children.' A group of ten kids.
Naferkal is a group of children who are at one place and they call them Naferkal.
Naferkal, ten.
This group of ten were there and then they made a garden, they planted everything, cabbage, taro, yam.
They were there and they looked to the sea and saw a big boat coming.
A big boat came. It came and

itorwak. Ale rusu pak elau.

Runa rusu pak elau, go runa rupakot, rupakot, tete rupakot kram tete rupakot masmes, tete rupakot safel, pik sernale nig talm̃at.

Pan pan me teesa sees, tenen ipi takrik ga ipaakot ga nalag nen ruto si, mouth organ, ga ipaaktofi.

Ale malen rupan na rukfreg talm̃at go tep̃afp̃of rupreg talm̃at rulao sernale. Me teses ne ga ito me ito si nalag.

Ito si nalag ga ne, panpan me ipiatlak nlak npak p̃ur iskei me ito. Nlak npak ipiatlak ntwam iskei ito em̃rom nlak npak.

Teesa sees nen ina ito si nalag, go ntwam nen inrog wi ki nalag. Ina inrog wi ki nalag go ito mai, ito nrus mai pak m̃eltig, panpanpan imai na ilek teesa sees ne go ina, 'Atrau nrog wi nalag gaag. P̃amer pregnrogo si.' Me teesa sees imer si nalag. Ntwam inrog wi ki. Ale ina,

'P̃apregnrogo tao kapregnrogo gaag si.' Ntwam ina isat nalag na isi, trau sati sef. Isati sef pan ale isil npak.

Ale teesa sees nen ito kai. Ikai pan pan go tep̃afp̃of runa ruto rumai paoski na, 'Iku kin kuto kai?' Go,

anchored. Ok, they went down to the sea.

They went down to the sea, and they bought, some bought axes and some bought knives, some bought shovels and picks, things for the garden.

Then a small child, the last child bought a mouth organ for them to blow, a mouth organ, he bought it.

Then they went to work in the garden, and the big ones made the garden, and planted things. But the small one stayed and played his mouth organ.

He blew on the mouth organ, and there was a big banyan tree there. There was a devil living in the trunk of the banyan. The child kept on playing a song, and the devil heard it and liked it. He liked the song and he came out closer and then he came to look at the child and he said, 'I feel good hearing your song. Try and blow it again.' And the small child kept blowing a tune. The devil liked hearing it. Then he said, 'Give it to me so I can try your mouth organ.' The devil took it to blow it, but he ran away. He took it and ran inside the banyan.

Then the small child cried. He cried until the adults came and asked him, 'Why are you crying?' And,

'Ntwam ito nlak npak ina imai isat nalag neu me kipe sef pa.'

Ale teesa nen runa ruto rupan stat, runa rukwat ntwam, me ntwam isil to npak, ale rutraf rutraf nako npak.
Tete rutai ki kram, tete rukli ki pik, pan pan npak nen ikano tarp̃ek.
Runa rutraf sees kai mer lag runa, 'Napag imarie rie, napag imarie napag imarie rie, napag inawe,

nawe, nawe nau tagisi.'
Ale inom go ruimer ruimer pregnrogo ruimer nri npak ne.
Ruimer nri npak me rumer nri npak, me npak ikano tarp̃ek, ale ruimer lag:
'Napag imarie rie, napag imarie napag imarie rie, napag inawe, nawe, nawe nau tagisi.'
Me npak ikano tarp̃ek ale runa ruto. Ale teesa sespal ne ina ito kin ipo pan tai kal iskei, kal altuk.

Ale itai kal altuk iskei. teesa p̃afp̃of runa me kal go ina imailumlum.
Komam upregnrogo ki kal p̃afp̃of me ukano nri npak. Me ag kusat kal nen ipi altuk imailumlum go kupo na p̃anri npak ki. Me ina, 'Kapregnrogo.' Ale rupo ga lag:

'Napag imarie rie, napag imarie rie, napag inawe, nawe, nawe nau

'The devil in the banyan came and took my mouth organ, and ran away.'
So all the children went to hit the devil, but the devil was inside the banyan, so they dug its roots.
Some cut it with axes, some dug with picks, on and on but it wouldn't fall down.
They dug more and then sang, [song] Napag imarie rie, napag imarie napag imarie rie, napag inawe,

nawe, nawe nau tagisi.
Finished, and they tried again to dig out this banyan. They dug it again and again, but it wouldn't fall down, so they sang again:
[song] Napag imarie rie, napag imarie napag imarie rie, napag inawe, nawe, nawe nau tagisi.
But the banyan would not fall over. The small boy decided to go and cut a digging stick, made of cabbage plant.
So he cut the cabbage digging stick. The big children said, 'But this digging stick is soft.'
We tried with a big digging stick, but we couldn't dig the banyan. You brought a digging stick made of cabbage tree, it is too weak and you will try to dig the banyan with it. And he said, 'I'll try.' And they sang for him:
[song] Napag imarie rie, napag imarie rie, napag inawe, nawe,

tagisi.'
Ale ina ilaoki kal altuk ga, ina inri go npak itarp̃ek.

Npak ina itarp̃ek. Ale, ntwam itaf ale rupuetsok ntwam ale rutaikot nanwen.
Natrauswen inom esa.
This is text 035.

nawe nau tagisi.
So he dug with the cabbage digging stick, he dug, and the banyan fell over.
The banyan fell over. Then the devil left and they held him and they cut his throat.
The story finishes here.

Harris Takau
Menal go katom, the barracuda and the hermit crab

The story of a race between the barracuda and the clever hermit crab.

Natrauswen ne ipi natrauswen ni, menal. Menal go katom. Menal ga ipi naik go katom, rato panpan go

This story is about the barracuda and the hermit crab. Barracuda is a fish, and the hermit crab, they were there and

menal inrik, menal inrik katom ki na,
'Takfo res.' Menal inrik katom ki na, 'Rakfo res.' Ale, katom ina, 'Iwi.'
Ale rato panpan. Ratil sef naliati kin rakfo stat, rares.

barracuda said, barracuda said to the hermit crab,
'We'll have a race.' Barracuda said to hermit crab, 'We'll race.' And the hermit crab said, 'Ok.'
So they stayed and stayed. They said which day they would start the race.

Me katom itae na ga ikano kraf pelpel, taos menal, menal itae spit.

But the hermit crab knows that he can't crawl fast like barracuda. Barracuda knows how to go fast.

Itae sef pelpel me katom ikano.
Naliati nen rakfo res wes me katom ipei usereki ser nagis.

He can run away quickly, but the hermit crab can't. That day they would race, but the hermit crab first went around every point.

Ipestaf aslen nen kin ruur ser nagis, ipestafir na naliati tefla,

He told his friends who were at each point, he said that day,

'Kofo, kofo redi me konrogo na menal kefios elau, go akam kofios euut.'

Naliati nen rana rastat, rares wes go, menal inrik katom ki na,

'Takstat nagis ne, takres panpan na tafak nagis kaaru. Ᵽanrogo kana, 'Wananatajo.'

Go kutae na atkal nagis nen kia, go ag if wel kin atkal nagis nen kin kineu atkos go ana 'Watetjo'.'
Ale menal, rastat, menal ina go ipan na itkal nagis pei. Ina, 'Wananatajo'.
Go katom ina 'Watetjo'

Rapan panpan ramer kop nagis kaaru panpan rapak nagis kaaru, go katom kin ipes kina, 'Wananatajo'. Menal ina, 'Watetjo.'
Panpan na rapak nagis, me katom nen kin mai ina, 'Katom nen ga ipi katom ᵽtae.'
Nlaken katom ᵽtae kin ito nagis kaaru, katom ᵽtae kin ito nagis katol.

Me menal ga iskei m̃as. Menal isef panpanpan na ipak nagis kaafat. Katom ina, 'Wananatajo.'

Go menal ina, 'Watetjo.' Me

'You get ready and when you hear barracuda call out from the water, you call out from the shore.'
The day that they said they would start, that they would race, and barracuda said to the hermit crab,
'We'll start at this point, then we'll race to the next point.'You'll hear me say, 'Wananatajo.'
And you will know that I have got to that point. And if you get to the point where I am you say, 'Watetjo'.
Then barracuda, they started, and he got to the point first. He said, 'Wananatajo.'
And the hermit crab said, 'Watetjo'
They went until they got to the next point and the hermit crab said,
'Wananatajo.' Barracuda said, 'Watetjo'
Until they got to the point, then the hermit crab who came said, 'This hermit crab, he is a different hermit crab.' Because there was a different hermit crab at the second point, and a different hermit crab was at the third point.
But there was only one barracuda. Barracuda ran until he got to the fourth point.The hermit crab said, 'Wananatajo.' And barracuda said, 'Watetjo.'

nmar menal kipe to m̃it. Ipan na ipak nagis iskei go katom ina, 'Wananatajo.' Go

nmar menal kipe m̃it, ina, 'Watetjo.' Pan na ipak nagis iskei, go katom ina, 'Wananatajo.'
Go menal ina, 'Watetjo'. Rapreg panpan nmaron im̃it. Nmaron im̃it, katom itae na menal nmaron kipe m̃it.

Raen pan, ipak nagis iskei go ina, 'Wananatajo'. Go menal ina, 'Watetjo'. Nmaron kipe m̃it. Panpanpan pak nagis mlaap

katom ina, 'Wananatajo'. Go menal ina, 'Watetjo'. Panpan nagis mlaap.

Go katom ina, 'Wananatajo'. Go menal ina, 'Watetjo'.

Go katom itae na menal, nmaron kipe m̃it. Ale ipak nagis mlaap wi go katom ina, 'Wananatajo'. Go

menal ina, menal ina ito trau, kipe mat, kipe ta pes mau. Nmaron im̃it go kipe mat. Go katom itae na menal imat go katom iwin.

Kin iwin na, nareswen, ale katom ipreg nafsan, ipreg nafsan ur ser nagis, nen kin katom

But barracuda's breathing was getting short. He went until he got to this point and the hermit crab said, 'Wananatajo.' But
But barracuda's breathing was short and he said 'Watetjo.'
Until he got to this point and the hermit crab said, 'Wananatajo.'
And barracuda said, 'Watetjo.'
They went until his breathing was short. His breathing was short, the hermit crab knew that barracuda was short of breath.
They went on, he went to this point and said, 'Wananatajo.'
And barracuda said, 'Watetjo.'
His breath was short. Until the last point and
the hermit crab said, 'Wananatajo.' And barracuda said, 'Watetjo.' Until the last point.
And the hermit crab said, 'Wananatajo.' And barracuda said, 'Watetjo.'
And the hermit crab knew that barracuda's breathing was short.
And he got to the last point alright and hermit crab said, 'Wananatajo.'
And barracuda was nearly dead, he couldn't speak at all. His breathing was getting short then he died. And hermit crab knew that barracuda was dead and hermit crab won.
Hermit crab won the race, then hermit crab sent word to every point to get all the hermit crabs

runomser mai pak naor iskei,
runa rusu pak elau ki menal
imat me itaasak to natik ntas.
Ale katom ru-, runa rupak natik
menal ki, kin go rupo preg lafet
kin go rupo pam silu menal.
Natrauswen nen inom esa.
This is text 036.

to one place to go down to the
water where barracuda died at
the edge of the water.
Then the hermit crabs went up
to barracuda and had a party
and ate barracuda all up. The
story finishes here.

Kali Kalopog †
ᴍaatleplep

ᴍaatleplep is the name of the snake who split the two small islands
of Kap̃um lep and Kap̃um rik..

Ipiatlak m̃aat iskei kin ga ipo-.
Iwelkia ipato elag Ep̃uf sanpe
kin ipo mai. Imai me imai kin
ipato teflan ga kin ifiskotkot
naur seserik nen kin rumai pan
pan pan tkal Ertap sanie.
Go naur inru kin ratu sanie,
rusos, rusos kaaru ki Kap̃um lep
ko kaaru ipi Kap̃um rik.
Go naur nra nen, me m̃aat ina
ifisktofir.
Ipiatlak nagis ni Eter ga ipi nagis
pram, me m̃aat nen kin ifisktofi.

There is this snake and it would-.
It was up at Pufa [behind
Montmartre] and it came. It
came
the small islands that come right
up to Eratap there.
And the two islands there, one
which they call Kap̃um lep and
the other is Kap̃um rik.
And these two islands, this snake
wanted to split them.
There is the point at Eter, it is a
long point, and this snake split
it.

Ipi nlaken kipe m̃it. Me nagis ni
Etmat m̃as kin ipram, nagis ni
Etmat kin akit tutkos to.

That's why it is short now. But
the point at Etmat is a long one,
the point at Etmat which is
where we are now.

Nagis ni Etmat. Me nagis ni
Emut kin ito, go nagis ni Eter
wan kin me iptau.
Nagis ni Emut nen kin ileg ki
naur sees nra ne. Nlaken kin
nakon, nakon wan ki kin nagis

Etmat point. But the point at
Emut and the point at Eter are
there.
The point at Emut which is in
line with the two islands there.
Because its face, its face, that is

South Efate Stories

ni Emut ne.
Me nakon kin. ᴍaatleplep ina nagi ᵐaat nen kin rusoso ki ᴍaatleplep. Ga kin ifisktofi kin rapi naur sees inru pato.
Rusoso ki Kaᵖum rik go Kaᵖum lep. Gawankia.
Nanre ni Erakor kin ato tli, me akano til nanre ni Ertap nlaken ga me ipi ntan ni naᵐer ni Ertap. Ore.
This is text 044.

this point at Emut.
Its face there. ᴍaatleplep is the name of the snake. He's the one who split them into two small islands there.
They call them Kaᵖum rik and Kaᵖum lep. That's it.
The Erakor side I can talk about. But I can't talk about the Eratap side because it belongs to people from Erarap.Eratap. OK.

Kalsarap Namaf †
Faat inru, the two stones at Ekasufat Rik

How the two stones at Ekasufat Rik came to be where they are, after having an argument about which one should move
down the hill.

Ipiatlak faat inru
Ekasufat rik. Rato puserek, faat nra nen rato puserek panpan go rakaitmer nrikirki na ramur rakpato elau.
Go faat sees inrik faat ᵖur kina, 'Ag ᵖafei.
Me kineu kafo inrok.'
Go raipreg ipi raitmer psaplilkir

panpan go faat ᵖur inrik faat, faat sees kina,
'Ag ᵖafei, ᵖafei pan pato etan, me neu kafo neetnpasilkik me takfo pan pato namos,
nen nataᵐol ruto palus, akit tato maloput'.
Malen rapreg kipi nafsaplilwen.
Faat sees inrik faat ᵖur kina, 'ᴇ,

There are two stones
at Ekasufat rik. They talked to each other, these rocks,
and they said to each other that they wanted to be at the sea.
And the small stone said to the big stone, 'You go first.
I will come behind.'
And they ended up arguing with each other
until the the big rock said to the small one,
'You go first down there, I will meet you, we will go in the ocean,
that people paddle out to, we will be in the middle.
Now they had an argument.
The small rock told the big

ag p̃afei me kineu kafo inrok.'

Go faat p̃ur inrikin kina, 'Ag ag kusees, me kineu atop.

Malen kin ag p̃afei pa, neu kafei, kainrok na kanpasilkik go takfo pa.'

Rapreg ipi nafsaplilwen. Panpan go faat sees ina, 'Orait, kineu kafo pei.

Go faat sees ito elag, imlil mai to etan.

Faat p̃ur ina imai ikano npasilki.

Go mees nen rato euut to to pan tuk mees.

Ipi natrauswen sees m̃as.
This is text 046.

---

rock, 'You go first and I will follow.'

And the big rock said, 'You are small, but I am big.

When you go first, I'll follow and I'll meet you and we will go.'

They kept arguing. Until the small rock said, 'Alright, I will go first.'

And the small stone stayed up high, it rolled down.

The big rock wanted to come, it couldn't meet him.

And they are still there until today.

It is only a short story.

John Maklen
Mantu the flying fox and Erromango

A story about a flying fox from Efate that laid eggs on Erromango and then returned to Ewor on Efate.

Natrauswen ni mantu, kafo traus mantu nen kin ito.

Ore mantu nen ito Erontp̃au teetwei ga ito pan, ito pak Ermag.

Ito esan to, pan pan imur kefak Ermag, kemer pak Ermag pa, go naliati iskei ipan.

Go kipiatlak na, atol, ipiatlak atol me,

ga, mantu nen, imai, ipsolki atol,

atol inru ipsolki atol inru.

The story of the flying fox, I will tell about the flying fox that is there.

Yes the flying fox that was at Rentapau long ago, it went to Erromango.

It was there until it wanted to go to Erromango, to go back to Erromango, and one day it went. And it had this egg, but

that flying fox, it came, it layed an egg,

two eggs, it layed two eggs.

Go gar atol nra nen rapato Ermag.

Go naṁer ni Ermag runa rukwatgi. Runa rukwatgi.

Go kitli na, 'Kafo gamus tao atol keto rakto san tok. Akam kofo teleekor atol, me kineu kafo mer ler pak naur ni Efat.'

Go mees imai to Efat.

Go mantu nen ito esan rusoso ki Ewor, ito mees ne.

This is text 048.

And those two eggs stayed at Erromango.

And people from Erromango wanted to hit him.

And he said, 'I will leave you the eggs. You will look after them and I will return to Efate.'

And today he came to Efate.

And that flying fox is still at the place they call Ewor today.

John Maklen
Asaraf

Asaraf was a giant who could walk from Efate to Erromango and who pushed Erromango away from Efate.

Asaraf ga ipi nataṁol ni teetwei

Go komam unrogo kin apu me ati nigmam ruto nigmam trausi na ipi nataṁol nen ipram, ipram kotkot.

Malnen ina kefak, itu sa imur na kefak Ermag.

Malnen isiwer ur ntas kin ipak Ermag, go ntas ipaṁor naputwen.

Esan mana ruta lom mau.

Me ina ipak Ermag pan kaimer ler mai go naliati iskei welkia Ermag, ipi, kutae to Efat go kuto lek Ermag.

Asaraf, he is a man from long ago.

We have heard our grandfather and grandmother tell us that he was tall, really tall.

When he wanted to go, he was there and he wanted to go to Erromango.

When he crossed the sea to Erromango, the sea came to his knee.

Here (indicating his chest) wasn't wet.

He went to Erromango and he came back, and one day, well, Erromango it was-, you could be on Efate and you could see Erromango.

Eṁeltig ṁas.	Just close.
Me teni Efat rupregi imaet	But the one from Efate made him angry.
Go itrau to nrus ki Ermag ipak inrus pa, me welkia ina ilao ki nṗaun pak ntas tefla.	And he went to Erromango, he went, and, well, he put his head into the water like this.
Me ipregi teflan ki nana go ntas ipo puk.	He did that with (his head) and the sea rose.
Welkia, ipreg na ṗaun pak ntas tefla me ipulki nṗaun tefla, nen kin ntas ina ifuk.	Well, he put his head in the water and he twisted his head like this so that the water rose.
Go, kupo kano lek Ermag.	And then you couldn't see Erromango.
Go malnen kin itu san to, itu Efat toto panpan malnen kin imat, go tiawi ni esan rupo tanki.	And now that he stayed there, he stayed on Efate until the time that he died, and the old people of that place buried him.
Me nlaken ipram top go rupo ṗelkin itol wes.	But because he was so tall, they bent him in three.
This is text 049.	

John Maklen
Mumu and Kotkot

A story about two traveling spirits, Mumu and Kotkot who punish wrongdoers.

Natrauswen ni Mumu go Kotkot, ga ita pi natrauswen ṗal mau, ga ipi natrauswen nen iṁol.	The story of Mumu and Kotkot, it is not an empty story, it is a story that is still alive.
Taos Mumu go Kotkot gar rato siwer userek ki nlaun nig Vanuatu.	So Mumu and Kotkot used to walk around Vanuatu.
Pan pak Banks pan pan kaimer ler mai pak Aneityum rato siwer tefla.	To Banks and then back to Aneityum, they would walk like that.
Me san kin ratkos ga ratok naur nig Etgo go Eṁae.	But the places they stopped at were Tongoa and Emae.
Rapi naur negar.	They are their islands.

Go sernrak rato ipitlak napu negar iur esa.
Kin imai kin iteflan panpanpan ileg pan.
Ur ntas kin ipanpan pak Ermag, pak Tanna, pak Aneityum.
Kaimer ler mai.
Go gar rapi tenen kin ratu teflan welkia ratok lek natam̃ol,
naat nen ipreg nawesien sa go rakfo watgi.
Tetenrak ratua ki sup̃tap̃,

rapregi ratua ki namsaki. Me rakfo mer pregi kem̃ol.
Me tete nrak rapregi nen kin kefo mat.
Kefo mat termau. Go nrak ilaap ruto paakorki natam̃ol.
This is text 050.

And everytime they have their road that goes along there.
They always have their road along here, it goes straight.
It goes along the saltwater, to Erromango, Tanna, Aneityum.
Then it comes back.
And they stay there, they look to see if
anyone is behaving badly and they go and hit him.
Sometimes they punish someone,
they make someone sick. But they make them get well again.
But sometimes they make them die.
They will be dead. And many times they appear to people.

John Maklen
Natopu ni Erakor, the spirit who lives at Erakor

The spirit of place, called 'maarik' or Mister out of respect, is still at Erakor, surviving the introduction of Christianity.

Natopu nen kin ito esan ga, ipi natopu nigmam.
Ser natam̃ol ni Erakor runomser mtaki natopu nen kin rusoso ki maarik.
Selwan kupreg sap̃ namrun, Maarik kefo pei tuok sup̃tap̃ sees welkia nen kin ituok kin ipregi kumsak.
Me ipitlak natam̃ol nen kin kefo mer gaag preg naul nkas nen

The natopu (local spirit) that lives here, it is our natopu.
Everyone from Erakor is scared of the natopu which they call 'maarik' (mister).
When you do something wrong, Maarik will give you a small punishment, like he makes you sick.
But there are people who will then give you leaf medecine to

ketuok p̃amingi, go p̃af mer m̃ol.

Natam̃ol ruto esan to rupiatlak naul nkas ni maarik.

Go maarik, teetwei malnen kin, mal ni nmalko, gar ruto- rupi nafet rupi m̃aau.

Maau rulaap, ruto preg nafkal toklos m̃aau ni Ertap, me Ep̃ag, me Em̃el.

Malnen kin ruto me kutae maarik ga inrus pi natam̃ol nen ipi na, kulru. Ipi kulru.

Kulru. Kulru imin se kleva.

Or, natam̃ol nen ipi kulru, welkia tenamrun kefo mai me ga kefo pei nrik nam̃er laap ki

Selwan ruto to pan pan welkia nalotwen ina kefo mai.

Go kinrik nam̃er laap ina, 'Ipiatlak tenmatun iskei. Kefo mai. Tenen ipi tenmatun wi iskei.'

Go akam kofo nomser pak, kofo nomser pak namrun nen kin kefo mai akam kofo nomser pakes.

Me kineu kafo gakit to nanre ni kastom. Tuk mees ne.' Go ga kin ipi maarik kin ita to.

This is text 051.

drink, and you will become healthy again.

People here have leaf medecine for 'maarik'.

And 'maarik', long ago, when, in the time of darkness, they were there, they were a group, they were warriors.

Many warriors, they had battles with the warriors from Eratap, from Pango, from Mele.

As they were there, you know maarik changed into a person who was a healer. He was a healer.

'Kulru' means a kleva (the Bislama term for a healer).

Yes, that man is a kleva, so that if something were to happen, he would have told all the people about it.

When they were there, then Christianity was about to come.

And he said to all the people, 'There is something. It will come. It will be a good thing.

And you will all go to this thing that will come, you will all go to it.

But I will stay inside custom for you. Until today.' And he is the 'maarik' who is still there.

Kalsarap Namaf †

Maarik Taap̃es

About how the Swamphen led a group of birds to take on the hawk and, in the end, kill him.

Amurin na kagakit traus natrauswen sees iskei.
Natrauswen nen ipaakor Maarik Taaᵽes.
Taaᵽes ipi man iskei nen kin nrak ilaap tutili na ito pregsaki nanr gakit.
Kulao nanr, taaᵽes kin kefo pan pami, me nametmatuan ga kin ipi nlaken kin amurin na kagakit traus.
Naliati iskei isos man laap rupak naor iskei. 'Me amurin na kafestaf mus nlaken
akit tupi man. Me itfale kin mal ito pregsaki kit, ito pam kit.
Tete naliati kefo pato eṁae.
Ilemis kit tuto. Imai ipregsaki kit.

Me akit tupi talpuk iskei.'
Ito nrikir kin na, 'Amurin na tukmai pak naor keskei me tuktai raru keskei'.
Go man laap runrikin kin na, 'Tkanwan tukfo tai?' 'Kineu kin kafo peiki mus kin tkanwan tuktai raru.'
Go rupak naor iskei go itli na rufan tai raru. Rupan tai raru. Rusol nkas, nkas nen kefo pi nel.

Rupanpanpan rupan pregi ruto naor iskei. Me ruwat,

rupkasai ruwat ne na, nkas nen ipi nel gar.

I want to tell you all this small story
The story is about Mister Taaᵽes.
Taaᵽes is a bird which, many times we say damages our bananas.
You plant bananas, taaᵽes goes and eats them, but his wisdom is what I want to talk about.

One day he called many birds to one place. 'I want to talk with you because
we are birds. But why does the hawk hurt us, it eats us?
Some days he stays away. He sees us here. He comes and hurts us.
But we are a group.'
He said to them, 'I want us to come together to cut a canoe.'

And all the birds said, 'How will we cut it?' 'I will show you how we cut a canoe.'

And they came together in one place and he said they would cut a canoe. They cut the canoe. They got the wood, the wood would be 'nel' wood.
They went and arranged it so they could be in one place. And they hit
they chopped the tree, their 'nel' tree.

Pan tkal kaaru katol kafat.
Rupregi panpanpan

itaos pot iskei, ito sal. Me itili nag,
'Mal teflan tukfo pakruk.'

Man laap rumai: mantu, sokfal,

taap̃es. Ga kin ipi naot. Ser man
laap nen runomser mai tu naor
iskei.
Go ina, 'Amur na kanrik mus ki na
tukfo kol.' Mapul ito p̃anrer,

too ito taar ser man runomser
preg na nawesien gar teflan kin
rutae, mantu ikai.
Malnen rupan tu raru gar nentu
go kinrikir ki na, 'Malnen tuktu.'
Ser teem̃ol nen ruknomser preg
naler kefak elag. Me kulek maal
ipes
ntaf. Itao ntaf mai. Kule perkati.
Malnen imaimai maimai kefo tao
nrir lfeki kit panpanpan inom.
Kefan pato em̃ae. Malnen iler
maimai maimai na,
imur na kekinki tefla. Go akam
kofrafer.
Me kefo lulki naknin rufak nmal
nanr pa.

Go ipi mal gamus nen kin itu
kop̃akro tukkrakpni.
Runrogo kaitu. Ruto kol mapul ito
kol me ito p̃anrer.

Ser man nen rupreg sup̃ nen ruto
pregi.

They hit it a second, third,
fourth time. They worked it
until
it looked like a boat, it floated.
But he said, 'This is the time for
us to come together.
Many birds came: flying fox,
owl,
and tap̃es. He was the chief. All
the birds came to stay at one
place.
And he said, 'I want to tell you
we should cry out'. The pigeon
cooed,
the rooster crowed, each of the
birds did their work as they
knew how, the flying fox cried.
Then they went to the boat and
he said, 'Now we'll stay here.'
Every animal called out at the
top of its voice. But you look,
the hawk started for
the hill. He left the hill and
came. You see, truly. Then he
came, flying around us until he
finished. He flew off a long
way. Then he came back,
he wanted to pinch us like that.
And you scattered.
But he would come and stick
his fingers in the middle of the
bananas and go.
And it is your time now, our
time to cover him, to kill him.
They heard him and stayed
there. They called, the pidgeon
shouted, but he cooed.
Each bird followed its habit.

Too ito taar, go maal itao ntaf. E maarik go kimai.

Rutu panpan panpan mai imai tu lfekir mai. Ito preg nrag naknin teflan kin kefo-
Ipo to peikir ki n pak etan teflan kefo nrakut tete pan pami,

malnen ipato emãe panpan po na ler na imai. Go taap̃es inrikir ki na,
'Kin kemai malfanen kemai kefo nrakut tete ki. Malnen kuleka iwel preg nrag naknir, rupak elag tefla,
malnen imaimai maimai pak etan. Go tukfa fserser me kefo lulki naknin nmal nanr.'

Go ipi mal gakit nen tukkrakpni. Ruleka go mal imai nrir lfekir panpan inom, pan pato emãe trau,

preg nafarun teflan traus nrir pe nrir me nrag naknin rupe pes.

Malnen imaimai maimai ipak m̃eltig na kenrakut tete kir teflan go rupaamaot
Me nrag naknin ilul pato na nanr to. Ipregnrogo nen kefreglua, me kipe kano nlaken nanr imailumlum,
pot ga nen kin imtalua. Imetmatu pregi.

The rooster crowed and the hawk left the hill. 'Eh, here he comes.'
They were there until he came down, came and put his fingers like he should.
He would show them his claws (to scare them) as if to show them how he would grab one and eat it.
then he went a long way, then he came back. And taap̃es said to them,
'As he comes now he will grab some. Then, you look, he will stick his fingers on top like this,
then he will come down, down, down. And we'll go our different ways, but he will put his fingers in the banana.'
And it is their time (for revenge), they kill him. They watched and the hawk flew down around them until he finished and flew a long way away
then he looked like he was going to fly but his fingers were ready.
Then he came close to grab some of them, and they scattered.
But his claws stuck in the banana. He tried to get out but he couldn't because the banana is soft,
that's the boat he chose. He got wise.

Malnen kin ilulki nrag naknin
rupato nanr ipregnrogo nen kin
inrir nen kefreglu nrag naknin
me ikano.

As he put his claws into the
banana he tried to fly away, but
he couldn't.

Go ipi maal nen rupakro, rutai me
mantu ikati. Me ser man nen
runomser pakro, go

And it is the hawk that they
covered, they cut him (and bit
him) but the flying fox bit him.
But every bird covered him and
his life was finished, he died.

namolien ga inom, imat.
Go ipi esuan natrauswen sees nen
ipaamau wes.
This is text 052.

And that is where this small
story ends.

Petro Kalman †
Katapel and Erakor Island
A longer version of the same story told several times in this
collection. Katapel can make seafood appear at a magic stone,
but only she knows how to work it. A man who tries to use the stone
causes a flood and Katapel dies trying to stop it.

Taos me ni lakun tiawi teetwei
ruto san kin Franis Roman
Catholic itkos.

As for the lagoon, the old people
before stayed up at the place
where the French Roman
Catholics were.

Franis Roman Catholic rusosoki
Momat. Me nafsan matu ni tiawi
rusosoki Epkat.

The French Roman Catholic
place, they call Montmartre. But
its real name, what our ancestors
called it, is Epkat.

Kaaru nen ito rumer sosoki
Epak. Epak kin po pak Epuf.
Me teetwei mal nen tiawi rutu,
ag kukano pak esanie.
Kafan kopei pemisen na kofo pa.
Kanrik naot kin me ifwel kin
afkop namurien neu pan rukfo
wat kineu,
rukfo pam kineu. Nlaken atap
ptuki nafsan.
Go malen kin rutu sanie,

Another place there they call
Epak. From Epak you go to Epuf.
But in those days, olden days,
you couldn't go to that place.
I would go and ask permission to
go there. I would talk with the
chief, but if I just followed my
own way, they would kill me,
and eat me. Because I didn't talk
to them.
And while they were there, there

South Efate Stories

ipiatlak lak itol.
Lak iskei rusoso ki lak Mpakur,
ga kin lakun nen ipo mai pak
esa.
Lak kaaru rusoso ki Ewotas, ito
saot is Efat.
Lak katol ga ito Eꝑuf rusoso ki
ᴍautul me Mautfer.
Me malen kin tenen ito esanie
naᵐer nen ruto Eꝑuf rumur
kapu.
Malnen rumur kapu go ruto gar
preg kapu.

Me ser nrak nen kin rufreg kapu
rupus altuk,
rupus sernale teflan me ati iskei
nen rusosoki Katapel. Ga ipi ati
nen ipiatlak faat iskei ito mai
nrea.
Malnen inrea tefla. Kimer sel
kai. Isel kai nen ito pregi kapu.

Go, malnen ipak nana pa. Me
selwan kin rupan teflan kin lak
tol ne, runomser pi ntas.
Go malen kin iku kia, ipreg nana
ipa. Go ati me apu nen rutu elag
Eꝑuf rupam ni ntas ne,
runrogwiki.
Go teetwei gar ruta pakot ki
mani, go ruta pakot ki tete
namrun ꝑet mau. Gar ᵐiit mas
kinruto ptuki,
go nawi, naꝑrai. Go ati nen ser
nrak nen kin rupa, ga ito sol
nafnag itop tol siluer.

Nlaken ga ito tanum kapu.

were three wells.
The first well was called Mpakur,
it is the one the lagoon came
from.
The second well was called
Ewotas, at south-east Efate.
The third well was at Eꝑuf, they
called it ᴍautul and Mautfer.
But then, they were there, the
people from Eꝑuf wanted laplap.

Then they wanted laplap and
they started to make laplap for
them.
But every time they they made
laplap they put island cabbage,
and other things in it, but one
grandmother, called Katapel. She
is a grandmother who had a
stone which she would turn.
She would turn it. She took
shellfish. She took shellfish and
she made laplap.
Then she went. But when she
wanted to do this for the three
wells, they were all saltwater.
She took the food and went. And
the grandparents they were at
Eꝑuf, they ate from the saltwater
and they felt good.
In those days they didn't buy
things with money, and they
didn't buy different things at all.
They gave mats only,
and yam, sugar cane. And this
grandmother, every time they
went, she got more food than
anyone else.
Because she put meat on the

Kai kapu ga ne, go runa, 'Me ag kupreg kapu gaag ikakas wi nlaken kin kusati ntas.'
Rupan pan pan rumaetki nlaken kin sernale nen kin kefan kimer sel nawi laap.
Isat nap̃rai laap, esum̃ ga ip̃ur mau ki nafnag.
Ati nen rusoso ki Katapel.

Pan go rutmer nrikir ki, 'E, tufo leperkat naftekin ito slati elau.'

Malnen kin rumai nen ruuut ntas nen rukfo pregi kefak naniu nen runroi kapu.
Go ke ona ke kukia.
Ga kefo inrok. Inrok ser nrak.

Malen kin ipo na imai tefla me ruipe preg naturiai iskei, kipe mai torakin to.
Malen kin ileka inre faat tefla, ipai kai pan pan inom tefla, naal na ipueti go iut ntas nen kefo pan nroi kapu ga.
Me malnen kin ipo na ipreg ga, naftekia, nana, teflan inom na itao,
go isiwer sak ki ntaf pak elag, malen ipan pan pan pak elag ntaf go inrog nai iser.
Malnen kin inrog nai iser teflan itarp̃ek ki napor naal ga ipato me itrau fit.
Malnen kin ifit mai mai mai mai legki san kia Korman me pak etan,

laplap.
Shellfish laplap,and they said, 'You make a sweet laplap because you get it from the sea.'
Until they got angry with her because every time she went she got lots of yam.
She got lots of sugarcane, her house was full of food.
This grandmother called Katapel.
Then they said to themselves, 'We should go and watch her taking things from the sea.'
Then they came to get saltwater to put with the coconut to milk the laplap.
And he, um.
And she came after. She came last every time.
When she came back, they made one young man go and wait for her.
Then he saw her turn the stone and fill up the basket with shellfish and take it and then pour seawater to milk her laplap.
But when she got all the, whatsit, and she left,

and walked up the hill to the top, when she was high up the hill then she heard water flowing.
When she heard the water flowing, she dropped her basket and just ran.
Then she ran and ran and came to where Korman stadium is, but down,

ipu tefla nagis nranru nen kin kepnut nai keta ser mau.

Ifit mai pak san, nai iskatur wes, mer fit mai mai pak san rusosoki Elaknap̃kas mer pueti me nai.
Imer fit mai pak nagis esanie nen rusosoki Emetp̃er go Efatp̃osfiu.
Malnen kin ientan tefla nen ke enkor ntas, ntas iskatur natuen.

Malen ntas iskatur natuen tefla, faat nra nen kin.

Iskatur natuen tefla, faat nra nen kin ratu. Iskatur natuen tefla gar ipi nra tu kaaru kin imakot mal ni Uma.

Me kaaru ita tu pan mees.
Rusosoki Efatposfiu.
Go naor Erakor teetwei ga itik.

Me malnen Katapel ientan teflan kin nai kin, me ntas ipo satktofi ipi naor.
Go malen kin ifit teflan mai mai imat. Ga kin itap̃o pato nametp̃agon nagis ne rusosoki Katapel. Nagis ni Katapel.
Go malen ip̃o, ser nafaswen nen gar kin runomser pi faat lfek naur to.

Go ipi nametp̃ag natrauswen ni Katapel.
This is text 058.

and she pulled the two points of land to try and stop the water from flowing.
She ran to the place where the water was flowing through, to the place they call Elaknap̃kas, to pull the water.
She ran to this point which is called Emetp̃er and Efatp̃osfiu.

When she lay down to block the saltwater, it went through her legs.
Then the water flowed through her legs, they became two stones.
It flowed through her legs, these two stones are still there. It flowed through her legs like that, they are two, one was broken during (cyclone) Uma.
But the other one is still there today. They call it Efatposfiu.
And Erakor island was not there in the olden days.
But when Katapel lay down to block the water, it broke off the island.
And when she ran like this, she died. She fell over at the point which is called Katapel. Katapel point.
And when she was rotten, each of the places she pushed at became stones around the island.
And that is the end of the story of Katapel.

Timothy Arsen
*ᴍaau inru, the two
warriors*

This story about the two warriors from Pango and Erakor was told
by Timothy Arsen when he was eight years old.

Nrakeskei ipiatlak na m̃aau ni,
m̃aau ni na Ep̃ag go m̃aau ni sa,
me
rato pan pan go m̃aau ni san
iparekina, e m̃aau ni sanpen
ipareki m̃aau ni sa,
m̃aau ni san imai tefla go, e
m̃aau ni sanpen imai tefla go

m̃aau ni esa, m̃aau ni esan ipag
to elag na nra mpak to.
Go m̃aau ni san imai teflan, go
m̃aau ni sanpen imai.
Go m̃aau ni san ito elag na mpak
teflan ale isok su mai ale

ratok rapan pan go ratmer ona
ratmer watgir, pan pan pan go
na na m̃aau kaaru iskei imai
teflan go iwat na, ipo fsei na
na m̃aau, nag m̃aau ni Ep̃ag, ale
m̃aau ni Ep̃ag ipo mat
Go tewan kin amur katli.
This is text 062 .

Once there was a warrior at
Pango and a warrior from here,
and
they were there until the warrior
from here came out and the
warrior from there came out
the Pango warrior came closer
and the warrior from here came
and
the warrior from here climbed
the branches of a banyan tree.
And warrior from here came and
the warrior from there came.
And the warrior from here was
up the banyan tree and he came
down from the tree
then they argued and they hit
each other, until
the other one, hit the one

the warrior from Pango was
dead.
And that's what I wanted to say.

William Wayane †
Falea and Toukou

A story about how the ancestors of Erakor people lived ad Rentapou
and then came to Erakor and were transformed into
places around Erakor.

Teetwei ipitlak tiawi inru rapitlak teesa ilates, nagi tiawi nranru nen ipitlak Falea go Toukou.	In the olden days two old people, called Falea and Toukou, had six children.
Teflan tiawi nigmam rupato Erontp̃au, mai pak naur Erakor.	Our old people lived at Rentapau come to Erakor island.
Tiawi ranru nen rapiatlak teesa ilates.	These two had six children.
Teesa pei nagien kin Apu Esel. Go Apu Esel, ipi nsel nai.	The first was called Apu Esel. And Apu Esel was a spring of water.
Nsel nai nag itok ser Mai sok ntas.	A spring that flowed. Down to the sea.
Tekaaru teesa kaaru ipi Apu Taf	The second child was called Apu Taf.
Apu Taf ipi nai nag iser pak namos,	Apu Taf is water which flows to the sea,
Teesa katol go ipi Ati Pako.	The third child is Ati Pako.
Ati Pako ipi pako kaitok sef	Ati Pako is a shark which ran away
reki naur sees Eraniao mai.	and came to Erakor island.
Tekafat ipi Apu Sal,	The fourth was Apu Sal,
Apu Sal, ga isal mai tkal naur Eraniao.	Apu Sal, he floated and came to Erakor island.
Teesa kalim ipi Apu Tfer. Ga ipi nao.	The fifth child was Apu Tfer. He was a wave.
Pako isal mai go nao itp̃er kin ipak euut Eraniao.	And the shark came floating and the wave picked it up and threw it onto the shore of Erakor Island.
Teesa klates ipi Ati Aas.	The sixth child was Ati Aas.

Go malnen kin nao itꝑerkin ipak
euut go ipi aas.

Go kimai pi aas. Ito panpan tete
ntau rumai go kiler mai pi faat.

Go faat nen ito Elignairo, naur
sees Eraniao.
Go natrauswen nen ipi
natrauswen ni tiawi nig Erakor,
nen kin ruto elag Erontꝑau mai
tkal naur sees Erakor. Ipi tesees
wan inom esa.
This is text 069.

And when the wave threw her
on the shore she was a coconut
crab.
And she became a coconut crab.
She was there for some years,
then she became a rock.
And the rock is there at
Elignairo, on Erakor island.
And this is a story from the old
people of Erakor,
who came from Rentapau to
Erakor island. This small story
is finished here.

Kalfaꝑun Mailei †
Katapel and Liportani

The story of Katapel, but in this version Liportani is a woman who
wanted to use Katapel's magic but fails, with bad consequences.

Ipitlak nmatu inru, rato elag
Eꝑuf.
Ale rato mai pak elau Emten.
Malen tiawi ruto sol serale.

Ruto sol serale pak nana,
naꝑlaki, nlauwen. Ale sernrak
rupa,
rusol serale. Tete rusol nawi,
tete rusol nmal, tete rusol nanr,
iskei ito sol ga kai.

Gar ruto namlas, nrak pei Emten
itik ki ntas. Ito sol ga kai.

Me gar rato esum̃ iskei, gar
Liportani, Katapel go Liportani,
rato esum̃ iskei.

There are two women, they
lived up at Bufa.
Okay, they came down to the
water at Emten. At this time the
old people carried everything.
They would take everything to
feasts and dances. So everytime
they went,
they took everything. Some took
yams, some took naos (hog
plums), some took bananas, one
took shellfish.
They lived in the bush, in those
days Emten had no saltwater.
She would get shellfish.
They lived in the one house,
Liportani with Katapel lived in
one house.

Ale, Katapel ipak elag isol kai, ipak esan kin faat itkos.

Ip̃elgat faat tefla isol kai. Inom ipa itao faat ip̃on. Ipak sum̃ ga pa, ipreg kai.

Ipan ipreg nafnag, rufam, ale Liportani ijaluskin a?
Ina, 'Me mtulep nen to ga ito pan sel nana, kai esua? Itik ki elau sa.' Ale ipaoski na, 'Ag kuto pan sel kai sua?' Ina, 'Ato pan sati elau'.

Liportani ipaoski, ipaoski, ipaoski. Katapel imal to tli. Nrak iskei Liportani ikuskor Katapel. Ikuskro to,

ileka Katapel ipan. Ifan inrea faat, isel kai, isati pan inom mer tao faat, ga isol kai pa.

Liportani ipa inre faat, inre faat inom, isel kai, me imetp̃akro nen kemer tao faat keler.

Ntas iser. Katapel ipato esum̃, go inrog ntas iser. Ifit. Ifit mai pak Ewenesu, itraem nen kepnuti kia kefueti nen kepnuti.
Kipe mten top, ntas kipe mten top. Imer tao, imai pak Elaknapuktao, me ntas, itikin, imaimaimai pak Elaknapuktao.

So Katapel went up and got shellfish, she went to where there is a rock.
She turned the rock and she got shellfish. Finished, she went, she left the rock closed. She went to her house, she carried the shellfish.
She got the food, they ate, then Liportani was jealous of her. She said, 'This woman, she goes and gets shellfish, but where from? There is no sea around here.' So she asked, 'Where do you get shellfish from?' She said, 'I get it from the sea.'
Liportani asked and asked and asked. Katapel didn't want to talk about it. One time Liportani hid from Katapel. She was hidden,
she watched Katapel go. She went and turned the stone, she took shellfish, she took it until it was finished, then she left the stone, she took the shellfish and went.
Liportani went and turned the stone, finished, she took the shellfish, but she forgot to leave the stone again.
Seawater flowed. Katapel was at home and she heard the sea flowing. It ran. It came to Ewenesu, she tried to stop it. It was too heavy, the water was too heavy. It left, it came to Elaknapuktao, nothing, it came and came to Elaknapuktao.

Kipe mten. Itao Elaknapuktao, me ifit. Imai mai mai pak, e Emetaikes.

Imer trae nen kepnuti, me kipe mten kaipe mten top. Ale inrog ntas. Imai mai mai ipak naur, ilaotu naur ale, ntas nen ina imai inran.

Kaaru iur nanre kaaru iur nanre. Katapel itu maloput. Imai mai mai mai na ipak nagis, nagis ni naur. Inrog ntas ga, ina, 'Ipi faat tap̃o.' Kaitu.

Ga kia ien nagis Elakatapel. Me ntas kipe ser kaipe pa. Ipi nametp̃agon ni natrauswen ne. *This is text 071.*

It was heavy. It left Elaknapuktao and it ran. It came to Emetaikes.

She tried again to stop it, but it was heavy, too heavy. Ok, she heard the seawater. It came and came to the island, then the water split into two.

One flowed on one side, the other flowed on the other side. Katapel was in the middle. She came and came to the point, the point of the island. She heard the water and she said, 'The stone has been turned'.

That is what is at Elakatapel point. But the sea flowed and went. It is the end of this story.

Kalfap̃un Mailei
The natopu around Erakor village

A description of some of the natopu (spirits) who live around Erakor and what they do.

Natkon ni Erakor, e ipitlak natopu inrus laap. Kulek naor nen itu elau to.

A, fei kia, Atumret, go Pakolep kin ratu elau to, rapi natopu tu kia.

Orait kumai pak e, esap kia Enainalop, san a Klan mana rupato. Faat inru kia ratu nmaota Enainalop go Emetp̃er.

Gar me rapi natopu tu kia, Flesaur, go Flep̃og.

Erakor village has many natopu. You look at the place down by the sea.

A, who now, Atumret and Pakolep were in the sea, they were natopu.

Alright, you come to, a, Enainalop where Klan and them live. The two rocks are between Enainalop and Emetp̃er.

They are natopu, Flesaur and Flep̃og.

Kupak Emetaikes, ipitlak naot gar kin itu es. Maarik kin itu Emetaikes.

Orait kupak, a, a, Elwaf, Elak Mparomwal, ipitlak mtulep iskei kin itkos to, ipi natopu.

Ale kumer pak Elak Napuktau, esan kin a, Radison ipato, ipitlak mtulep iskei itu san. Ipi nmatu.

Nanre knen pak nanre gakit, ipitlak natopu iskei itues.

Teni naflak namkanr. Teni teesa nen rutu, nana natopu gar a? Ale kupan panpan

kupak e, esap. Kupak Ekoftau nen pato. Ipitlak natopu iskei ituwes. Ekoftau.

Me natopu ne, ga isiwerki mp̃agon. Nlaken itik ki natuen, ga isiwerkin.

Me ipi natopu, ale, kupak e elag esan kia rupreg redio stesen foum wes.

Ipitlak Lagtatalof itu wes. Ga ipi natopu iskei.

Ale kunrookot tefla, kupak e Elakles kin kaipaakor nanre ni Ertap ki.

Me rupi natopu nen rulfekor Erakor. Iskei itu esan, ale kaimai pak naor na ipato, Atmowit. Go m̃asei gar, kin rato elau Ekap̃um.

Gar me rapi natopu tu kia, esan, natopu rulfeka, a?

(NT) Go ag kumas preg nafte,

You go to Emetaikes, there is their chief who is there. The gentleman who is at Emetaikes.

Ok, you go to Elwaf, Elak Maromwal, there is a woman spirit there, she is a natopu.

Ok, you then go to Elak Napuktau, the place where the Radison is now, there is a woman spirit there.

From that side to our side there is a natopu there.

Those of the namkanr clan.

Those of the children who are here, it is their natopu. Ok, you keep going until

you get to that place. You go to Ekoftau. There's a natopu who lives there. Ekoftau.

And this natopu, he walks on his bottom. Because he doesn't have any legs, he walks on it.

It is a natopu, ok, you go up to the place where the new radio station is.

There is Langtatalof there. He is a natopu.

Ok, cross over like that, you go to Elakles and I come out at the side of Eratap.

They are the natopu who are around Erakor. One is there and he comes to the place where Atmowit stays. And their stars are at sea, at Ekap̃um (island).

They are the natopu of the place; natopu all around it.

(NT) And what must you do? To

olsem blong lukaotem ol samting ia. Yu mas mekem wanem?

(KM) O oli stap nomo, olsem oli lukaotem. Welkia rulekor kit a, iwelkia.

Gar ruto, rupi, rupi natopu nen kin rupi naflak, a?

Naflak ne, naflak ne, naflak ne, ipitlak kram, ipitlak namkanr,

(NT) If wel ag kupreg nafte, nanrogpirwen?

(KM) Ore if wel kufla maetki naat, ag kupan, p̃afo preg, taosi rutil nfak.

Kupreg ipak natopu. Natopu itrapelpel nrogo, kefo wat naat ne

(NT) Me ag kuto ni naflak, olsem pitkaskei ni natopu? Natopu ito lekor ag?

(KM) Ore welkia, akit tuto nalekoren ni Atua. Me gar gar rupi teni emermen.

Me Atua ga ipei. Ga kin ilekor wou. Me gar rupi natopu teflan to me gar ruta preg namrun mau, ruteflan m̃as to.

Me iwel kia rulekor natkon a? Rulekor natkon,

(NT) Rutap preg nawesien sa mau?

(KM) Toklos natam̃ol, itik. Ruta preg nawesien sa mau.

Me iwelkia olfala nen ipato esanpe Emetaikes, ga kin ga ipi naot, ipi naot ni ser natopu ne.

Me wel kin tete natopu ifla mur na kewat naat, kefei paoskin ki.

look after these things?

(KM) They are just there, they look after things, they look after us.

They are there, they are natopu that have a clan, eh? This clan, this clan, this clan, there is the clam clan, the namkanr clan.

(NT) What if you disobey?

(KM) Ok, well if you are angry with someone, you go and get, like, they call it a 'nfak'.

You take it to the natopu. The natopu will quickly hear, he will hurt that person.

(NT) But are you in the same naflak as the natopu, does he look after you?

(KM) Yes, so, we are all in God's care. But they (natopu) they belong to the world.

But God is first. He looks after me. They are just natopu, they can't do much, they are just there.

But they look after the village, eh? They look after the village.

(NT) They don't do bad things?

(KM) Regarding people, no. They don't do bad things.

But for example, the old man at Emetaikes, he is the chief, the chief of all natopu.

And if a natopu wants to hurt someone, they must first ask

Wel ga ketil, 'Ore', go kefo watgi, me wel itli na, 'Itik', ukano.

(NT) Go natopu rupiatlak tete teeṁol, nen ruto?
(KM) Ore taos teeṁol gar, ore. Taos, tenen kin gar ruto ntas a?

Natopu nen rupi tenen ruto ntas. Go serale nen ruto ntas, gar rupi serale gar.
Taos pislama, taṁra, star, me naik, me serale ne ipi serale gar.

(NT) Me ita piatlak sikskei mau, olsem wanwan natopu ipiatlak,

(KM) Ga serale, e.e. Gar rumaui pitlak serale teplan ne, go ipitlak naik. Kumurin paoski naik kefo tuok ki.
(NT) Maat olsem blak and waet snek (KM) A takwer.

(KM) Takwer ga ipitlak, ipitlak tete naat nen kin ipi natopu gar.

Me ita top go ita laap Erakor mau, nlaken naṁer laap rumtaki.

Naṁer laap rumtaki takwer. Maat ni euut ipo pitkaskei, ṁaat ni namlas. Naṁer laap rumtaki.

(NT) Me malpei, tiawi rupreg tete nanromien sees rutuer natopu?

(KM) Teetwei tiawi, tiawi ni

him about it.
If he says, 'Yes', then he can kill him, but if he says, 'No', we can't.
(NT) And do these natopu have any animals with them?
(KM) Yes, like their animals? So, those that live in the sea, ah?
These natopu are the ones that live in the sea. And everything that lives in the sea is theirs. Like bêche-de-mer, starfish, fish and everything like that is theirs.
But they don't each have their own one (animal, familiar), like each natopu?
(KM) No, they have everything. They all have something like this, like fish. If you want to ask for fish, he will give it to you.
(NT) Snakes, like the black and white snake (sea krait). (KM) Yes, sea snake.
The seasnake has some people that are-, it (the seasnake) is their natopu.
But not many, not many at Erakor, because many people are scared of them.
Many people are scared of the seasnake. Snakes from the shore or the bush too. Many people are scared of them.
(NT) But before, did the old people take presents and give them to the natopu?
(KM) Before, the old people, old

teetwei teetwei, gar ruta lotki Atua mau, gar rulotki natopu.

people from long long ago, they didn't pray to God, they prayed to the natopu.

Wel rufla mur na rukfak nafkal ko. Rupreg nanromien tu natopu. Natopu kin ipeikir pak nafkal.

They may want to go to battle or something. They prepare a present to give to the natopu. The natopu is the one who leads them into battle.

Ko iteflan tefla. Rufla mur namrun, rupaoski natopu ki. Ale rupreg tete nanromien.

Like that. They may want something, they ask the natopu about it. OK, they make a present.

(NT) Rupsi esua?
(KM) A rupan, rufla psi welkia rutae san rutkos, rufla psi ntas ko rufla psi sa.
Gar rumai, me gar rupo pan leka.

(NT) Where do they put it?
(KM) They go and put it, well they know where the natopu are, they might put it here. They come, and they will go and look at it (the natopu).

(NT) Go ni natkon ipitlak tete ntwam rutokos?
(KM) Natkon, e, teetwei. Ataeki teetwei, ipitlak tete ntwam, me.

(NT) And are there some devils that live in the village?
(KM) In the village, well, long ago. I know that long ago there were some devils, but.

Iwel kia naor kipe kipe top me, rulakor to me rukus. Rulakor to me rukus.

Well, the place got bigger and bigger and they may still be there, but they are hiding. They may be there, but they are hiding.

This is text 073.

Toukelau Takau
Koaiseno
A small boy called Koaiseno is born from the sea and is adopted by a family, but then returns to live in the sea.

A, kagaag traus nmatu iskei, go nanwei iskei, rato. Me ratik ki teesa.
Me ipiatlak teesa iskei ipaakor

I'll tell you about this woman and this man. But they had no children.
But a child appeared in a rock in

faat elau.

Teesa nen ipaakor faat, mal nen gar rapak elau pa, rapamŏor teesa nen itu.

Go rapaos kin ki, 'Gaag tmam go raitom wa?'

Teesa nanwei inrikir ki na, 'Kineu apaakor faat'.

Go ratli na, 'Komam ratik ki teesa, me ag kutae skot komam?' Go teesa nanwei ina, 'Kineu atae skot akam'.

Go rapo plake pa, rapregi ipi teesa gar.

Rapo lekor wes pan go ipi teesa p̃ur.

Rapregi ipi teesa wi gar, ranromi. Me nrakeskei go papa ga ifsei.

Ipuet nkas me ifsei. Teesa ina ikai go kiler mro pak esan ga itkos mai.

Ina ito, kaistat siwer raki elau, go tmen ipios.

Nagi teesa ne, Koaisen.

Isiwer raki elau, ga imro ki esan ga ipaakor wes.

Go tmen ileka go imrotae. Isiwer raki elau go kipios, 'Koaisen p̃aler'.

Koaisen isiwer. Go imer pios, 'Koaisen p̃aler.'

Koaisen, isiwer pan pan go kikam ntas.

Ikam ntas go tmen imer pios,

the sea.

This child appeared in the stone, then these two went to the sea and found the child there.

And they asked him, 'Where are your father and mother?'

The boy said to them, 'I came from the rock.'

And they said, 'We haven't got any children, can you come with us?' And the boy said, 'I can come with you.'

And they took him and went, they made him their son.

They looked after him until he became a big boy.

They made him into a good boy, they loved him. One time the father whipped him.

He got some wood and he whipped him. The child wanted to cry, and he thought back to the place where he came from. He was there, and he began to walk to the sea, and his father called out.

The name of this child, Koaisen.

He walked to the sea, he was thinking about the place where he was born.

And the father saw and he realised. He walked to the sea and he called out, 'Koaisen, come back.'

Koaisen walked. And he called again, 'Koaisen, come back.'

Koaisen walked until he walked to the water.

He came to the saltwater and his

'Koaisen p̃aler'. Ipan kam ntas
go ipo lag ipreg nalag:

'Koaiseno koaiseno seno, nato
wawa nato wawa meremo,
koaiseno seno.'
'Koaisen p̃aler.' Koaisen ipan
ikam ntas, go ntas ipamau
nap̃utwen.
Tmen imer pios, 'Koaisen p̃aler
mai.' Go inrus pak elau, ntas
ipamau esa.

Tmen ipe nromi itop. Tmen
inromi itop imer soso, 'Koaisen
p̃aler mai'.

Koaisen inrus pa, go ntas
ipamau esa.
Me ileka na, tmen inromi itop
go isursur tmen.

Inrik tmen kin, 'E nasum̃ gakit
isor.' Malen tmen itmen nrea,
ile pak euut.

Go Koaisen itut pak ntas, go
kipuel.
Go tmen ipo lag: 'Koaiseno
Koaiseno seno,
Nato wawa, nato wawa,
meremo, Koaiseno seno.'
Olsem singsing ia, hemi olsem
hemi krae, hemi krae, hemi sori
long hem hemi krae, hemi tok
tok long hem olsem
Nafuserekwen ne inom esa.
This is text 074.

father called again, 'Koaisen,
come back.' He went to the sea
and he sang, he sang this song:
'Koaiseno koaiseno seno, nato
wawa nato wawa meremo,
koaiseno seno.'
'Koaisen come back.' Koaisen
went into the water, and the
water covered his knees.
His father called again, 'Koaisen,
come back.' And he went into
the sea, the water covered up to
here.
His father had loved him greatly.
His father loved him too much,
he called out, 'Koaisen come
back.'
Koaisen moved away, and water
came up to here.
But he saw that, his father loved
him a lot, and he tricked his
father.
He told his father, 'Hey, our
house is burning.' Then his
father turned himself around, he
looked to shore.
And Koaisen dived into the
water and disappeared.
And the father sang: 'Koaiseno
Koaiseno seno,
Nato wawa, nato wawa, meremo,
Koaiseno seno.'
This song, it is like he is crying,
he cries, he is sorry for his son,
he saying this to him.

This story finishes here.

South Efate Stories

Toukelau Takau
Litong

Litong is a woman given to be the wife of a Natopu.

Ore ipiatlak natopu nigmam ni esa.

Yes, we have a natopu.

Nigmam natopu nigmam ni esa, ga kin ito, ito ito pan, ito teetwei paakor mees.

Our natopu, the natopu from this place, he is the one who is there, who has been there from long ago until today.

Me ito, mal ni tiawi ni teetwei, malen natopu nigmam ito.

He was there at the time of our ancestors.

Go iptal, iptal nmatu. Iptal teesa nmatu, na ruktua teesa nmatu keskei.

He would ask for a woman or a girl, he would ask that they give him a girl.

Go rupo tua teesa nmatu iskei.

And they would give him a girl.

Malnen imur na teesa nmatu ne, teesa nmatu ne nagien ipi Litog.

Once he wanted this girl, her name was Litong.

Me imur teesa nmatu ne go ito tp̃olu na,

He wanted this girl and he would send a message, saying

tenen rusel nafsan ga, ki taosi kin, [..] itp̃olu polis ga.

that they (his police) take his message. [A natopu has assistants to do its work and they are called its police.]

Olsem hemi sendem polis blong hem, a? Itp̃olu polis ga, olsem, ol smol smol samting we oli stap long sol wota, a?

[Bislama] So he sent his police. He sent them with a message, all the small creatures that live in the sea.

Ipiatlak, na, pislama, kufa.

There was bêche-de-mer, shellfish.

Malen tiawi rulemsi rutae, na polis rupa raru teesa nmatu ne, rumai ruler pa.

When the ancestors saw it they knew they were the police. They took the girl in the canoe, they came and they returned.

Tete nrak tañra, rumai tiawi rutae.

Sometimes starfish come and the old people know.

Rupi police ga, rupa reki nmatu. Ipregi panpanpan naliati iskei.

They are its police, they go to get a woman. Until, one day,

go runa, 'Tukga kraksoksok me tukfan psi.' Go rupo pan ga psi im̃ol.

Malen kin ruga pregptaki m̃it, ruga preg ptaki nkal, panpan inom rutatweki raru, rumsagi raru me rupa.

Nlaken esum̃ ga, ipato elag esanpe. Ruga msag serale nen plake pa me rupan me ga kipe pi nskau p̃ur iskei a?
Ipaakor to, ito elag nam̃oru. Rupa rupam̃or nskau nen ito rutae na rukfo psi esa.

Go rukoi psi, ruga sat serale pan psi pan inom, ale rulaoki.

Puet nmatu, Litog, rupsi ilao skot serale tu, me rukoipak em̃ae.

Malen rupak em̃ae itaos nao iskei, a?
Imai mai mai mai, p̃aakor faat ne. Inom. Iplake im̃ol pa.

Go iplake im̃ol to, go im̃ol to tup̃ mees.
Ito paakor tup̃ mees. Litog. Nlaken ipi nmatu ga, ilakor pi, kefo to panpanpan emermen kefo plake puel, tefla.
Natopu nigmam ni esa, rutua nmatu, me rutua kin im̃ol.
Go ga kin ito, ito tup̃ mees. Ale

they said, 'We will prepare things for her and we will put them there.' And they put her there alive.
Then they prepared mats and cloth for her, and when they were done they put them in a canoe and took them to it (Litong)
Because her house was up there somewhere. They took her all this stuff but the natopu's house was the big reef.
She had appeared, there out in the deep sea. They went and found the reef and they knew that they would put their presents there.
And they put it there, they took her everything until there was no more, they stood it up there.
They took a woman, Litong, they put her there, she was standing with all the things, but they went away.
When they went away it was like a wave came up, do you see?
It came and came, over that rock. Finished. It took her, alive, and went.
It took her alive and she is alive to this day.
She keeps appearing today. Litong. Because it is his wife, she will disappear with the world.

They gave the natopu a woman, they gave him a live woman.
And he is still there, until today.

itefla.
Taos ni natopu nigmam ni esa,
ratua malen imur nmatu, rutua
kin im̃ol

It's like that.
Like our natopu from here, they
gave him the woman, when he
wants a woman they give her to
him, alive.

This is text 075.

Toukelau Takau
Lisau, a natopu
Lisau is a natopu who lives around Tassiriki.

Ipiatlak, Etasrik, Ratison. Etasrik
ipiatlak mtulep iskei itkos.

There is (a natopu at) Tassiriki,
the Radison. Tassiriki has a
woman spirit there.

Ga me itkos. Nagien ipi Lisau.
Ga me itu lekor ga esa.
Rupi natopu me rutae nam̃er,
rutae natam̃ol ni natkon, lekor
ptaki natam̃ol.

She is there. Her name is Lisau.
She looks after this place.
They are natopu but they know
people, they know the people of
the village, look after the
people.

Tenen kin ipreg tenamrun itakel,
rufei kin kin teflan kin itae na
ipreg namrun itakel, ifei kin ki.

Anyone who does something
crooked, they show her so that
she knows that he is doing
something crooked, she shows
him it.

Go natam̃ol ito mrotae na tenen
kin ipregi, ita wi mau.
(NT) Me ipiatlak natam̃ol nen
rutuer tete nanromien?
(TT) Or. Or. Wel, namroan sa ni
natam̃ol, natam̃ol imrosaki tete
natam̃ol imrosaki tete aslen,

And the man will recognise that
what he did is not good.
(NT) But are there people who
give them some presents?
(TT) Yes. Yes. Like, evil
thoughts, if a man wishes bad
things on someone, he wishes
bad things on some friend,

isel tete nanromien ipan tua ki.
Ina, 'P̃afo neu, p̃afo neu watgi.'

he takes a present, he goes and
gives it to her. He says, 'You will
hit him for me.'

Kefo pregi taosikin, taosikin
natam̃ol nen isel nanromien ipan
tua ki.

She will do it, as that man
brought a small present and
gave it to her.

Malen kin natamol kaaru nen ifla tu msak, nlaken kin tekaaru kipe pan tu natopu ki.

Then that other man might get sick, because the other one went and gave the natopu a present.

Ifla tu msak, panpan ale ilel na, tete munwei nen ketae ga pamor nlak namsaki ga.

If he is sick, eventually he will go and see a healer who will be able to find out for him the cause of his sickness.

Pan kefo tli na, kefo tae nrikin ki na, 'Ga kin itu natopu kik'.

Then he will tell him, 'He is the one who gave you to the natopu.'

Go ga kefo mer tae nrikin ki na, 'Pamer sel tete nanromien mai tao kin, me kineu kafo pan ga psi, me kafo plakek ler.'

And he (the healer) would then be able to tell him, 'You go now and get a present and give it to me, and I will go and give it to her and I will come back with you.'

Tefla. Ipitlak tete natamol nen kin namroan gar itakel, ruto.
Me ita pi sup̃ wi mau, ipi sup̃ sa.

That's it. There are some people who don't think straight.
But it is not a good way, it's a bad way.

(NT) Me natopu ipi natopu sa, ko iwi?

(NT) But is the Natopu good or bad?

(TT) Iwi inrom, inrom ser natamol, me malen kin naat iskei imaetki aslen, me ipan tua tete nanromien ga kefo pregi taosi kin nanromien nen rupan tua kin

(TT) She is good, she loves all people, but when a man gets angry with his friend and he gives her a present, she will do as he wants. (Lit: she will follow the present that they gave her)

Itefla. Natopu itefla.

It's like that. The natopu is like that.

This is text 077.

Toukelau Takau
Too go taap̃es, the chicken and the swamphen

The chicken steals the swamphen's comb and the swamphen then hides its shame in the bush.

Too go taaρes rapiatlak, ratmer pi asel kir. Rato ur naor iskei.

Me nrak iskei go ratli na rakfan los.
Kotfan nrak iskei go ratli na rakfan los elau.
Ale rana rato rapan los elau.

Me nlaken nser ne. Nser nen too isuun to. Nki.

Ga teni taaρes, ipi nser ni taaρes, tene, ipi teni taaρes.
Me tene ipi teni too. Gawanki.
Ale rato rapan los elau.

Me nlaken too kipe lewiki kom ni taaρes.
Malen rapato los pan, go too inrik taaρes kina, 'Ag ρafei to me kineu kafei sak.'

Ina ipa na ikalki nkal ga inom.
Me imailum pnaklu kom ni taaρes, ipaskin nρaun

Isef kaipa, me taaρes ipen los, ipen los panpan na imai na ikalki nkal ga pan inom.
Me ilel kom ga me kom ga ipuel, nlaken too kipe pnakon pa. Me ni too kom ga ito.

Taaρes inrogtesa. Too ipnak kom ni taaρes.

The chicken and the swamphen were friends. They stayed at one place.
Then one time they said they would go for a swim.
One afternoon they said they would go and swim in the sea.
So they wanted to go for a swim in the sea.
But because of the comb. That comb that it put on its head. That one.
This one is the swamphen's comb.
But this one is the chicken's.
Like that. Okay they went and swam in the sea.
But because the chicken liked the swamphen's comb,
When they went swimming the chicken said to the swamphen, 'You stay here first and I'll get out.'
He wanted to go to dress in his clothes. Then he quietly stole the swamphen's comb and put it on his head.
He ran away and went, then the swamphen swam there until he came to get dressed.
Then he looked for his comb, but it was gone, because the chicken had stolen it and gone.
But the chicken's comb was still there.
The swamphen felt bad. The chicken stole the comb from the swamphen.

Isemsem wes go kipe to ur esuñ ur narmal, itu fekfek ki kom, nlaken kin ipnakon,

He was happy because of it, and he went around the house and the yard and he showed off, because he had stolen it.

kom ni taaꝑes. Me taaꝑes ina ipan na ikal su, me ileka ki kom ga ipuel.

the comb from the swamphen. And the swamphen wanted to get dressed, but he saw that his comb was missing.

Me kom ni too, ito. Go ina isati kaipsi nꝑaun me inrogtesa.

But the chicken's comb was there. And he wanted to get it and he he put it on his head, but he felt bad.

Imaet go kisef pan kus namlas, ipan kus namlas, go kito ur namlas.

He got angry and he ran away to hide in the bush, he hid in the bush, and he wandered in the bush.

Go mees kutae parñor too kin ito ur esuñ, nlaken kin ipnak kom ni taaꝑes.

And today you will find that the chicken stays around the house because it stole the swamphen's comb.

Taaꝑes imalier kom ni too, nlaken isees go kisef pan kus namlas.

The swamphen is ashamed of the chicken's comb because it is small and he runs and hides in the bush.

Nafuserekwen ni taaꝑes go too itefla.
This is text 078.

The story of the chicken and the swamphen is like that.

Jinane †
Barracuda and hermit crab story

This is another version of the same story told elsewhere in this volume of a barracuda being tricked into losing a race with a hermit crab.

Kafo traus teñol inru. Teñol inru. Kaaru ipi tenen itrapelpel, me kaaru ipi tenen ifrak.
Ale tenen itrapelpel ipi naik, naik

I will tell about two animals. One was a fast one, the other was a slow one.
Ok, the fast one is a fish, this

ne nagien na,
ipi nagi leg m̃as me ametp̃akro.

Ale kaaru ipi katom.

Me ag kuto lek naik itrapelpel,
me katom ifrak.
Ale malfanen rapuserek pan pan
pan, ratli na rakfes nawesien gar.

Nen rakfregnrogo nen kin,
rakfregnrogo nen rak, raktae
trapelpel nen rak-.
Fei kin kefo trapelpel go fei kin
kefo frak.
Ale rapregnrogo me katom ipi
tenen ifrak ale i-, is-, ipuserek kin
iseki nafsan ga pak katom laap
na katom laap ruk-, ruk-,
rukfregnrogo nen rutau em̃eltig
nen kin,
ifwel naik ke-, naik ke-, naik
kesosor, me rukfo trapelpel pes
nre nafsan.
Ale malfanen rapuserek pan
inom, go ratli na rakfregnrogo
Ale malfanen naik, naik isef. Ipan
pan pan na ipak nagis iskei.
Ale ipo pes, 'Ag kuipeto ko?' Go
katom ipo pesp̃tae naik ina, 'Neu
kaipe pei to me ag kuipo inrok.'

Ale ramer, imer sef pan pan pan
pan pan na, ipak nagis kaaru,
imer soso, 'Ag kuipe to ko?'
Go katom ina, 'Neu kaipe pei to
me ag kupo inrok.'

Ale imer pan pan pan pan pak

fish, it's name
it has a name but I can't
remember its name.
And the other one was the
hermit crab.
But you see that the fish is fast
and the hermit crab is slow.
Okay now they are talking,
talking, then they say they will
start their work.
That they tried to be able to go
fast.

Who would be the fastest and
who would be the slowest.
So they tried, but the hermit
crab, the slow one, said
to the many hermit crabs
that the many hermit crabs
should try to stay close,

if the fish called out they
should hurry to answer him.

So they talked and they said
they would try.
He went and went until he got
to the first point.
Then he said, 'Are you there or
what?' And the hermit crab
said to the fish, 'I was first but
you came behind.'
So they went again and he got
to the second point and called
again, 'Are you there?'
And the hermit crab answered,
'I was first and you came
behind.'
So he went on to the third

nagis katol, imer preg nfaoswen, 'Ag kuipe to ko?' Katom ina, 'Neu kaipe pei to me ag kupo inrok. Pan pan pan pan rapregi preg pregi pan pan pan naik ipan pan pan go kikano, go naik imat. Naik imat elau ale ntas ipo slati mai pak euut,

npakin ito nmalawen. Ale katom ipo to euut po mai pamlu namten. Go ipi nametꝑag natrauswen neu. *This is text 080.*

point and asked again, 'Are you there?' The hermit crab said, 'I came first but you came behind.' They kept going until

the fish couldn't keep on and he died. He died in the sea and the sea carried him onto the shore, threw him onto the sand. Then the hermit crab came to the shore and ate the fish's eyes. And that is the end of my story.

John Kaltaꝑau †
Tabu stones

A story about sacred stones that are used to ensure that food will be plentiful

Me faat nen ga taos rusosoki, nana, faat Lelep a? Tenen kin rupreg potut ki. Rutfagi pak elag. Faat ꝑrakot nen pato ita kerai mau, me tenen ga ikerai top. Tenen kutaiki kraus kram gaag itai sa me ga ipitkaskei ito.

Ikerkrai. Ipitlak faat nen itol, kulek inru rapato nlak nkas sanpen to? Tenen aslati Aneityum, nlaken akit tutiki esa.

(NT) Aneityum? (JK) Aneityum.
(NT) O, a.a.
Ipato natik nai a? Ga ipi faat nen kin ipaakor nai, ga ita paakor

And that stone is called Lelep. That's what they made an altar out of. They built it up there. Other stones aren't hard, but this one is really hard. This one you cut with your [kraus] axe it cuts badly and the stone stays as it was before.
It is hard. There are three of these stones, you see two over there at the tree? I got those from Aneityum, because we don't have it here.
(NT) Aneityum? (JK) Aneityum

It was on the river's edge. This is a rock that came out of a

ntan p̃rakot mau. Ga wankin
aweslua wes.
Me ga ipi faat, ne ipi, faat ipi
msal. Ipitlak tenen kin ipi teni
nafnag.
Taosikin rulao nawi kupan psi
talm̃at, kupsi talm̃at, malnen kin
ina iwel nawi rustat pak elag, go
kunrea itarp̃ek.
Me malpei, kupan lao kulaoki,
kulao kipi tu ntan. Kala, imten!
Kulaokin itu leg tu. Malnen
nafnag ina ipan panpan kuleka go
kunrea ipan tarp̃ek.
Nafnag rutu wi. O, nafnag itop.
Mm. Ipitlak faat ni nawi, ipitlak
faat ni nanr, ipitlak faat ni ntal,
teni apregnrogo rupitlaken.

Gawankia. Malpei, mal ni natap,
ga, ipitlak natap iskei, ga atap tae
mau puul ruto wok elag.

Gar rupreg ipi natap ga ipi
natam̃ol, go imaag teflan to.
Malen us iwo, kulek nawen ip̃ur

Man iskei kia rusosoki oknait,
sokfal, ga ipan laotu wes tu ne ito
min nkanron pan ga inrogo
namanrewen inom. Kimer nrir pa
me ip̃ur tu, me ipi faat.
Faat p̃ur. Kineu aleka me mees
nen puul iwok kulekor pregsakir.
Itu san rusosoki Em̃elfat
nametp̃agon leg. Faat p̃ur me ipi
natam̃ol.
Kupan leka ntwam me kuleka
kumtak kusef. Me malnen kuta

river, it is not from any ground.
That's where I got it from.
But that stone is different.
There is that one which is to do
with food.
When they plant yams, you put
them in the garden when yams
start to grow and you turn it, it
falls.
Before you would stand up a
rock like this. Oh it is heavy! [JK
lifting the rock] You stand it up.
Now the food would go on and
on, and you turn the stone.
Now, the food would be good.
Too much food. There was a
rock for yams, for banana, for
taro, whatever you wanted they
had a rock for it.
Long ago, in the time of idols,
there was one idol, I don't
know, bulldozers have worked
up there.
They make him an idol, he is a
person, and he is open. When it
rains you see the sand is piled
up.
This bird that they call owl, it
comes and stands on it and
drinks until it satisfies its thirst.
It flies off again but it is a stone.

A big stone. I saw it, but today
bulldozers have worked there
and damaged it. It's at the place
calle Em̃elfat, right at the end.
A big stone, but it is a man.
You see this devil, you see it
and run away. But now you

mtak mau, kofo pak m̃eltig me natam̃ol ko nafte?
Ko wan p̃afam̃ori na natap kin ruilaotu. Tewan rusosoki natap kia.
(NT) Me natap ita pi natopu?
(JK) E, natopu tep̃tae. Natopu, ga tenen kin ga ilakor pi tenen na Atua ga kipe preg ito emermen to. Ga ipi natam̃ol me ipi spirit p̃otae. Ipi naaten p̃otae.
(NT) Me natap ipi?
(JK) Natap ga imsal. Natam̃ol ki na ipreg natap.
Me Atua kin ipreg naaten, naaten p̃otae, naaten nen kin ipi naaten nen kin iwel ag kurog, go kefo watgik, a?
Atua ikano mai watgik mai tu natap tu na natap, naftemena, natopu nag kin to. P̃afan iskei.
Me ipo mer preg nalkis kenen, Iwel. Komam tete utae. Tete naat rutae. Malnen kin kuna kumsak go natam̃ol nen kin kefo gaag preg naul nkas taos meresin.

Kumingi kefo nrikin na, 'Ag kupan mes, e, mau ni na, natopu nen pato. Kukraksm̃anri imaetki kia kefo sm̃anri.
Ale imer puetlu kuler ta msak mau kumer m̃ol tkanwan nawesien ipanki. Or, teni nanre ni Melanesian, a, gawanki Natopu, natap, go potut go rumsal. Rumsal ruta pitkaskei mau...
This is text 092.

aren't scared, you go close, 'But is it a man or what?'
You find that it is an idol (natap) standing there. What they call an idol.
(NT) But the idol is not a spirit?
(JK) Natopu is different, it is what God made and put on the Earth. He is a man but a different spirit.

(NT) But what is the idol?
(JK) The idol is different. People made the idol.
God makes the spirit, different spirits, and if you do wrong he will punish you, eh?

God can't hurt you, he gives the spirit that to do. You go to one.

And he will make bush medicine for it. Some of us know. Some people know.
When you feel you are getting sick, this man will make leaf medecine for you.
You drink it and he will say, 'You go today, the natopu is there.'

He takes away your sickness. You are alive. That is his work. It is the Melanesian way.

Natopu, natap (idol) and potut (altar), they are all different. They are not the same.

John Kaltaβau †
A devil at Nguna

A devil at Nguna who makes everyone afraid and unable to cook in the daytime. A woman who runs away has a son who then challenges the devil and shoots it, and their dog chases the devil away.

Ana katraus natrauswen ni Egun.

I want to tell you a story from Nguna.

Egun nrak pei, ipitlak natamol kin naur Egun, nen Peter Milne ipakes pa.

On Nguna before, there was one of these men on Nguna island, where Peter Milne went to.

Ipitlak natamol, me ipitlak ntwam iskei ito. Me ito fam. Natrauswen tilmori nen kineu ato trausi. Akano traus natrauswen psir.

There were people and there was a devil there. It used to eat. This is a true story I am telling. I cannot tell a false story.

Nfaag ntwam nen ito fam. Ito fam pan me, ipan na kefam nmatu iskei, me nmatu nen itrau fag.

The story of the devil who ate. He ate until he wanted to eat this woman, but she had sores on her body.

Ipitlak nfag ru- namolin. Ina, 'O, me ag kufag ag βafo pi temlaap kafei pam tenen kin aleka na naskon imalmal wi, kin me kafo inrok mai pamik.'

She had sores all over her body. He said, 'Oh but you have sores, you will be the last, I will eat the ones whose skin I see is clean and then I will come and eat you.'

Me nmatu nen ito. Ito me kipe mtaki maarik ntwam ne. Ito pan pan, ntwam ito gohed fam ito fam, ito fam.

But the woman stayed. She was scared of the devil. She stayed and the devil kept eating and eating.

Nmatu nen ito pan imtak me ipitlak kori sees iskei. Inrik kori sees ga nen kin na, 'Taksef'. Rapa raru me rasef. Ramai mai rapalus mai, mai, mai mai mai.

The woman was scared and she had a little dog. She said to her dog, 'Let's escape.' They took a canoe and escaped. They came, they

Ramaos. Rato sal namos. Raimer palus pan ramai sak esan rusoso ki Krikai. Rasak Krikai. Rasak pak elag ntaf.

Rasak pak elag ntaf, rato ntaf to. Me rato panpan go nmatu nen ito pan pan me ipitlak teesa iskei.

Ipitlak teesa me teesa nanwei. Rana ratkos to panpan go teesa ga nen kito to me plakori ga nen ruto. Teesa ga nen ito to pan panpan kaipi natamol.
Me inrik mama ga ki na, 'E, mama, me tkanwan kin ag kuto maet kuk p̃og tefla?' Go mama ga ina, 'E me neu akano kuk aliat. Kakuk, akuk p̃og'.

Nlaken teesa ga ileka kuk ni p̃og me rupami p̃ulp̃og pami dina, me rapami kotfan. Me kefo mer kuk p̃og reki matool.

Ina, 'Iku kin komam uto pam nafnag mlaanr?' Go mama ga ina, 'Nlaken akano kuk aliat nlaken kin ipitlak ntwam iskei kin ito pam kit, nanre ni naur Egun'.

Kakuk aliat, kelek nuasog kefak elag kefo mai, kefo fareki. Me ina 'A, Me ikano mai', Teesa ga nen itli na, 'Itik ga, ikano mai.'

paddled and came and came. They were tired. They drifted on the ocean. They paddled some more until they landed at Krikai. They landed at Krikai. They climbed to the top of the hill.
They climbed up the hill, and stayed on the hill. They were there and the woman had a baby.
She had a boy. This boy and this dog, they stayed, then the child became a grownup.

He said to his mother, 'Hey, mother, why are you scared of cooking at night like this?' And his mother said, 'I can't cook in the day. If I cook, I cook at night.'
Because her child saw her cook at night and they ate it in the morning and they ate lunch in the afternoon. And she would cook again at night for the next day.
He said, 'Why do we eat cold food?' And his mother said, 'I can't cook in the daytime, because there is this devil who eats us, this side of Nguna island.
If I cook in the daytime, he will see the smoke rising, he will come because of it. And he said, 'Ah no, he can't come.' And her child said, 'No,

'Kefo mai tfale?' Go ina, 'Ᵽafo leka, kamer kuk aliat, me atli na, kafo tli na akano kuk.' Go inrik teesa ga inrikin ki na 'Okay, if wel kukano kuk aliat, upan upreg nas keskei'.

Ina, 'Kagaag preg nas. Kafo gaag preg nas.' Ina 'Ᵽafregsi nas, ᵽaneu tua ki timen kelim.' Aro. Timen kelim.
Ale ipreg nas kina inom, bow, inom, aro ipa. Imer ga preg timen ilim ina, 'Mama malfanen', Ina, 'Malfanen kapreg, ᵽakuk.'
Ᵽakuk aliat, me tufo nrogo. Malnen, ito, ikuk ina, 'Ᵽafo leka ᵽamer kuk aliat, ᵽafo nrog ntwam kefo pes'.

Me malnen ikuk panpanpanpan nuasog kipe pak elag. Inrogo ina, 'O ey naᵽkas inom mees kafo pam wes.' Kuleka?

Ntwam nen kin ipios. Malen mama, ni teesa ina, 'Ᵽanrogo, ᵽanrog nalen. Itli na mees kefo pam kit.'

Go teesa ga ina, 'Ᵽata mtak mau.' Me inrik kori sees ga nen kin na, 'Takfak sanpe me tak-. pan ᵽawelu wou me uta preg tᵽer. Kafreg fanis keskei, tᵽer keskei. Me kapreg, nana, nmet wes. Kapreg nmet wes me takfo pan kus tokos to.'

he can't come.'
'How will he come?' And she said, 'You will see, if I cook in the daylight, he will come, but I say I won't cook.' And her child said to her, 'Okay, if you can't cook in the daytime, we will go and make a bow.'
He said, 'I will make you a bow.' She said, 'When you have made the bow, make me five arrows.'
So he made the bow and arrows. He said, 'Mother, I'll make it so now you can cook.'

You cook in the daytime and we will listen for him. Then, she stayed, she cooked, he said, 'You will see, if you will cook again in the daytime you will hear the devil speak.'
And then she cooked until the smoke rose high. It smelled it and said, 'Oh the meat is ready, today I will eat you.' See?
The devil was calling out. Then the mother of the child said, 'Do you hear, do you hear his voice? He says that today he will eat us.'
And her child said, 'Don't be scared.' And he said to his small dog, 'We'll go over there. I'll make a fence, and I'll put a door in it. I'll put a door in it and we'll go and hide in it.'

Ag p̃afo to etan na ket me kineu kafo tu elag, kafo tp̃a ki nas.

Ina, 'P̃amer kuk.' Mama ga ikuk go imer pios, 'O ai'. Imer ler ipakelag pan, 'Ka- mees kafo pam wes, apam̃or nap̃kas iskei.

Me ito pes me ito palus, imai mai mai na isak elau Krikai

Go inrogo go ntwam nen imer m̃la. Im̃la pak elag, inag, im̃la a? 'O ai.' Ina, 'P̃anrog kin imer m̃la. Nalen kin ipak elag.

Kitli na kefo sak mai. Malnen ita pi twei mau go ipaakor ntaf.

Ipaakor ntaf tefla. Me ga itafnau kori ina, 'Malen kemai ag kin p̃akati'. 'P̃akati.' Me itli, 'A, itik p̃ata kati mau me p̃aneu tao me kafo tp̃a.

Kafo tp̃a'. Malnen ina itp̃a ki timen pei ntwam itnoli. Itp̃a ki timen kaaru. Ntwam itnoli.

Kaatol, kaafat, kalim, itnol silua. Go inrik kori kin ikati. Kori ikati ikati panpan inrog saki.

Natu iskasok skasok panpan inrogsaki natu kori isef pak elau ipa raru.

You will be down below at the gate and I will be above, I will shoot arrows.
He said, 'You keep cooking.' Her mother kept cooking and the devil called out again, 'Oh, ai.' He was coming up. 'I will eat here today, I have found some meat.'
And he talked and paddled, he came and came and landed at the beach at Krikai.
And she heard the devil growl and call again. It growled loudly. 'Oh ai'. She said, 'Do you hear that it is growling again. Its voice is loud.'
He said he would land. Not long after that he appeared on the hill.
He appeared on the hill like that. And (the man) taught his dog, 'When he comes you will bite him.' Then he said, 'Oh, no, don't bite him but leave him for me to shoot.'
I will shoot.' As he shot his first arrow the devil swallowed it. He fired his second arrow. The devil swallowed it.
The third, fourth and fifth, he swallowed every one. So he told the dog to bite him. The dog bit and bit until it felt bad from it.
The leg jumped around because its was sore, he ran back to the sea and paddled

South Efate Stories

Isef pak elau, me itoktan to raru to me ito maag, ito lek napu teflan po leka mau, kori ifit paakor.

Kori ifit paakor. Imtaki kori me isaiki raru. Ipalus panpanpanpanpan ga ito namos me imaos. Inpaki nawes elag na nakiat

Me ito marmar pan pan pan ikrokur. Kori kin iwat nrookot, pan pa pak natik raru ina, imtaki kori me imer ser, imer palus

Ipan pan na isak natkon Taalo, san kin isi pakes ina isal, isak wes. Ito marmar.

Ito marmar teflan panpanpan go ileka go kori ipaakor m̃eltig. Imtaki kori ifit. Ifit pak sum̃ ga me kutae, kros ni nmet ne, kros ne, ifit pak nmet ga go kros kaaru itan me ina itop po mer

ito etan tefla me ito toluki esum̃, ki em̃rom. Me ito ler pak ektem. Ito leka teflan panpan me ilelkau kori me kori itap leg ki napu mau. Me kori, iur naor p̃otae

Ilfek mai mai mai trau paakor natik

its canoe.
It ran back to the sea, it sat down in the canoe and it looked around (in fright). It was looking at the road as the dog appeared.
The dog came running. He was scared of the dog, and he pushed the canoe, he paddled and paddled until he was on the ocean, and he was tired. He threw the paddle on top of the cross-wood (of the canoe) and he rested.
He rested, then he was surprised. The dog had swum across to the side of the canoe. He was scared of the dog and he paddled again.
He went on to the other village, Taalo, the place that he went down to, he drifted and landed there. He rested. He rested like that until he saw the dog appear close by. He was scared of the dog and he ran. He ran back to his house, but, you know, the top of the door. He ran to his door and the other crossbeam was low and he was tall and then. he was below, and he turned his back on the inside of the house. And he went outside. He looked and looked but he didn't see the dog, but the dog wasn't right on the road. The dog went a different way. The dog went around and

nmet. Ipaakor natik ne tefla me ntwam ileka me ina kesok. Me isok, me ifrak.

Isok me ikrel nana, nkas ni kros. Trau tau sal tefla.

Itrau sal itrau sal me kori iwokim kati panpanpanpan itarp̃ek. Ina itarp̃ek pak etan go ikatktof na

ikatktof, nana, ikatktof, nana, pol, na, p̃ura ga. Ikatktof p̃ura ga. Ipo komkomki. Ntwam itarp̃ek kaimat pe.
Me ini ntwam komkomki na p̃ura ga pa. Iolwe me ipan los nrookot. Ipan panpan pak elag Krikai,

pan lek kano sees ne plak mama ga. Me ipak natkin teflan me ilai.

Ilai na p̃ura ni na ntwam ne. Me ina, 'Ga ki. Kaipe katpuni.

Malfane tupo ler.' Kin ruler, gar rupak Egun pan kin go im̃ol im̃ol ipo mer ftomki natam̃ol.

Kin panpanpan kin mees nen kin natam̃ol rupo laap naur Egun. Tenen ga ipi natrauswen tilm̃ori. Anig teesa nen rutu trausi.
This is text 094.

came just to the edge of the door. He appeared at the edge there, and the devil saw him and wanted to jump. He jumped, but he was slow. He jumped and grabbed the wood of the top of the door. It just hung there.
He hung there and the dog bit him and bit him until he fell down. When he fell down the dog bit off
he bit off, he bit off, his balls. He bit off his balls. He sucked them. The devil fell down and died.
And he sucked the devil's balls and went. He swam all the way across, and came ashore at Krikai,
he went to see this small man with his mother. He went to his side and he spat.
He spat out the devil's balls there. And he said, 'Here it is, I bit it and killed it.
Now let's go back.' They went back to Nguna and it was healthy and would again have more people.
Until today when lots of people live on Nguna. That is a true story. I tell it to the children here.

Toukelau Takau
Litapurong and Ati Tam̃am

A story of a girl, Litapurong, who lived with her mother and grandmother but who is abducted by a ntwam or devil.

Natrauswen ni sa, ipiatlak, imer piatlak na, ati iskei go mama iskei.

The story from here, it has a grandmother and a mother.

Rapitlak teesa nmatu iskei iskotir to. Teesa nmatu ne, temen ga kipe mat.

They had one girl who lived with them. The girl's father had died.

Me mama go ati kin raplaker ruto, ruto pan nrak iskei go

The mother and grandmother stayed with them, until one time and

runa rukfreg kapu, runa rukfreg kapu.

they wanted to make laplap, they wanted to make laplap.

Go runrik-, mama go ati ranrik teesa ki na, teesa nmatu ki na, 'P̃afan gakit sao ntas elau.'

And they said, the mother and grandmother said to the girl, 'You go and get saltwater from the sea for us.'

Nlaken malpei, ga sol ga ntas, ruta pakot sol taos mees mau.

Because in those days they got saltwater, they didn't pay for salt like today.

Pan gakit sao ntas, me tukfo pi naniu gakit, ko tukfi kapu gakit.

Go get us saltwater, then we will pour it on our coconut and pour it on our laplap.

Teesa ipa, isat botel ipak elau pa, islat las naniu, ipan na kesao ntas.

The child went, she took a bottle and went to the sea, she took a coconut shell so she could get salt water.

Ina ipan kaipuel, me ipiatlak mtulep iskei, ga ito nmal napu.

She went, then she disappeared, but there is a woman (a spirit woman) who is there, halfway along the road.

Mtulep nen itaos na, ipi na setan, ga itaos ntwam.

This woman is Satan, like a devil.

Ipi ntwam, me ipiatlak erfale ga ito, teesa nmatu nen ina ito,

She is a devil, but her cave is there, the girl is there, she went

ipak elau pan na iler na imai.
Go ntwam kipuetsoki, ipuetsoki
kaipsi ranru to eṁrom, rato nfal
faat.
Mama go ati rato panpan ki
teesa nmatu ipuel, rapan
panpan ler pak elau, pan.

Ra-, mama ga-, raiten ipak elau
pan ilerekin ipuel elau, go itae
nen kin, kipe mai kon nmal
napu ki.
Ina ito kaipa, ipan, ipaṁori na
ga kin ito erfale esa.
Go ilag isoso, nagien Litapurog.

Me tenen ito nfal faat nagien
Taṁam, nagien Taṁam.
Me tetau nmatu ne nagien
Litapurog.
Raiten ina ipa, me itraem soso,
ilag: 'Ƥataf eṁae e, ṗataf eṁae e.

Litapurogo, Litapurogo ṗataf
eṁae e, ṗataf eṁae e.'
Ale Litapurog ipes, ipes eṁrom,
ipo pestaf raiten pak elag.

Anag kataf me ati Taṁam, ifla
miawe, ifla miawe.

Tefla itefla, a.a.
This is text 096.

to the sea, and was coming back.
And the devil held tight and put
them both inside a cave.

The mother and grandmother
stayed until the girl didn't come
back, they went to the sea to
look.
Her mother went to the sea, but
she was not at the sea, and she
knew that she had got stuck
along the road.
Then she went and saw that her
daughter was in this cave here.
And she sang, she called out, her
name Litapurong.
But the one who was in the rock
was called Taṁam.
But this woman's child was
called Litapurong.
The mother wanted to go, but
she tried singing: 'You go far
away, you go far away.
Litapurongo, Litapurongo, You
go far away, you go far away.'
So Litapurong spoke, she spoke
inside, she talked to her mother
up above.
I want to get out, I want to get
out but Nana Taṁam might
miao. (?)
Like that, it's like that, yes.

Metu Josef †
Agel ni Ermag, The angel from Erromango

A woman who could fly between Erromango and Efate but whose
wings are stolen by a man who then lives with her and she

has his children. Eventually they find her wings and she is able to return to her home, leaving them.

Ruto los ena, ruto pan los Ermag me gar,

The washed there, they would go and wash at Erromango, but they,

rupi nana, rupi nafet nmatu m̃as.

they were a group of women.

Nmatuerik. Me kin rulaoki nafarur runrir. Runrir mai pak e rupak e- Ermag pan rupan los. Me ruto pregi ser nrak. Rupan los panpan inom tefla. Kin, p̃ata preg tenen mau. Me katraus teflan tukpe pei nrogo. Ina rupa, rupan me ru-.

Young girls. They would put on their wings and fly. They flew to, they flew to Erromango to wash. And they do this every time. They went and washed until it was enough. You don't do that. And I'll tell it how we first heard it.

runa- ruto elag sanpe e ilakor pi

He said, they go, they go, but they they are far up there, it might be,

rupato-, rupato e Ep̃uf me,

they are far up there, it might be, they were there, at Bufa, and they wanted to go and wash over there.

rumur na rukfak, e, rufan los sanpe.

Rutrau stat nrir trau pa. Rupa.

They just started to fly and went. They went.

Malen kin runa rukfa, rutmer, rutmer, runa runa rutmer mai p̃onkir panpan inom tefla, rutmer fer panpan inom. Rutm̃alu.

When they wanted to go, they ...

they closed their wings until they were ready, they counted each other. They left.

Rutm̃alu, kainrir panpanpan rupan lao Ermag.

They left, they flew until they landed at Erromango.

Rupan lao Ermag, rulao tete nai nen kin, nai ito-, itop Ermag, me ata tae sef nai kin rupakes mau.

They stood up on Erromango, at a river. There's lots of rivers on Erromango, but I don't know which water they got to.

Ale rupan na, rulos, rulos teflan pan inom.

Then, they went in order to wash, they washed until they

Me, kano iskei ga ikus to, ikus to leker.
Me rulos panpan inom teflan rumai
pak euut teflan, ru- kutae ru= pre- jenj panpan panpan go go inom.
Tefla. Rupreg na,
rulaoki nafarur tefla, me runrir, runa ruknrir.

Me iskei me iskei nafarun ipuel.
Go inrogtesa wes. Ruileles panpan me rukano wes.

Me kano nen kin ikus to israkor na nafaru-, na teesa nmatu ne.
Go mal tefla nen kin al ipak etan teflan, me tenen ruipa.
Me nmatu, na- teesa nmatu nen nmatu nen ito kait na, nafarun.
Ikaiten panpan.
Ruito, runa, 'Ag p̃ato me mam ko-, kofan me.'
Runa ruto kaipa me, ga ito.
Ito panpan go natam̃ol nen israkoro ipo mai.
Imai na ina, ipo psir na, 'Ag kupo-, kuto lel nafte?' Go ipo tli,

'E, Me nafarum ga ilakor to, ko naat ifla wesi.'

Me ga iwesi.
Ipregkoro ito panpan mal skei mau nen kin.
Gar rukui mai go ina, 'E, naat ilakor srakor, nana nafarum.

finished.
But this man hid, he hid and he looked at them.
They washed and washed then came
to shore like this, you know they changed.

Like that. They did that,
they put their wings on like that, and they flew, they wanted to fly.
But one was missing her wings.
And she felt bad because of it.
They looked and looked but they couldn't find them there.
But the man who was hiding hid the girl's wing.
And that time, the sun was going down, and these ones all went.
But this girl cried for her wings.

She cried for them.
They were there, they said, 'You stay, but we will go.'
They left, but she stayed.
She stayed and stayed until the man who was hiding came.
He came to say, he was going to lie, 'Are you looking for something?' And he said,
'Hey, but your wings might be here, or someone might have taken them.'
But he had taken them.
He covered them up for all this time.
They all came and he said, 'I think someone hid your wings.

Akit talakor pan nru pan matur.
Go kiplake pa, kiplake pan,
ranru matur.
Iplake pan ramatur panpan
panpan, kipi nmatu ni kano nen
to.
Panpan go, ita p̃okoro ki puur
lisan ito.
Me israkor wi ki, me ito panpan
go ipitlak teesa inru, teesa
nanwei inru.
Teesa ni kano ne. Kano nen ina
ito pan go ina, 'Koto me kamer
pak talm̃at pa.'

Malnen kin ipak talm̃at pa, ipato
panpan imalik, mai ki nmatu
nen ito.

Me ruta pam̃or namrun nen
mau, me ito pan kaipe pi nmatu
ga to, me
ito mroki- to mroki nam̃er ga
nen kin ruipe pa.
Ruto mai traem panrogo me,
ina, 'Nafaruk ita puel. Kapei to.'

Ito pan panpan
nrak iskei go
teesa sees nra nen, rato pan me
ratili na rukgar preg nas a?

Go rata tup̃, go ratup̃ na. Go nas
a go
teem̃ol seserik nen kin ruto sil
sil na, e, panpan.
Teem̃ol iskei ina, Kutae ofag?
Ina isef pan trau sil puur lisan
ne.

You and me should go to sleep.'
And he took her and went, he
took her and they both slept.
He took her and went, they slept
until she became that man's
wife.
On and on and he still covers
them with a giant clam shell.
But he hid it well, and she stayed
on until she had two children,
two sons.
Children of this man. The man
stayed on, then he said, 'You
stay, and I will go to the garden
again.'
When he went to the garden, he
stayed there until dark, he came
back to the woman who was
there.
But they didn't find this thing
(the wings), and she stayed until
she became his wife, but
she still thought about her
people who had gone.
They came and tried to go but,
she said, 'My wings are still
missing. I will stay here.'
She stayed and stayed until
one time, and
the two children said they
wanted them to make them a
bow.
And they kept shooting, they
shot-. And the bow.
And they shot small animals that
go inside-
This animal, you know geckos?
It wanted to escape and it ran
inside this clam shell.

Malen kin kaaru ipo na inrea teflan trau pam̃or tenamrun p̃ur ni Mama ga.

Me maarik nen ga kipe pak talm̃at pa.

Ipak talm̃at pan pato talm̃at tu me,

teesa ne ipam̃ori me itrau slati pan:.

Inrik iak ga ki na, 'He, e.'

Apap-, ore iak ga ki na, 'Apam̃or namrun iskei me itrau wipewi.'

Ale ipeikin kin teflan go itrau mur me ina, 'O atrau semsem lek namrun go.'

Go itrau na, malfanen kaigar preg nafnag ki, me kafo traem wes. Ilakor ta wi to ki.'

Igar preg nafnag panpan, nen kin ketaor ki.

Igar preg nafnag panpanpan rato fam.

Isol kutae tenamrun ni tiawi nen kin ruto- runa ntae a?

Ilofir kin panpan rawi to.

Ipregi ralos panpan inom me rapo ipo gar pregi.

Pan inom ina, 'Raknrokof nafnag gamus to, me kineu katraem nana, namrun ne, katraem wes. Ilakor ta wi to ko?'

Malen kin ipo traem teflan itrau tae nrir a?

Isemsem wes, me, ina imai

When the other one turned like this he just found this big thing of his mother's.

But the husband had gone to the garden.

He had gone and stayed at the garden, but

the child discovered them and just took it and went.

He told his mother, 'Hey.'

his father-, his mother, he told her, 'I found these things and it is really beautiful.'

So he showed her and she laughed and said, 'Oh I am glad to see this.'

And she said, 'Now I'll make their food, but I'll see if these (wings) work. Maybe they still work.'

She made food for them, that she would leave for them.

She made food for them, and they ate.

She took, you know this thing the old people had that they call 'shit'?

She rubbed them with it until they were good.

She made them wash until they finished, she did it for them.

When they finished she said, 'You finish your food, but I will try these things (wings). Are they still good?'

When she tried them, she could fly.

She was happy about it, and she

kaimer mai
imai sog nañer nran ne, inakin,
'Kafo tao mus ki.
Me raktoreki apap gamus to.'
Me maarik nen ipato me inrogo
teflan kin
al ito pañas, me iwelkia tfa ito
kat.
Go ina, 'Mes nen tfa kin ito kat
neu me al ito pa.'
Me mtulep ga ito p̃or na, ntali
p̃ur iskei ito em̃au ga a?

Me ito krakp̃orp̃or namrun ne,
nen kin kenrogo me kemai.
Pregi panpanpan inom tefla, na
nra ntali ien

Me mtulep kipe pa, a? Maarik
nen imai mai mroki na ipo taos
sermal
Po na imai ki tenran rato, ina
ilek, ileka teflan kin rapi na,
ntae ito a?
Rupam̃or namrun nen, mtulep
nen pan kipak nam̃len pa.

Malen kin imai,
imai na inrikin ki tefla, go
ranrikin kin na na, 'O Mama
nigmam kipe pa.'
Kipe pak nam̃len pa.
'Me fei kin ipam̃ori?' Go rana,
'Komam, komam rapam̃ori.'

Go itraem laokin kia kunrog na,
nra ntali nen ien kia ruto
m̃altelit. Go ina

came
and kissed the boys and she said,
'I will leave you.
But you wait for your father'
But the man was there and he
heard how
the sun was shining but there
was the sound of thunder.
And he said, 'Today there is
thunder, but the sun is shining.'
But his wife was breaking the
branches of the big natapoa
(tropical almond tree) that was
in her yard.
She broke them so he would
hear it and come,
So that when she finished, the
branches of the natapoa lay
around.
And the woman was gone. The
husband came and he thought it
would be like every other time.
He came to the two boys,
he saw that there was 'shit'
there.
They found this 'shit'. This
woman had gone back to her
place.
And when he came,
they told him, 'Oh, our mother
has gone.'

She has gone back to her place.
'But who found them (the
wings)?' And they said, 'We
found them. '
And she was trying to put them
on and you could hear her
breaking all the natapoa

'O anrogo me amroki nana tfa ito kat, me al ito pa.'

'O, I heard it, but I thought it was thunder, but the sun was shining.'

'E ga kia ipregi.'

'She did it.'

Panpan kipa. Ipan pan tuk mees ne.

Until she went. She went and is gone until today.

Kipe pak nañlen pa.

She went back to her place.

This is text 098.

John Kalfau
Ririel and Ririal

The same story told elsewhere in this collection, but here it is told by a nine-year old

Nagi kineu John Kalfau Ana katil na kastom stori ni natkon.

My name is John Kalfau. I want to tell a custom story from the village.

Me taitel, taitel knen, taitel taetel knen ina, ipi teni Ririel go Ririal.

The title of it is Ririel and Ririal.

Me gar rato siwer pan, rasiwer pan ale ratrau lek ntali ale ramai.

They were walking and they saw an almond tree.

Rapagsak ki ntali Ririel ga ipagki ntali ne, me ipag pato elag,

They climbed the almond tree, Ririel climbed this almond, he climbed high.

Ale ruto le, le ntali panpan ina inom.

They looked for almonds until they were done.

Ale ito npakin isu mai pak etan ito tu Ririal kin. Me Ririel ina ipuetsok nrankas iskei.

So he threw them down to Ririal. But Ririel wanted to hold on to a branch.

Ale me imer pus natuen nranru ipak nkas nñarteu ale ina ito teflan trau þrai nkas teflan trau tarþek mai pak etan.

He put both his feet on a dry branch and broke the wood, and fell to the ground.

Trau mat nrak iskei. Ale Ririal itrau kai teflan ale ikai pan ina ilag pan pan pan inom.

He died straight away. Then Ririal cried and cried, then he sang until it was over.

Ale rusati elag mai mer us napu mai mai mai pak esumĩ. Ale imai lek mama mana.

Ok, they took him and followed the road and came back to the house. Then he came and saw his mother and others.

Ale gar rukaiten pan na inom. Rupus nafumĩnkas kin pan inom. Rupo tankin nanre, nanre nasumĩ gar. Ale ipo nom
This is text 100.

They cried for him until they stopped. They put flowers on him. They would bury him by the side of his house. And that's the end.

Toukelau Takau
Wit go kusu, the octopus and the rat

The rat wants to cross back to Efate and asks the octopus to ride on its head. They have an argument and the octopus uses its ninth tentacle to whip the rat who grabs the tentacle and it becomes the rat's tail.

Amurin gaag puserek, Nick, kafo gaag pusereki kusu go wit.

I want to tell you, Nick, I'll tell you about the rat and the octopus.

Naliati iskei, elau imat. Elau imat, itrau mat pe mat pe mat me. Ipiatlak nskau ienkot naur iskei.

One day, it was low tide. It was low tide, a really low tide. There was a reef that lay around an island.

Naur sees iskei ito elau me elau imat. Malen elau imat kerkrai, mat top, go nskau igar userek

This island was in the sea, but the tide was out. When the tide was really low, very low, the reef was dry right around

pan tkal naur sees. Me kusu, kusu iskei, ito Efat.

right up to the small island. But the rat, this rat, it was from Efate.

Ileka na elau imat top. Isemsem imur nag, isiwer ur nskau.

It saw that the tide was out. It was happy, he wanted to walk along the reef.

Ipi nlaken kusu isiwer, ipan pato siwer ur nskau panpanpan ipak naur sees.	That's why the rat walked along the reef, until it got to the small island.
Ipak naur sees. Isiwer panpan inrogo kin nlag.	It walked to the small island. It walked and it felt the wind.
Inrogo kin nlag na nanre naur sees ne, go	It felt the wind along the side of the island, and
ipen marmar	it rested there.
Ipato marmar panpan panpan panpan panpan me elau kipe to mu.	It stayed, rested for a long time, and the tide started to come in.
Elau kipe to mu, me selwan kin ipen sat nlag panpanpan imroki nen keler.	The tide came in, but as he felt the wind, he thought he would return.
Me imai me elau kipe mu top.	He came, but the the tide was too high.
Elau imu top go, ipregi kipe kano nrookot.	The tide was too high so that he couldn't cross.
Nlaken kin elau kipe mu top.	Because the tide was too high.
Nao kin kipe to mai pa go kipe tu fit lefek.	A wave came in and it (the rat) ran around.
Itu fit lefek imurin na inrookot me kipe kano.	It ran around, it wanted to cross, but it couldn't.
Go, malfane, wit wit imai.	And now the octopus came.
Wit imai me ileka kin ito fit lefek.	The octopus came and saw that he was running around.
Go wit kipaoski na,	And the octopus asked him,
'Me ag kuku? Kumurin na kufak nanre ko?'	'But what are you doing? Do you want to go to the other side?'
Me ina, 'Ore, kineu amatur, natowen neu ato nanre.	And the rat said, 'Yes, I sleep, I stay on the other side.
Ato Efat.	I stay on Efate
Me amai marmar esan me.'	But I come over here for a rest.'
Ale, kusu ito fit lefek, ito fit lefek, ki naur me wit kipe leka.	So the rat kept running around the island, but the octopus saw the rat.
Selwan wit ina imai,	When the octopus wanted to

imai pak euut me ipan soksoki
ina, 'Me ag kuku?'
Me ina, 'Neu natowen neu ato
Efat.
Me alek elau imat wi.

Ato siwer ur nskau mai mai,
anrogo kin nlag ni naur sees, go

kaipe to marmar panpanpan
malfane.
Namroan neu amroki nen kafei
ler me elau kipe mu top.
Go, kineu kaipe kano nrookot
nlaken kin elau kipe mu top.'
Go wit ipaoskin ki, ina, 'Me
kumurin na kawelu ag?'
Go kusu ina, 'Me wel kin
kuwelu wou iwi top.'
Ina, 'Ƥamai totan nanuak.'

Ƥamai totan nanuak, me kineu
kafo fan nrookot.'
Malfane, kusu ipan totan.
Na wit, me wit iofa nrookot nen
kefan psi na, Efat.
Me malen kefan to namos me
nao kipe top.
Nlaken nao imai na, islatir epak
elag tefla.
Go nƥau wit kimer tul

Nƥau wit itul tefla, go kusu
inaito imer murki.

Kusu ito murki nƥau wit.

Go wit ina ito me ina, 'Me ag

come,
it came to the shore and it said,
'What are you doing?'
And the rat said, 'My life is on
Efate.
But I saw that the tide is really
low.
I walked over the reef and
came, I felt the wind from the
small island, and
I stayed and rested until now.

I thought I could get back but
the tide was too high.
And I couldn't cross back
because the tide was too high.'
And the octopus asked the rat,
'Do you want me to help you?'
And the rat said, 'If you would
help me it would be very good.'
It said, 'Come and sit on my
neck.'
Come and sit on my neck and I
will go across.'
So the rat sat down.
The octopus carried the rat
and put it on Efate.
But when it was in the ocean
the waves were too big.
Because the wave came and
took them up high.
And the octopus's head was
swaying.
The octopus's head was
swaying, and the rat decided
he wanted it.
The rat wanted the head of the
octopus.
And the octopus said, 'What do

kuto murki nafte?'
Go kusu ina, 'E ato mur kin nao
isat, kitau pakelag kaimer
paketan.'
Rapanpan na rato na nmal
namos.
Me nao kipe kerkerai.
Islatir teflan go nɡ̃au wit kimer
tul.
Go kusu kimer mrosm̃anr na

nɡ̃au wit, go kimer mur, go ina,
'A me kumurin nafte kin?'

Ina, 'E, itik amur kin ki nao ito
slat kito pakelag me imer
paketan.'
Me gar rapanpan panpan rapak
natik euut.
Kusu ileka na itae sok pak nmal
nawen.
Ikam nɡ̃au wit trau sok.

Isok pak na nmal nawen pan, na
ilek wit pak elau, me inrik wit
ki na,
'Kineu ato murki nɡ̃aum kia.'
Ito murki nɡ̃aun nlaken kin na,
nao islat na,

islatki tefla go nɡ̃aun kimer
farfar kimer tul.

Ina, 'Ato murki nɡ̃aum.'
Me wit kipe maetki.

Me na, imaetki kusu teflan go
ipuetlu nlaɡ̃wen me ifis,

you want?'
And the rat said, 'I wanted the
wave to take us up and down
again.'
They kept on going until they
were in the middle of the sea.
But the wave was strong.
It took them like this and the
octopus's head swayed again.
And the rat again thought
about
the octopus's head, and
wanted it, and the octopus
said, 'What do you want?'
The rat said, 'No, I want the
wave to take us, it was up high
but it went down again.'
And they kept on going until
they got to the shore.
The rat saw that it could jump
into the middle of the sand.
It stood on the octopus's head
and jumped.
It jumped to the middle of the
sand, and it saw the octopus in
the sea and said to the octopus,
'I want your head.'
The rat wanted the octopus's
head because the wave had
taken,
it had taken it like this, and the
head had continued to move
about, to sway.
It said, 'I still want your head.'
And the octopus got angry
with the rat.
It got angry with the rat, and it
took off a tentacle and
whipped,

South Efate Stories

ipulkin pak kusu.
Ipul kusu ki go, gawankin nlap̃ wit, naen wan kin ipuki napu kusu to.

Nlap̃ wit ipi, wit ipiatlak nlap̃wen ipi naen.
Me ina ipuetlu iskei na ipul kusu kin. Go kusu iof napuen iskei ipi napuen me,

ga ipiatlak na nlap̃wen rupi eit.

Go natrauswen gar kipe nom esa.
This is text 101.

it slung it at the rat.
It slung the rat with it and that's the octopus's ninth tentacle, that he made the rat's tail.
The octopus had nine tentacles.
But it wanted to take off one of them to sling it at the rat. And the rat put on its tail, it became its tail,
(The octopus) it had eight tentacles.
And their story finishes here.

Kalsarap Namaf †
Litrapong and Kaltong

The story concerns Litrapong, a natopu or spirit. Kalsarap tells of his son, Kaltong, who was sick and needed custom medicine.

Akit tumaui tae esan ipi, go Litrapog ne, amurin na kanrik mus ki,
Litrapog ne, ipi naflak ni apu.
Gar apu rato puserek ser tete nrak.

Ser nrak rato puserek, rato ur naor iskei. Atae naliati iskei

komam upak elag ntaf. Aplak teesa nen upa, upan Kaltog isees. Kaltog kipe pi natam̃ol p̃ur, me
malran una upa, go Litrapog me imai. Imai ilakor mai saof apu

We all know that place, and this Litrapong, I want to tell you about her.
This Litrapong, she is of grandfather's clan. Those two, grandfather and Litrapong, would talk every now and then. They would always talk, they would be at the same place. I know one day
we went up a hill. I went with my child. Kaltong was small. Kaltong is already a big man, but

when we went Litrapong came. She might have come to visit

sanie nlaken gar rapi nametrau
iskei naflak kram.

Ralakor, ilakor mai lemsi, mer,
na keler. Mam upak talm̃at pan
go ipuetsok Kaltog.
Umai na kofak esum̃ Kaltog
imsak. Alereki nen kin
kenrogtiawi, uga preg nalkis.

Ser naor wes napu, na, aga preg
nalkis ikano nrogtiawi.

Me natam̃ol iskei ipi natam̃ol ni
Banks, rusoso ki Selwin.
Naliati ne, natam̃ol nen iskot
Paul go Alick to, elau Emtapenr,

apan leka anrikin ki na, 'E
amurin na p̃amai ni Kaltog preg
nalkis, if wel kuf tae pregi.' Go
ina, 'O iwi.'

Go ipo mai, anrikin kin, 'Kaltog
kin to me imsak.
Atap tae nafte if pi nlaken kin
imsak mau.
Amurin na p̃atraem ga preg tete
nalkis gaag, nen ag kutae.'

Go ipo pregnrogo ina, 'Iwi.' Ipan
neu wes nalkis mai, tu Kaltog
kin imingi. Me ipo lek, nalkis
nen ipo pregi ipo siwer.

Malnen ipa, ipak Ertap pa, ipan
pato, ipan, ipan Kaltog ito erfale
nen ato tli.

Grandfather
over there, because they are the
same naflak (clan), naflak kram,
the clam clan.
Maybe she came to see him, then
go back. We went to the garden,
and she was holding Kaltong.
We came to go to the house,
Kaltong was sick. I waited until
he felt better, we got him herbal
medecine.
every place on the road, I got
him medecine, but he didn't feel
better.
There was this man from the
Banks Islands, called Selwin.
At this time, that man was with
Paul and Alec by the sea at
Emtapenr.
I went to see him and I said,
'Hey, I would like you to come
and make some medecine for
Kaltong, if you can do it.' And he
said, 'Okay.'
And he came, I told him,
'Kaltong is there but he is sick.
I don't know what caused his
sickness.
I want you to try to make some
medecine for him as you know
how to.'
So he tried, he said, 'Okay'. He
went and brought leaf medecine,
gave it to Kaltong to drink. And
he looked, the medecine made
him walk.
When he went, he went to
Eratap, he stayed, he went and
saw Kaltong in this cave that I

Isiwer ki nalkis nen pa, ipam̃ori na, mtulep nen kin ipreg Kaltog imsak.

Ipi nlaken ipa, ipan me mtulep nen ipato esan kin ato tli. Ipato mp̃agon, maumau.

Polis ga rato na, nmet, me ga, ga ipato mp̃agon.
Ipregnrogo nen kin kefan, me mtulep itap trok nen kin kefo pan mau, ina, mtulep nen ileka go ina, 'Mees kin apo pkaskei lemisik.'
Inrik Selwin kin teflan, go Selwin ina, 'Kineu amai, apa reki Kaltog.
If wel kuf tae trok wes go kafo plake ler.' Go mtulep inrikin ki na,
mtulep nen inrikin ki na, 'Atap trok nen p̃afo plak Kaltog mau.'

Ito mro panpan inom. 'Kafo pregnrogo.' Ito ipan lek nmarit sees iskei.
Ipuet nmarit nen, me iur elag faat pan pato elag

me ipo pusfifki faat nen ipak etan pa. Nmarit nen ipak etan.

Malnen ina ipregi ipan go Kaltog ina ito etan imer le sak tefla, go Selwin inrikin kin na,

'P̃afuetsok nmarit.' Malnen

am talking about.
He walked about because of the leaf medecine, and he found out that this woman (Litrapong) made Kaltong sick.
That's why he went, he went and this old woman (Litrapong) was in this place I talked about. She was right at the end of it.
Her police were at the door, but she was at the end of the cave.
He tried to go, but the old woman didn't want him to go, she said, this old woman looked at him and said, 'It is just today that I see you.'
She said this to Selwin, and Selwin said, 'I come on behalf of Kaltong,
If you agree to it, then I will take him back.' And the old woman said to him,
the old woman said to him, 'I don't agree that you take Kaltong back.'
He stopped and thought and thought. 'I'm going to try.' He went and saw a small vine.
He pulled this rope, and he climbed above, a stone that was up above.
He threw the rope down. The rope went to the bottom (of the cave).
When he had made the rope go down, Kaltong was down, he looked up again like this, and Selwin said to him,
'You take hold of the rope.'

Kaltog ina ipuetsok nmarit go

Selwin imailum pueti imai mai mai mai. Mtulep ne itu preg namurien ga, itap tae teflan kin Kaltog itaf mau.
Ikrokur kin Kaltog kipe pato elag. Selwin inrikin ki na, 'Ƥakel ntakuk.'

Malnen rakel ntakun, go Kaltog ikel ntak Selwin teflan go rakailer mai pak esum̃, Erakor.

Go ipi nametp̃ag natrauswen neu. Kaltog im̃ol tuk mees
This is text 103.

When Kaltong took hold of the rope and
Selwin slowly pulled he came and came. The old woman was doing her own things, she didn't know that Kaltong got out.
She was surprised that Kaltong got up out of the cave. Selwin said to Kaltong, 'You hold my back.'
Then they held his back, and Kaltong held Selwin's back like this and they came back to the house at Erakor.
And it is the end of my story. Kaltong is alive to this day.

Harris Takau
Ririal and Ririel

Ririal is a story about two brothers who go to gather fruit. Ririel climbs a nakavika (Syzygium malaccense) tree and Ririal catches the fruit. Ririel falls and dies. Ririal sings a song asking first a pig, then a horse then a flying fox to take a message back to this parents. The first two ignore the request, but the flying fox takes the message and the parents come to take their son and bury him.

Ipiatlak nmatu iskei,
nmatu tiawi iskei ipiatlak teesa inru rana rato panpan.

Go, teesa nra nen nagier kaaru nen ipi Ririel go kaaru ipi Ririal.
Rana rato panpan go teesa nen rana rakfan lel nkafik, mal ni nkafik.

There was this woman,
this old woman, she had two children and they lived and lived.
And these two children, their names, one was Ririel and one was Ririal.
They stayed and then these children wanted to look for nakavika fruit, it was the

Nkafik imam, rana rapa.

Ale, kaaru ina,
Ririel inrik Ririal ki na, 'Ag
p̃afei. Ag p̃afag.'
Go Ririal imer nrik Ririel ki na,
'Tik, ag p̃afag.'
Rana rapregi panpan go Ririel
kin ipo pag.
Ipagki nkafik pak elag, me
Ririal ito etan.
Ina israf trau m̃el, itarp̃ek.
Itarp̃ek mai pak etan.
Ina itarp̃ek mai pak etan trau
mat.
Ale Ririal ina isatsok, ina islati
kaipe to tag.
Ito tagsi panpan go
nana wak iskei imai, wak ina
imai go
Ririel inrik wak ki na, 'P̃afa neu
ona,
p̃afa neu nrik mama neu go
papa neu ki na,
Ana, 'Ririel ina itarp̃ek me
imat.'
Ale ga ipo laga ipi nalag:
Wak e p̃a ginau rogorogo ki
tete go mame.

Ririel o kitiroa matetoko.
Ririal eselatia toko tagisi ae.

Ririel o, ririel o, riel o, i!
Ale wak ina ipan me ita ler
mau.

season for nakavika (Syzygium
malaccense).
The nakavika were ripe, they
went.
So the other one said,
Ririel said to Ririal, 'You go first.
You climb'.
Then Ririal said to Ririel again,
'No, you climb!'
They wanted to get it and Ririel
was the one to climb.
He climbed up the nakavika and
Ririal stayed down below.
He missed it and fell down
He fell back down to the ground.
He fell down to the ground, like
he was dead.
So Ririal took him, he carried
him and he cried.
He cried for him until
a pig came by, the pig came and

Ririel said to the pig, 'You go,

You go and tell my mother and
father this for me,
I said 'Ririel fell and he died.'

Then he began to sing this song,
[Song. The words are in a North
Efate language (Ngunese), but
translate as 'Pig, you go and tell
my father and mother for me.']
[Ririel has fallen and died]
[Ririal has taken him and is
crying for him.]
Ririel o ririel o riel o. i.
The pig was going, but he didn't
go back at all.

Ita pa nrik, ita pa nrik mama ga go papa kin mau.
Ale ina ito panpan go, hos imai hos ina imai. Ale imer nrik hos ki na
hos kefan nrik papa ga go mama ki, ale itli ipi nalag ina:

Hos e p̃aginau rorogo ki tete go mame.
Ririel o kitiroa mate toko.
Ririal Eselati atoko tagisi ae.
Ririel o Ririel o Riel o i

Ale, hos ina ipa ita pan nrik temen go raiten kin mau. Me ina ipan kaipe pa.
Ale islati to panpan go mantu imai.
Mantu ina imai go imer nrik mantu ki:
Mantue p̃a ginau rogorogo ki tete go mame.
Ririel o kitiroa matetoko
Ririal eselatia toko tagisa e

Ririel o ririel o riel o. i.
Ale Mantu ina ipanpan kir po nrik temen go raiten ki. Ale, temen go raiten rana rato go rapo mai,
mai na ruslati kin po pan tanki.

Go natrauswen nen inom esa.
This is text 104.

He didn't go and tell the mother and father about it at all.
OK, so he stayed there then a horse came by so he

told the horse to go and tell his mother and father about it, and he sang this song.
[Horse, you go and tell my father and mother for me.]
[Ririel has fallen and died]
[Ririal has taken him and is crying for him. Ririel o ririel o riel o. i.]
So the horse was going but didn't go and tell his father and mother about it.
So he carried him on and a flying fox came by.
The flying fox came by so he sang to the flying fox:
[Flying fox, you go and tell my father and mother for me.]
[Ririel has fallen and died]
[Ririal has taken him and is crying for him.]
Ririel o ririel o riel o. i.
Then the flying fox went to them and told his father and mother about it. And his father and mother came,
came in order that they take him and bury him.
And that story finishes here.

Toukelau Takau
Natrauswen ni of go makou, the heron and the prawn
The young heron's leg is held tight by a prawn while the tide

rises. A turtle offers to help and bites off the prawn's leg. The heron returns to its mother who had warned it not to go out because it was too small but who has now learned its lesson.

Amurin na kagaag traus natrauswen ni of.
I want to tell you the story of the heron.

Teesa ni of,
The child of the heron,

akit tutae na
we know that

of, malnen elau imat.
the heron, when the tide is out

elau imat kefo to
When the tide is out, it will be there.

panpanpanpan elau imat panpan
until, the tide is out, until

emeltig nen kin elau kemu, ko, elau kipe to mu.
just until it starts to turn, or, the tide would start to come in.

Go ipo pi malnen of ipak elau me ilel naik.
And it would be the time the heron would go to the sea to look for fish.

Go, naliati iskei, naliati iskei
And one day, one day

of iskei ito, me iplak teesa ga ranru to.
this heron was there, and with its chick they were both there.

Me elau imat.
But the tide was out.

Panpanpan me, elau kipe mat pak kotfan.
On and on and the tide was out in the afternoon.

Malen of ileka na elau istat mu
Then the heron saw that the sea was starting to come in.

Go ipaoski mama ga, ipaoski raiten kin, itli na,
And it asked its mother, it asked its mother, it said,

'Kineu me ana kafan lel tete naik elau.'
'I would like to go looking for fish in the sea.'

Go raiten itli na, 'Itik, ag kukano pan nlaken ag kusees.'
And the mother said, 'No, you can't because you are small.'

Me kipe pi kotfan. Me elau kipe to mu.
But it was the afternoon. And the sea was coming in.

Go teesa ni of itli na, 'Itik, kineu amurin na kafan lel tete naik.'
And the heron's chick said, 'No, I want to go and find some fish.'

Go raiten itli na, 'Itik, kineu atap trok na ag p̃afan mau.'
And it's mother said, 'No, I don't agree that you go there.'

Me teesa ni of ikerkrai. Imurin na kefak elau.

Me, ina ito go raiten kitao kepa. Ipak elau pa.
Ina ipa go kita mur natik ntas euut mau me ipan namta elau.
Me elau kipe to mu.

Me teem̃ol sees iskei, ipi tenen ito namta.
Ito nskau. Go ipitlak ga nfalen ipram pak, etan. Ileg pak etan.

Teem̃ol ne rusoso ki makou.

Rusoso ki makou go ipiatlak ga npatin inru rapram.
Kaaru ipa go kaaru ipa. Malnen elau imu ga me ipo to paakor nlaken elau imu.

Isaiki npatin rapram pato.
Me malen of itu lel naik itu leser.
Of sees itu le ser panpan ita lek makou mau.
Ipan ipalag leg ki nfal ni nana makou, me makou kipe saiki npatin rato.
Malen ikam leg ki nfal ni makou go makou ipuetsok natuen, ikatsok natuen.
Me malfane ikano puetlu natuen.
Nlaken, makou kipe puetsoki.

Itraem na kepuetlu natuen me elau kipe to mu.

But the heron's chick was strong. It wanted to go to the sea.
It wanted to go and its mother let it go. It went to the sea.
It wanted to go, not just to the edge of the sea, but to the end of the reef. And the sea was coming in.
And this small animal is one who is at the end of the reef.
It stays on the reef. And it has its hole, a long hole that goes straight down.
This animal, they call it a prawn.
They call it a prawn and it has two long claws.
One goes one way and the other the other way. When the tide is in the prawns will come too, because the tide is high.
It pushes its long claws.
And as the heron looked for fish, it looked everywhere.
The small heron looked around and didn't see the prawn.
It walked straight over the prawn's hole, but the prawn pushed its claws out.
When it walked right on the prawn's hole, the prawn grabbed its legs, it held them.
But now it couldn't pull its leg out.
Because the prawn had hold of it.
It tried to free its leg, but the sea kept rising.

Of sees ikano.
Istat, nlaken ileka na elau kipe
to mu.
Go istat kai. Ikai me ipreg ipi
nalag.
Go nakaiwen ga ipreg ipi nalag
itefla.
Ina, nalag ga nen ina,
[song] Seseria seseri,
nalomatarere, naempiripiri,
alolipu karia, Lawo kowa sai
koroko,koro namaloko, ekatia
ekatia oo pa, ekatia ekatia oo pa

Me, elau ito mu.
Ito mu me makou ipuetsoki,
ipuetsok kerkrai ki nen to

Ina ito pan kaimer lag.

Welkia nalag nen ipi nakaiwen
ga.
[song] Seseria seseri,
nalomatarere, naempiripiri,
alolipu karia, Lawo kowa sai
koroko, koro namaloko, ekatia
ekatia oo pa, ekatia ekatia oo pa

Me afsak iskei, ito waf me isik
nน̃aun, ilek of kin itu.

Inruน̃ pak etan inrus mai isaiki
nน̃aun me ileka kin of itu.

Me elau ito mu.
Afsak inruน̃ pak etan,
imaimaimai ipak natik of.
Isak pak elag me ipestaf of. Itli

The small heron couldn't.
It started, because it saw that
the tide was coming in.
And it started to cry. It cried,
and it made it into a song.
And its cry, it made it into this
song.
It said, its song said,
[song] Seseria seseri,
nalomatarere, na empiripiri,
alolipu karia, Lawo kowa sai
koroko, koro namaloko, ekatia
ekatia oo pa, ekatia ekatia oo
pa
But the tide was rising.
The tide was coming in but the
prawn held the heron, it held it
tight.
It wanted to go and it sang
again.
So that song is his crying.

[song] Seseria seseri,
nalomatarere, naempiripiri,
alolipu karia, Lawo kowa sai
koroko, koro namaloko, ekatia
ekatia oo pa, ekatia ekatia oo
pa
But a turtle was swimming and
raised its head, it saw the
heron there.
It dived down. it came and
pushed its head out of the
water and it saw that the heron
was there.
But the tide was rising.
The turtle dived down and
came up next to the heron.
It went up and talked to the

na, 'Ag kuku?'
Go of inrikin ki na, 'E, kineu
amai lel naik.
Alel naik, me makou ipuetsok
natuok.
Akano nrus, me elau kipe to
mu.'
Go afsak ipaoski na, 'Me kumur
na kawelu ag?'
Go kina, 'Ifwel kufmer welu
wou kefo wi top.'
Go afsak ipo nruρ̃ pak etan.

Inruρ̃ pak etan kin po kati. Ikat
npat nana, makou.
Go makou ipo tao natuen.

Ale afsak ipo tu of pak elag.

Itu of natuen pak elag malen
ileka na itae tao.
Go itao ntas. Inrir pa.
Ipo nrir pan lek raiten.

Go raiten ipaoski na, 'Iku
kin kumai [mei] malik? Ita pi
malen kuna ρ̃amai weskin mau.

Me ipo nrikin ki na, 'O, raitok
kuipe nrik wou ki na
kata pan mau, me kineu apsig.
Apan me apo paakor
nanrogtesan, me
afsak iwelu wou, ipam̃or wou,
go iwelu wou.
Ineu kat makou go makou ipo
tao natuen.
Slat wou pak elag, ga kin apo
mai.'

heron. It said, 'What's up?'
And the heron said to it, 'I
came to look for fish.
I looked for fish and the prawn
grabbed my foot.
I can't move, but the tide is
coming in.'
And the turtle asked it, 'But do
you want me to help you?'
And it said, 'If you could help
me it would be very good.'
And the turtle then dived
down.

It dived down and bit it. It bit
the prawn's claw.
And the prawn let the its leg
go.
Then the turtle gave it to the
heron above.
It gave the heron the leg when
it saw that it could let it go.
And it left the sea. It flew away.
It flew and went to see its
mother.
And its mother asked, 'Why
did you came so early? It's not
the time you come to work
here.
But it then said, 'Oh my
mother, you told me that
I shouldn't go, but I disobeyed.
I went, and I got into trouble,
but
the turtle helped me, it found
me and it helped me.
It bit the prawn for me and the
prawn lost its leg.
Took me up, that's how I
came.'

Go ipi nametp̃ag ni
nafuserekwen gakit.
This is text 105

And that is the end of our
story.

Kalsarap Namaf †
Litrapong

Litrapong, a natopu, has policemen who guard her cave. Kalsarap
tells of the time when he saw her and managed to pray enough to
get away.

Amurin na kanrik mus ki. Akam,
teesa, teesa ni mees,
utap lek esan kin Litrapog itkos
mau, me kineu aleka ki namtak,
go asil wes, apan to natkin.

I want to tell you. You, children
of today,
we don't see the place where
Litrapong lives, but I have seen
it with my own eyes and I went
into it and was there on the
edge of it.

Litrapog, esan kin amurin na katli
nlaken mees teesa akam uto pa.

Litrapong, the place I want to
tell about, because today we go
there

Uto pan me uta lek erfale ni
Litrapog mau. Kineu aleka ki
namtak, ipi nlaken amurin kanrik
mus ki.
Naliati iskei kaipe mai to Erakor
to, kin me apo pa ana kalel aas.
Go san kin apakes pa, nap̃lel
rutmer tfagir, tefla, akano nraf.

We go, but we don't see
Litrapog's cave. I have seen it
with my own eyes which is why
I want to talk to you about it.
One day I came to Erakor, I
went to look for coconut crabs.
The place that I got to was
overgrown with the hibiscus, I
couldn't get through.

Apan alek aas rutu, aas p̃afp̃of
nen kin atap leka tete nrak mau.
Me ato Erakor pa.

I went and saw that coconut
crabs were there, big ones like I
had never seen before. But I
went on to Erakor.

Malen apan pan pan, atu sol aas
pan kaimotir panpanpan inom,
me ato nraf, ato nraf pa.
Ilakor pi, namroan neu kipi tefla,
amrokin ilakor pi Litrapog kin

When I went, I took coconut
crabs and bound them and I cut
through the bush, I kept going,
It might have been my will but
I think it was Litrapong who

ipregi nen kalek nfalen.
Malen apan panpanpan na asok,
asoki erfale ne. Ale tefla, alek
polisman ga kin ratu nmet.

Me Litrapog ipato ito m̃pag na,
nfal faat. Alek polis kin rateflan
tu.
Polis ne rusoso ki Tap̃ar go
Nrotik. Malen kin apa, ana, 'O me
mees kaipe mai paakor esa, kafo
pan le soksokir'.

Ipi nlaken apo nraf panpanpan
apan pato me ato leka. Apei-,
tenen apregi, apei lot. Alot
panpan na inom.

Kin me apo pa, amailum pan to
m̃aak leka, panpanpanpan inom.
Aler mai na asol aas kaimai pak
elau Epakor, na asaiki raru,

Kin po mai pak Erakor. Ipi
nametp̃ag natrauswen neu,
apsawiki mus.
This is text 107.

made me look into her cave.
Then I went and jumped, I
jumped into this cave. I looked
around, I saw the two
'policemen' at the door. (*natopu*
always have policemen who are
their guards)
Litrapong was there at the end
of the cave. I saw the police
standing there.
These police were called Tap̃ar
(Sin) and Nrotik (Stupid). As I
went I said, 'Oh, but today I
have come out here, I'm going
to have a good look around at
them.'
That's why I broke the bush
until I got in and looked
around. What I did, first, I
prayed. I prayed and prayed
until it was finished.
Then I went I slowly went and
looked until I finished. I
returned and took coconut
crabs to the sea, at Epakor, to
go by canoe.
Then I came to Erakor. That's
the end of my story, thank you.

Kalsarap Namaf †
The spring at Epakor

The spring at Epakor had its source at Elakmamiel and if you pushed a stick into the water there it would come out at Epakor. Today the spring is blocked.

Ipitlak nai iskei ito Ertap.   There is a spring at Eratap

Nai nen rusoso ki Epakor.
Akam telaap ni esan uleka, me
nai ne, ipi nai nen kin iser totur
faat.
Me kineu aleka ipi tenmaagwen
neu nen asees leka.
Go amurin na katrausi, akam,
akit tukfo tu tae.
Selwan nai nen ito, ipitlak faat
iskei itu kor nameten.

Me namten ipan pato elag
Elakmamiel.
Nlaken, kineu asees tu Ertap, go
atae esan kin namet nai nen
itkos.
Teetwei ifwel kumur p̃asol
nalenan knen,
p̃afo mas nkas, nap̃rat keskei me
p̃afaskin Elakmamiel,

me selwan kupaski, malen kumai
pak elau Epakor,
kulek nap̃rat sees nen kipato sal
elau, iplak nmaagwen, ipi
nmaagwen p̃ur.
Go aleka ito panpan tuk mees.
Me Tata Sailas, ipreg talm̃at wes.

Go nai-, naor nen imsai to ip̃on.
Go natam̃ol rumer kano- rutap
tae san itkos mau. Me
komam nen kin utae, teesa ni
maarik Sailas, gar rutae.
Me nam̃er laap, ni Ertap rutae

tete rutae, me tete rutap tae
mau. Me Tata Sailas ipreg talm̃at
go talm̃at nen, ilao na nafis,

This spring is called Epakor.
Many of you from here have
seen it, but this spring is one
that flows through a rock.
But I have seen it, it amazed me
when I was small and saw it.
And I want to tell you about it so
that we will know about it.
When this spring was there,
there was a rock that covered its
source.
But the source was up at
Elakmamiel.
Because I was small at Eratap
and I knew the place where the
spring was.
Long ago, if you wanted to find
out the truth of it,
you would cut a tree, a Nap̃rat
tree, and you would push it in to
Elakmamiel,
and when you pushed it, when
you come to Epakor,
you will see the small piece of
Nap̃rat floating in the sea, it is
amazing, it is really amazing.
I have seen it, and it is still there
today. And Tata Sailas made a
garden there.
And the place where the hole
was is closed. And people don't
know where that place is. But
we who know, the children of
Mister Sailas, they know.
And many people from Eratap
know,
some know, and some don't
know. And Grandather Sailas
made a garden and in this

go kutae nafis, ipi tenmatun
iskei nen kin ipu ntan naor laap.

Go mees namet nai nen kiρon
kumer kano pam̃ori.
Ipi natrauswen sees m̃as, go
apsawi ki mus nen kofo nrogo.
This is text 108.

garden, he planted Nafis (Fijian
asparagus)
and you know Nafis, it is
something that grows all over
the ground.
And today the spring is blocked
and you can't find it.
It is just a small story and I
thank you for listening.

Kalsarap Namaf †
Nkapmat go Nkapfag

The story of two holes that used to have magic fire before the time
of Christianity.

Ore kafo gaag tili,
nkap, malfane kamer traus,
Nkapfag go Nkapmat. Kato
Ertap
teetwei malen kin tiawi ruto,
ruto pa.

OK, I will tell you,
fire, now I will tell about Nkapfag
and Nkapmat. I would be at
Eratap
in the olden days, when the old
people were there, they would
go..

Me Nkapfag go Nkapmat nen
malen kin tiawi ipa iρurki ifla
sol tete ntankep, nen kin kefo
preg nkap.
Me selwan ipan imetρakor
ntankep nen kefreg nkap, kefo
pan si nfal nran rato.
Kefo si panpan nkap kefo
paakor kaaru. Kaaru imat me
kaaru ito fag, go rato panpan
tuk mes ne.

And Nkapfag and Nkapmat, when
all the old people went, if they
got a firestick so they could make
a fire.
When he went, he forgot the
firestick to make fire and he blew
on the two holes.
He would blow until the fire
came out of the other hole. The
fire in one of the holes died but
the other one was growing. And
they are like this right up until
today.

Rata puel mau, me rato, rato
faat, nfal inru rato faat, go

The two holes have not
disappeared, they are still there,

ramol to panpan tuk mees. Me malfane itaosi kin nalotwen imai,

go rakaimat. Me selwan kupan si, kusi nfal kaaru, kunrogo iwelkia nkap imat, kusi kaaru, kunrogo welkia nkap ito fag,

Me rekin nkap kemer saof wes, itik.
This is text 117.

they are on a stone, those two holes are in the stone and still exist up until this day. But today now that Christianity is here, the fire holes have died, but if you blow on one of them you feel that it is dead, but when you blow on the other one, you can hear that it is still alive and burning.
But for the fire to actually come out it is no longer possible.

Kalsarap Namaf †
Inglis polis, the English Police

Kalsarap talking about his time with the English Police in the 1930s.

Amurin nag katil na natrauswen sees iskei.
1933 selwan ato, komam uto Inglis polis.
Natamol nen ipi distrik ejen to Esanr, Hog Haba rusoso ki Mista Solsbri.
Janweri 1933, Charlie Naot, ipi lanskoprel. Iplak Ruben, Simeon, Kalsaopa, go kineu Kalsarap.

Utao Efil upak Weso, Emlakul go SS.Morinda ikon. Go utu naliati mau Weso, eMlakul.

Rupreg tete kaku ni raru nen ruto nakpei rupak nakoinrok Morinda.
SS.Morinda, go selwan elau imu go raru imel, go utu tmalu raki

I want to tell this small story.
1933 when I was, we were in the English Police.
This man who was the District Agent on Santo, Hog Harbour was called Mister Salisbury.
January 1933, Charlie Naot was the lance corporal. Together with Ruben, Simeon, Kalsaopa and me, Kalsarap.
We left Vila and we went to Weso, Malakula and SS Morinda got stuck. And we stayed that whole day at Weso, Malakula.
They took some cargo from the front and put it at the back of the Morinda.
SS Morinda, and when the high tide came in, and the boat

Tangoa, Santo.

Utok Santo. Utorwak me kipe
malik. Ƥulƥog go rutao mam
Tangoa, naur.

Utap tae fei kin kefo mos mam
pak ist Hog Haba mau.
Namba faef Janweri 1933 ol Linsi
Makmilen, ipa lons nega mai po
mos mam pak Kanal.

Namba sefen utu Sak Bei aliat
Mandei, go upo tkal Hog Haba.

Namba totin, fotin, Saint Andre
imai torwak Hog Haba.
28 Janweri 1933 go rusi busman
iskei
rusi elag. Mista Solsbri itkos.
Aliat tap ruslati mai pak elau.

Go na naot nigmam itli nag,
'Kofo pan psi hospitel go kofo
pan psi hospitel, Kanal Santo.'
Namba 27 Fraide, aliat Fraide, go
nafsan imai tli nag Limok Erakor
imat.
Namba fo Febrari 1933 kopan
sari naor ni Linsi, ito nmaota
Hog Haba, go Pot Olri.

Ipi nawesien nigmam nen kin
tete naliati weswes tete naliati
upan sari.
Janweri 1933 iskei nen, Hog
Haba, Febrari faef go Laperus
itorwak Hog Haba.
1933, go SS Makambo, imer mai

floated and we left for Tangoa,
Santo
We stayed at Santo. We
anchored, and it was dark. In the
morning they left us, Tangoa
island.
We didn't know who would take
us to east Hog Harbour
January fifth 1933, Lindsay
Macmillan took their launch and
came and took us to Kanal
(Lugainville).
Namber seven we stayed at
Shark Bay on Monday and we
reached Hog Harbour.
On the fourteenth the Saint
Andre anchored at Hog Harbour.
28 January 1933 and they shot a
bushman
in the hills. Mister Salisbury was
there. Sunday they carried him
down to the seaside.
Our boss said, 'We'll put him in
the hospital at Luganville'

Friday 27th and word came that
Limok died at Erakor.

The fourth of February 1933 we
went to visit Lindsay's place
between Hog Harbour and Port
Olri.
This was our work, some days
we worked, some days we went
walking about.
January 1933 this was, February
fifth, La Perouse anchored at
Hog Harbour.
1933, and the SS Makambo

torwak Hog Haba.
Torwak, Febrari namba 12, Pot Olri,
Maj namba eitin, go SS Morinda imer mai torwak Hog Haba April wan go tu go Laperus imer torwak Hog Haba.

Naliati ilim inom, ipi us m̃as.
Komam tete naat ita pak nawesien mau unom go ser to esum̃ to.
Go namba naen go naot itu mam tanmaet iskei kopan tp̃il naik.

Upan pan pato oraik ur elau panpan tp̃il fotisiks kaitao rumat.
Namba naentin Mei, SS Makambo imer mai torwak Hog Haba.
Twante Mei, upan lek naor iskei ipi Blu Wota.
Me Jun namba fo 1933, utao Hog Haba nen koler mai pak Efil.

Aliat tap us itop, umai matur Sak Bei namba faef, mo siks umatur Mafea naor.

Namba seven uto Tangoa me namba twelf uto Efil upa SS Morinda mai pak Efil. Ipi nametp̃agon.
This is text 021.

anchored at Hog Harbour.
Anchored, February 12th, at Port Olry.
March 18th, the SS Morinda came and anchored at Hog Harbour. April 1st and 2nd the La Perouse anchored at Hog Harbour again.
On the fifth day it was raining. Some of us didn't go to work, we finished and all stayed at home.

And on the ninth the boss gave us a dynamite so we dynamited fish.
We went fishing in the sea until we had dynamited 46 karong.

The 19th of May, SS Makambo came and anchored at Hog Harbour.
The 20th of May we saw this place, Blue Water.
Then, on June 4 1933, we left Hog Harbour and we came back to Vila.
Sunday it was raining heavily, we slept at Shark Bay on the fifth and on the sixth we stayed at Mafea island.
On the seventh we were at Tangoa, then on the twelfth we stayed at Vila, we took the SS Morinda to get to Vila. That's all.

Kalsarap Namaf †
Kalsarap's time in the English Police

Kalsarap read this text from his diary, which is why he mentions Erakor, Eratap and Malakula on the same dates. He tells of the role of the police in suppressing those on Malakula who were fighting.

Amurin nag amertil naliati nag komam utok plisman. Komam nen upak Emlakul, 1934.
Lans koprel, Jimmy Takaye, Praivet Jon Lisbet, go Naser. Rupi teni Hog Haba, Santo.

Praevet Ruben, Ben, Kalsrap. Komam upi teni Erakor.
Sem go Kalfao, rapi teni Eﬁag.

Utao Efil namba eit September 1934.
Upan ntan Busman's Bei. Ulek mista Adam go mista Harrison ranru to esuﬁ ni mista Adam.
Namba naen September ipi miting ni Efil.
Namba ten, upato Petenter, Emlakul.
Namba fitin Oktober, upak Lakaskas.
Aliat toknak, kineu, Kalfau, Reuben, upan lel naik, Krapei.

Namba sikstin, miting ni Efil.
Namba naentin September, Jimmy Takaye, Jon Lisbet, Sem, Ruben,
Sem, Ruben, Kalfau, Kalsrap, Naser.
Aliat toknak Ruben go Ben go

I want to tell more about when we were police. We went to Malakula in 1934.
Lance corporal Jimmy Takaye, Private Jon Lisbet, and Naser. They were from Hog Harbour, Santo.

Private Ruben, Ben, Kalsrap. We were from Erakor.
Sam and Kalfao were from Pango.

We left Vila on the eighth of September 1934.
We landed at Bushman's Bay. We saw Mr Adams and Mr Harrison at Mr Adams's house.
On the ninth of September, there was a meeting at Vila.
On the tenth we stayed at Petenter, Malakula.
On the 15th October we went to Lakaskas.
On Saturday, I, Kalfau and Reuben went looking for fish, for Krapei.
On the sixteenth there was a meeting in Vila. Number 19 September, Jimmy Takaye, John Lisbet.
Sam, Ruben, Kalfau, Kalsrap, Naser.
Saturday, Ruben and Ben and

Kalfau rupan sari.
Namba twentetri, 1934 aliat tap,
miting ni Eratap.
Namba twentefo aliat Mande, utu
Ajen. Ufak nananre, nort
Emlakul.
Namba twentesiks, SS Makambo
itorwak Ajen, utu naor naliati
nen aliat tap.
Namba torti, miting ni Erakor.
Utu raki utu Ajen raki

Ions kefo mos mam pak nanre ni
nort Emlakul.
Namba wan Oktober, go utao
Ajen, raki nort wes of Malakula.
Upan torwak Tontar, naor ni
Malapar namba wan.
Namba tu Janweri raru upak
Tanmaru.
Namba siks, Espigel Bei, Emlakul
go Malua Bei.
Namba siks, Ruben, kineu go Sem
ulek natam̃ol malik inru rusir
ramat to elau. Utao rato me
tuipan utap tankir mau nlaken
ranap̃o top. Natam̃ol malik nen
rutakot natuen kaaru. Utap tae
mau ruslati pan pami ko?

Esuan rususoki Spigel Bei. Namba
siks rutp̃il nasum̃ ni nam̃er taar
nlaken SDA itokes. Nam̃er malik
nen rusu mai, rutp̃il nasum̃tap ni
SDA, rutp̃il, ruporp̃rai

pija rol, go slet, paipol, ipi

Kalfau went walking.
On the twenty-third, 1934,
Sunday, meeting at Eratap.
On the twenty-fourth, Monday,
we were at Atchin. We went to
the side, north Malakula.
On the twenty-sixth, SS
Makambo anchored at Atchin,
we stayed there on Sunday.
On the thirtieth there was a
meeting at Erakor. We waited at
Atchin for
the launch to take us to north of
Malakula.
October first we left Atchin to
go to north-west of Malakula.
We anchored at Tontar, at
Malapar, on the first.
On the second of January, the
boat got to Tanmaru.
On the sixth, Espigel Bay
Malakula and Malua Bay.
On the sixth, Reuben, Sam and I
saw the two heathen who had
been shot dead on the beach.
We left them there, but we
didn't bury them because they
stank too much. The heathen
cut the leg off one of them. We
didn't know if they took it to
eat it or not.
The place they call Spigel Bay.
On the sixth they burned the
white people's houses because
the SDA were there. These
heathen came down and burned
the church of the SDA, they
burned and broke
the picture roll, the slate and

nanrogtesan p̃ur. Natam̃ol kenen rupak Aore, nlaken nanrogtesan ipi nanrogtesan p̃ur. Namba seven Oktober, ipi miting ni Ep̃ag, go usak pak Tanmaru, natkon ni nam̃er malik.

Go usak pak Tanmaru, natkon ni nam̃er malik. Utao Dinamit go umatur Dinamit. Ipiatlak ntawot natam̃ol ruto esan umaturwes. Utokleg p̃ulp̃og, go upak Makawe, natkon kia nag katli. Makawe, Piter, go Amok.

Amok, ipi np̃aur, ipi hedkwota nig natkon nran ruentafkir. Go Mista Adam inrik mam kin nag, 'Kofai polet sisi negamus.' Selwan tukfan paakor kotap to naor keskei mau, me tukfan ifwel rukfei sisi go ipi mal negamus.

Utao Amok go Mista Tam inrik Kali naot ni Amok kinag, 'P̃atu mam tete naat kefei ki mam pak Lefenpis.' Selwan upan kailek nra. Go natam̃ol nen inag keler go naot itli nag, 'P̃atap ler mau.'

Go inag, 'Malfanen aletae nra ita pi wak mau me ipi nra natam̃ol.' Go Mista Tam ipulu sisi sees ilaukin ntakun. Natam̃ol ne kipei selwan upa paakor natkon ulek naot ni Lefenpis itarp̃ek to esum̃ nega to nlaken utaptae fei isi

the bible, it was a big disaster. These people went to Aore, because it was such a big disaster. On the seventh of October there was a meeting at Pango and we landed at Tanmaru, a heathen village. We left Tanmaru and we slept at Dinamit. There were human bones around the place where we were sleeping. We stayed until day break and we went to Makawe, the village I spoke about. Makawe, Piter and Amok. Amok was the main village, headquarters of the two villages. And Mister Adams told us, 'We'll put bullets in our guns.' When we appear, we will scatter [so we're not an easy target] then we'll go, if they pull out guns then it will be every man for himself. [Lit: it will be your time]. We left Amok and Mister Adams told chief Kali (chief of Amok), 'You give us some men to guide us to Lefenpis.' When we went we saw blood. And the man said he would go back and the chief said, 'Don't go back.' And he said, 'Now I can see that this is not pig's blood but it is human blood.' And Mr Adams took out his revolver and put it to the man's back. This man led us when we came to the village we saw the chief of Lefenpis

mau go koimatur skoti.

Ƥulƥog go rupo sol naot nega mos
pak elau. Rupau naul naniu ipi
napor go rupo pai naot
negarwes. Raru imai msagi pak
hospitel ni Kanal Santo.

Namba ten, utao naor ni Apon,
natamol fnau iskei, Mista Paton,
ipregi mai. Upak Tuwalo,
Lamlasi, Nefenaila, esan ipi
natokon itol, rupi esuan Big
Nambas inom wes. Go merler
mai. Umatur Lampumpu. Ƥulƥog
ur lanis imai mos mom uler mai
pak Tontar naor ni Malopar.

To Lampumpu to. Namba 12, uler
mai pak Mtanfat, naor ni
Malopar, Tontar. Namba 12 usak
pak elag natkon ni maarik
Medon rusosoki Tanmililip.

Upan ƥog utkal natkon gar
ƥulƥog rik. Selwan rupilo rulek
mam tete rusef me utli nag, 'Kota
sef mau!'

Unrikirkin nag upa raki natamol
iskei nagien Charlie. Go rutli nag
ipan pato matur erfale iskei.

Go Ben go kineu (Kalsarap) rapo
parekin pan natamol iskei ipeiki
mam ki napu. Me upa me ipuel.

Go ramer ler mai nrik gafman ki

fallen at his home, but we didn't
know who shot him. We stayed
there with him.
In the morning they took the
chief to the coast. They wove a
coconut leaf basket for him to
lie on. The boat came to take
them to the hospital at Kanal
(Luganville).
On the tenth we left Apon, the
missionary, Mister Paton, came.
We went to Tuwalo, Lamlasi,
Nefenaila, these three villages,
they are where the Big Nambas
villages finish. And back. We
slept at Lampumpu. In the
morning the launch came and
took us back to Tontar,
Malopar's place.
Stayed at Lampumpu. On the
twelfth we came back to
Mtanfat, Malopar's place and
Tontar's we landed up at Mister
Medon's village called
Tanmililip.
We went at night and got to the
village in the early morning.
When they woke up they saw
us, some ran away but we said,
'Don't run away!'
We told them we were looking
for a man called Charlie. They
told us he had gone to sleep in a
cave.
And Ben and I (Kalsarap) went
for this man who went ahead of
us on the road. Then we went,
but he wasn't there.
And we went back to tell the

go uler mai pak elau Tontar.

Be namba tortin, upak elag, naor ni ... naor iskei rusosoki Tanmililip.
Rutli na ipi naor ni maarik Medon.
Me p̃ulp̃og, ita malkolik to ulefekor natkon negar, selwan rupilo, rulekmam, tete rusef, me

komam utli na, 'Kotap sefmau, nlaken upareki natam̃ol rusosoki Charlie.'
Go rutli ito matur, nfalfat iskei, go komam Ben rafopan leka natam̃ol iskei. Iptanki mam upan me ipuel go

umer ler. Selwan umer mai kailer mai pak elau.
Elau Santo rusosoki... preg kamp nigmam itkos rusosoki Tontar.

Namba fiftin, go uler mai pak Busman's Bei. Uto Busman's Bei twentewan deis,
go umer pak tete natkon, naor utok elag Busmans Bei.
Namba 22 October, upak natkon rusosoki Rakatambol, Tanmari, Atolpilak.

Umaturwes naliati iskei, go p̃og iskei. Go Malawut, naot negar, inrik Mista Tam kin nag, 'Natam̃ol iskei, nagien Teptep, ito pregsaki nam̃er nigneu nag amragir itosir me nega ipuel. Go

government and we came back to the coast at Tontar.
But on the thirteenth we went up to the place of ... this place they call Tanmililip.
They said it was the place of Mister Maden.
Then, in the morning, before dawn, we went around their village when they woke up, they saw us, some ran away, but we said, 'Do not run away because we came for a man called Charlie.'
And they said he was asleep in a cave and we (Ben and I) we went to see this man. He came with us then he (Charlie) was gone and
we returned. When we came back, we came back to the coast. The place at Santo where we made our camp was, they call it Tontar.
Number 15 and we went to Busman's Bay. We stayed at Busman's Bay for 21 days, and we went to some villages up from Bushman's Bay.
On the twenty-second of October we went to the villages they call Rakatambol, Tanmari, Atolpilak.
We slept there that day and that night. And Malawut, their chief, told Mister Adams, 'This man, called Tetptep, is causing trouble among my villagers, and he is shooting them, then he

Mista Tam inrikirkin nag, 'Naot negamus kafo pueti pak elau Busman's Bei.'

'Ifwel Teptep iftap mai mau naot negamus kefo pak kalbus Efil. Me ufpaṁor Teptep kofueti mai go kafo tao naot gamus keler. Me naot Malawut ito pios go Mista Tam inag, 'Ko tupaakor nataṁol nen kutap pestop mau.'

Go komam Sam, rapa pueti me ikelsok nig namet nega go nasuṁ ipi ṁeltig nag ketarp̃ek.

Go Mista Tam inag raktao go rapotao nataṁol nen ipan.

Go rupo plak Teptep mai pak elau p̃ulp̃og kenen. Go Mista Tam ipo tau naot negar ruplake ler pak natkon negar pan. Me Teptep ipak esuṁ malik. Ulermai marmar naliati ipat.

Me namba faef November, aliat Mande,
Kalfau go kineu Kalsrap, rapak Unua, naor ni mista Paton.
Namba naen, upak naor ni Per Krekov, go upan nag, 'Kulek nataṁol nig Jermani, iskei, nagien mista Prubak?'
Me rutli na kimer ler pan. Go umer ler mai pak Krekov.
Utok Krekov, upak Ranon, ipi Ambrim,
upak naor ni Ranon, Makam go

disappears.' And Mister Adams said to him, 'I will take your chief to the coast at Bushman's Bay.'
'If Teptep doesn't come, your chief will go to gaol in Vila. But if we find Teptep, we take him, I will leave your chief to return.'
Then chief Malowut called out and Mister Adams said, 'We will make this man come, don't you shout so loudly.'
And Sam and I went to grab him, but he held on to the window of the house and the house was about to fall down. And Mister Adams said they should leave and they left the man to go.
And they took Teptep to the coast that morning. Then Mister Adams let their chief go with them to their village. But Teptep went to the gaol. We came back and rested for four days.
But the fifth of November, Monday,
Kalfau and I went to Unua, Mister Paton's place.
On the ninth we went to Per at Craig Cove and we asked, 'Have you seen that German man, Mr Prubak?'
But they said he had gone. And we returned to Craig Cove.
We stayed at Craig Cove, we went to Ranon, on Ambrym, we went to Ranon, Makam and

ipi natkon ni Amprim.
Esan ures. Namba ten, upak
Pentekos, Melsisi, umatur
Lonoro. Namba eleven go twelv
Laone, me namba 13 utau Laone
mai pak Busman's Bei.

Namba 24, komam Ben rapan
puet prisen prisona iskei isef
nagien Sulun. Namba 14 go
komam Ben rapareki natam̃ol
iskei isef.
Ramai puetsoki p̃og, mai pak elau
Busmans Bei, uler pak Efil,
namba 30 November. Natam̃ol
nen praivet Ruben kin ipi prison
gad ilekor wer me isef aliat ipan
kaitok natkon nega me itap
matur esum̃ mau me aliat ito
matur nafrofur.

Me p̃og go imai pak natkon ga.
Rumai preg repot pak Mista Tam
go itli nag, 'Komam Ben rakfo
pan pueti p̃og go rapopan me atli
nag Ben kefo pan puetsoki me
inag kineu kin kafopan pueti.'

Go aponrik natam̃ol nen imai lek
mam kin nag, 'Ag p̃afei me kafo
nrokosik selwan takfan go
p̃atulegkin go p̃afak em̃ae me
kineu kafo puetsoki selwan
rapan natam̃ol nen ipan tu leg
kin kaipak em̃ae
Go kineu apuetsoki go masmes
nega nen ipueti to im̃el. Selwan
apuetsoki aslen nen rumau to
rusef. Ipiatlak naum sees iskei ito

it was a village of Ambrym.
On the tenth we went to
Pentecost, Melsisi, we slept at
Lonoro. On the 11th and 12th
at Laone, then on the 13th we
left Laone to go to Bushman's
Bay.
On the 24th, Ben and I pulled
the prisoner out and set him
free, his name was Sulun. On
the 14th Ben and I went for this
man who ran away.
We went to get him at night,
came to the sea at Bushman's
Bay and we came back to Vila
on the 30th of November. These
men, Private Ruben had been
guarding, but then they escaped
in the day back to his village,
but he didn't sleep in his village,
that day he slept in the bush.
That night he came to his
village. They came to make
their report to Mister Adams
and he said, 'Ben and I went and
I said to Ben to go and get that
man but he told me I should and
get him.'
And I told this man to come and
see us, saying, 'You lead but I
will follow you when we go and
you will go a long way, after I
will hold him when we go this
man will stand up and go away.

And I held him and his knife
fell. When I held him his friends
all ran away. There was a small
river and when his friends all

selwan aslen nen rusef rutaos naik iskei rusosoki kaitau.

ran away. There was a small river and when his friends ran away they were like a fish which we call Karong ('Trevally' in Bislama). It chases sardines.

Ikop napel.
Komam rapo plak prison nen mai pak elau Busmans Bei rapei pan lek Mista Tam plak prison nen nagien Sulun tu Mista Tam kin.

We took him to prison to the coast at Bushman's Bay, we led him to see Mister Adams, with the prisoner whose name was Sulun, to Mister Adams.

Go Mista Tam ism̃anri ki naot puluk nrak itol go ramer plak em̃ae pak parik. Ruwatgi go kaitp̃okrorwes.

And Mister Adams hit him with a bullock's pizzle whip three times and we took him to the barracks. They hit him and I told them to stop.

Utu Tangoa, namba 1 Disemba, Ampai namba 2, Aliat toknak Umai pak elau Busmans Bei, uler pak Efil, namba 30 November, utu Tangoa, Disemba namba 2, Efil, aliat tap, ipi nametp̃ag nafsan.

We stopped at Tangoa, number 1 December, Ambae number 2, Saturday, We went to the sea at Bushman's Bay and returned to Vila, 30th November, we were at Tangoa, December number 2, Vila, Sunday, that's the end of the story.

Ipi nametp̃ag nafsan.
This is text 022.

That's the end of the story.

Kalsarap Namaf †
The fire at Ballande

What happened when the Ballande store burned in 1927.

Amurin nag katil tete natrauswen nen kin aleka, selwan api teesa.
Alek tete nam̃er taar nen ruto mai pak esa.
Iskei rusosoki mis Trasi.

I want to tell a story about what I saw when I was a child.

I saw some white people who came here.
One was called missionary Trasi.

Natam̃ol nen, teni Ertap ruto
pan sor kai, go rusor pan
pamkin, go rutua pret.
Slati mai pami esum̃ mer taf.

Ipi natam̃ol iskei nen kin teni
Ertap rufafatwes teetwei.
Atap tae ntau ipi ito Eum̃ mau.

Tekaaru, rusosoki Tekrila,
kaatol, rusosoki Lekog, nam̃er
nen ruto Eum̃.
Kafat ipi Telaplan, ga me ito
Eum̃.
Nam̃er nen ruto Eum̃. Nrakpei
raru nen kin ito mai pak Eum̃
gar mos kopra, rusosoki Perfas,
St. Michel,
nagi raru, me nam̃er taar nen,
rupiatlak raru ruto mai gar mos
kopra Eum̃, teetwei.
Aleka ki namtak. Ipiatlak nam̃er
taar nen amurin nag kagamus
trausi konrogo.
Ipiatlak natam̃ol taar iskei ito
Pelfi teetwei.
Rusosoki Larso.
Larso ito panpan itm̃alu Tekraus
imer to nam̃len ipuet imer to
nam̃len. Selwan Tekraus ipuet
Pelfi go ipi mal wan nafkal
ipaakor, 1942. Teni Amerika
rupreg Pelfi ipi Bes Ospitel.
Komam telaap ni Efat umaui
weswes Pelfi. Saot pak Not
umaui weswes ur Pelfi. Go ipi
namagwen p̃ur nigmam. Tenag
uleka kafo til tete me akano til
silua. Natam̃ol nag rumat go

This man, those from Eratap
sold shellfish, pumpkin, and
they gave him bread.
Took it, ate it at home and came
out.
It was a man who those from
Eratap believed in, in those days.
I don't know how many years he
was at Teouma.
The other, called Tekrila, the
third, Lekong, these men were at
Teouma.
The fourth was Telaplan, he was
at Teouma.
These men were at Teouma. In
those days the boat that came to
Teouma to carry copra for them,
it was called Perfas, St Michel,
the name of the boat, the white
men took the boat to Teouma to
get copra for them in those days.
I saw them with my own eyes.
There is a white man that I want
to talk to you about, you listen.
There was a white man at
Belview.
His name was Larso.
Larso stayed and then left and
there was Tekraus at that place.
When Tekraus had Belview it
was the time of the war, 1942.
The Americans took Belview to
be their base hospital.
Many of us from Efate went to
work at Belview. From the south
to the north we all worked at
Belview. And we were very
surprised. We saw some things
but I can't tell everything. Some

tenag ruṁol ruto slatir mai psur ospitel ni Pelfi. Marine, army, go navy.

Selwan uto weswes uleka ipi namagwen p̃ur. Nigmam tenag uleka itop. Nmaten itokos, tete nataṁol rumat, me tete ruṁol mai pak ospitel nen.
Tenag rumat rutfeir go rupu nmarter ipan me rupregi ikal ki nakal nega go rupregi iler pak nafanu nega pan. If pi marine, ko if pi navy, ko if pi army.
Tenag ruṁol rulekor wer tenag ipi mankotik rupak esuan ipi naur ni dokta kefo wesweskir.
Tenag rumat ruplak naṁler go tenag ruṁol me negar me rupak esuan dokta itokos.
Nataṁol nen kin ruto natikin iskei rusosoki Rossi.
Rossi mees ipreg hotel taon Efil. Ipiatlak tempalun itol.
Nataṁol nen kin ruto taon iskei kin rusosoki mista Mi, nega itṁalu Efil, ipan pak Esanr.
Ko ito Esanr to panpan imat Esanr, selwan ito Efil, ito Efil pak Esanr, go ipan to Totel Bei.
Ipi esuan naṁolien ga inom wes.
Iskei rusosoki Kipe, Kipe ipreg sto Efil taon.
Nataṁol taar iskei rusosoki Tersat, Franisman, ga ipreg sto go ipiatlak wof, taon Efil.
Nataṁol nen kin rupreg sto p̃ur, iskei rusosoki CFNH, Efil taon.

men were dead, others were alive, they put them in the hospital at Belview, marines, army, or navy.
When we worked there we were always surprised. For us, what we saw was too much. There were corpses and wounded people at the hospital.
When they died they dressed them in their uniform and they took them back to their country. It might be marines or navy or the army.
Some lived, some were wounded, they went to the doctor who worked on them. Some died and they went back to their place.

The man who lived at the side of Belview was Rossi.
Rossi today has the hotel in Vila. He had three brothers.
The man who stayed in town they called Mista Mi, he left Vila and went to Santo.
He was there until he died there, at Turtle Bay.

That was where his life finished. This one they call Kipe, he had a store in Vila.
This white man was called Tersat, a Frenchman, he had a store and wharf in Vila.
This man had a big shop, called CFNH (Comptoirs Français des Nouvelles-Hébrides) in Vila.

Ipiatlak wof go BP, ipiatlak wof
ipreg sto p̃ur taon Efil.
Natam̃ol nen kin rapreg sto p̃ur
taon Efil.
1927, go sto p̃ur Balan nen isor.
Tete natam̃ol kin rumat wes.
Selwan rupregsi sto nen, utap
tae naftekin ipiatlaken kin sto
nen inkap ipami mau.
Me selwan natam̃ol nen rupakes,
rumroki na rukfan sol tete mane
em̃rom sto.
Selwan rupan go rulakor preg
tete namatun ito leg ki esuan
mane itkos itefla o atap tae mau.

Me selwan rupak em̃rom pan go
tenamrun im̃alit, malnen im̃alit,
nam̃er laap kin rumat wes.
Nam̃er laap nam̃er laap perkati,
atai tli, 1927 kin namrun esum̃
p̃ur nen isor, esum̃ ni Palan isor.
Tenmatun iskei namrun nen
isor, isfeki aian iskei iur elag pan
ipan na ip̃rai nmet klas
nasum̃tap ni Efil imap̃or.
Ipi stori ni teetwei.
Selwan p̃ulp̃og komam uto Ertap
pa.
Upan lauto uto maag nasum̃.
Uto maag natam̃ol ruto slati
rupa pak ospitel. Tenen rumat
tenen rupi mankotik. Ipiatlak
natam̃ol ni Ampai iskei, rusosoki
Tokolu, ipi Inglis Polis me
selwan rukfiit pan,
go namrun nen im̃alit go aian
iskei ipregkot natuen atap tae
natuen maur ko matu mau, me

He had the wharf and BP, the big
store in Vila.
These men had shops in Vila.

In 1927, Ballande caught fire.
Some men were killed there.
When they destroyed the shop,
we didn't know how the shop
was completely burned.
But when these men went, they
thought someone had taken
money from inside the shop.
When they went and maybe
they were getting something
that was right where the money
was, or, I don't know.
When they went into the
building, something exploded
and many men were killed.
Many men, I can tell you, in
1927, when the Ballande burned.

When this place burned, it threw
iron high and it broke the glass
windows at the church in Vila.

This is a story from before.
When we were going from
Eratap early in the morning.
We stood and watched the store.
We watched them carry people
to hospital. Some were dead,
some wounded. There was an
Ambae man called Tokolu, in the
English police, but when they
ran,
this thing exploded and the iron
hit his leg, I don't know if it was
his left leg or his right leg, but

natuen imakot.
Apo pa pan pam̃ori 1933 ito ni,
ipa ni Kulog weswes Esanr, Sak
Bei nanrup̃ naniu ni Kulog.

Mista Mi nen selwan komam
upan ulauto etan me ga ipag kin
nasum̃ nega.
Me nasum̃ ne smen ki ipi kava
ga.
Selwan isol kamra ga ipan ipak
elag pa.
Ipato elag go ikamp̃rai kava ne,
smen ne malnen itarp̃ek mai
imatmal.
Ruslati esum̃ ga rupak Franis
ospitel.
Dokta iwesweskin panpan imer
m̃ol, imai torik kin po pak Esanr
pa.
Go ipi natrauswen sees perkati.
Ipi tenag ana kanrik mus ki nen
kotae.
This is text 030.

his leg was broken.
I went and found him in 1933, he
went to work for Kulong at
Santo, Shark Bay on Kulong's
coconut plantation.
Mister Mi, when we stayed down
there, but he went up to his
house.
But his house had a cement roof.

When he got his camera he
climbed up.
He went up and he broke the
cement roof and fell through
and nearly died.
They took him from his house to
the French hospital.
The doctor worked hard on him
and he got better, then he went
back to Santo.
And that is this small story.
That is what I wanted to tell you
so you would know.

George Zachari
*A story about George
Zachari's life*

George Zachari talks about his life and the training he has had at
Bible College.

Apaakor 1949, naur sees.

I was born in 1949 on the small
island.

Apaakor naur Erakor 1949,

I was born on Erakor island in

Erakor, rutil Eraniao.
Kineu ato naflak nawi mai.

Me kineu apaakor namkanr.

Namkanr ipitlak nafrofur iskei
ito ftom talm̃at mana.
Kuleka na inrus pitlak nafte
nelepleptau ko nafte itkos.
Go ipitlak temiel go ipitlak
tetaar.
Me komam upaakor namkanr
taar.
Or, nlagwat ni 1959 go
government itili komas tato
naur sees mau, naur Eraniao.
Koler mai pak esa.
Komai pak naur p̃ur nanre.

Go malnen kin umai apitlak ntau
ten ata pi teesa.
Ntau astat skul malen kin, ore,
ata mrotae sef ntau kin astat
skul wes mau, me atae kin malen
kin apitlak ntau ten.
Go amai atato skul.
Go askul ni Franis, elau Ep̃ag.

Go amai askul sa.
Me askul sa, na afnes ki skul sa.
Go askul Franis pan pan inom.
Go inom skul.
Aweswes tete mal.
Apei weswes ata mrosok sef ntau
mau, aweswes British kafman.

Malen mal ni Condominium
itato.
Ore malne ina inom, me

1949, it is called Eraniao.
I am from naflak nawi (the yam
clan).
But I came out of namkanr (the
wild arrowroot clan).
Namkanr has a bush that grows
in gardens.
You see it has some spots on it.

There is a red one and a white
one.
We come out of the white one.

After the cyclone of 1959 the
government told us we couldn't
stay on the small island.
We should come over here.
We came to the side of the big
island.
And when we moved I was ten, I
was still a child.
Then I started school, I don't
remember which year it was,
but I was ten.

I came, I was still at school.
I went to the French school at
Pango.
And I came to school here.
I schooled here, then I finished.
I was at French school, finish.
No more school.
I worked some times.
I worked, I don't remember
what year, for the British
government.
When the Condominium was
still here.
Then I got to think I wanted to

kaipiatlak namroan nen amur kafak Bible College.
Teni Assembly of God.
Go apak Bible College stat nawesien ni nasumtap.
Go apak Bible College ntau itol.

Ana afnes ki nakte skul, go kaisat diploma nen kin ni Bible College inom.
Me apei pitlak kos nen kin ato satir, nen kin korespondens nen kin rusent kin ovasis.
Ito America mai, Philippines, go Australia. Ale apas nafet na correspondence nen runeu sent ki, me ato pregi me ato pak skul, pak na Bible College, ale welkia atlasi nen amai pi pastor iskei.
Go ruodeinki wou.
Natamol imat atae tan ki, atae preg naftourien. Apreg Lord's Supper.
Gawanki.
This is text 033.

go to Bible College.

Of the Assembly of God.
And I went to Bible College to start doing Church work.
I went to Bible College for three years.
I wanted to finish my school so I took my diploma from the Bible College.
But first I had correspondence courses which they sent from overseas.
It came from America, the Philippines and Australia. I passed the course that they had sent me, and when I had enough of Bible College I became a pastor.
They ordained me.
When someone dies I know how to bury them, or do weddings. I can do the Lord's Supper.
That's all.

Kalfapun Mailei †
A story of Kalfapun's life

Kalfapun joined the French police and stayed until 1955, then worked around the village.

Ale, namolien neu, askul naur.

Askul naur inom, apak IDS. IDS malen kin rustat wes.

Okay, my life, I went to school on the island.

I finished school on the island and I went to IDS (Iririki District School). IDS had just started.

Ito Iririk, esuñ ni dokta Frayter
elag. Go misis ni dokta Frayter kin

iplaksok mom. Ale uto to to
panpanpan unom. Ale kaipe nom,
kaipe mai tu.
Panpanpanpanpan tupreg
nawesien seserik. Panpan 1941,
go apak plisman.
Ni franis polis. Ato 1941,

inom apak Esanr. Ato atlag iskei
Efil, apak Esanr pa, kaipe pato
Santo to, me seken wol wo ipo
maag.
America rumai me apato Esanr.
Go kineu kin apo tu plak America
ur
ser naor, upreg napu me upan.
Askotir atlag itol, uto Suranta.

Pan pan runrik wou ki, 'Kufiar
nen p̃afak Solomon?' Ana,
'Idipen',
nlaken kaipe saen reki Army.
Nafkal me apa,
ifpi nmaten. Amat kat kantri. Ale
Franis kafman inrogo,

ale imai msag wou Suranta.
Apiatlak sot plisman,
kamer plake ler. Ale amai tu,
tutu panpan 1945 go anom.
Anom na amai pak Efil, atlag iskei
inom go amer pak Tanna.

Tatsman pak Tanna. Apan pato
Tanna, ntau inru, go atlag ilates.

It was on Iririki, Doctor
Frayter's house up there. And
Doctor Frayter's wife
taught us. We stayed on there
until we finished. I finished
then I came back.
We stayed and were doing a
little work. Until 1941,
I joined the police.
The French police. I was there
in 1941,
finished, I went to Santo. I
stayed a month in Vila, then
Santo and the Second World
War broke out.
America came, and I was at
Santo. I took the Americans
around
all over the place. We made
roads and we went. I was with
them for three months, we
were at Suranta.
Then they said to me. You
aren't scared to go to the
Solomons? I said, 'It depends',
because I had signed with the
Army. If there is a war I will go,
maybe I will die. I die for my
country. The French
government heard this,
and they came and took me me
to Suranta. I had a police shirt,
I went back with it. I came,
and then in 1945 I finished.
I finished and went back to
Vila, one month, then I went to
Tanna.
Attachment to Tanna. I went to
Tanna, for two years and six

Go amer tao Tanna mer mai pak Efil.

Polis. Atutu panpanpan 1948 kin go apo lak Liaal. Ga ipo mat ntau ne, March.

Ale uto Lamelis to, 1948 nen alak, me ato plisman lak.

Inom ale upato panpanpan 1949, 1950,
1952 pak 1955 go anom plisman.

Amer ler mai pak naur.
Uto naur to panpanpan nlag iwat 1959. Nlagwat p̃ur.

Go umuf mai pak menlan. Mai to menlan to. Tototo panpanpan.

Ale rumer wou apan lekor skul etan sanie. Alekor pablik skul etan sanie,
ntau ilaru apan, me 1973 to pan 1980 malen ruindipenden, ale komam unom.
Nlaken iwelkia Franis kipeto muf ale komam unom mai pak elag sa,

mer lekor Sante skul esa. Nafet tija plak Sante skul,

amer lekor wer ntau ilaru, nen amer lekor teesa skul esa.

Go api tija ni devosen, tija ni devosen ato mal mai.
Iofa ntau ralim inru, kin ato moning devosen.

months.
And I left Tanna and came back to Vila.

Police. I stayed and then in 1948 I got married to Liaal. She was to die this year in March.

We went to Lamelis, 1948 when I was married, I was a married policeman.

We stayed until 1949, 1950,
1952 until l955, then I was finished as a policeman.
I came back to the island.
We stayed on the island until the cyclone of 1959. A big cyclone.
And we moved to the mainland. Came to the mainland. Stayed on.
And they told me to go and run the school there. I ran the public school down there
for seven years, 1973 to 1980, time of Independence, then we finished.
Because the French were leaving so we finished and came back up here,
to run the Sunday School. All the teachers at the Sunday School,
I looked after them for seven years and the children at the school here.
And I am the teacher of devotion, from then.
Over twenty years I did morning devotion.

Apan pan pan ntau naentin
ntau pei nen pa, 1994. Ruling elda
imer mai lek wou na,
'Ƥamer sel nawesien nega.
Kamarmar nlaken tupiatlak
tefsofus rulaap.'
Malfanen tefsofus rusel naṁle kit.
Neu kato me askot mus nafte
weswes ki.
Askot mus. Kin ato esuṁ to.
Tototo panpanpaan go olfala neu
ki nƥaun ita leg mau.
Ale rato esuṁ ntau inru rata pak
tenaor mau. Rato esuṁ to, ato
lekor nmatu neu nlaken nƥaun ita
leg mau.

Ito esuṁ to, ipi tenen ito fam ṁas.
Aga preg nafnag kefam.
Panpanpan ntau ne.
Maj namba faef go ipo tṁalu. Rato
esuṁ ntau iskei ntau inru.

Kin ga kipe mat ga, me neu kin
kaipe kano kaipe pi tiawi, kaipe
kano pak talṁat.
Ato lek nawesien me kaipe kano
weswes. Nlaken nafitiawian totur
namsaki nlaken neu me apo to su
maroṁit.

Asmok teetwei me mai mai pak
malen ato lekor skul etan. 1977
apak hospitel pa go dokta itƥokor
wou sikaret. 1977 mai pak mees
atap smok mau.

Ale naminwen kineu api nataṁol
iskei nen amin.

I stayed until nineteen,
las year, 1994. The ruling elder
came and said to me,
'Take some of his work.
I'll rest because we have too
many young people.'
Now the young people are
taking their place. I will stay
and support the work you do.
I am with you. I will stay at
home. I stayed until my wife
went a little bad in the head.
We stayed in the house for two
years, we didn't go any place.
We both stayed at home, I
cared for my wife because she
wasn't well.
She stayed at home, she only
ate. I made her food to eat.
Until this year.
Until the fifth of March when
she died. We stayed at home
for one or two years.
She died, but I am old, I can't
work in the garden.

I see work (that needs to be
done), but I can't work
anymore. Because of sickness
I have got old, because I have
asthma.
I smoked long ago then I ran
the school down there. In 1977
I went to hospital and the
doctor banned me from
smoking. From 1977 to today I
haven't smoked.
Drink, I am a man who can
drink.

Oh, nataṁol itik nen itol neu naminwen.
Malen aᵽelgat botel tefla alaokin nkanrok, anpaki botel.

Nmalok ato mingi, me atli reki alkol nrak pei.
Nrak pei ga naat ita tol kineu naminwen mau. Amin me asmok, paket inru naliati iskei.

Me malen amin, paket itol. Me 1977 dokta ina, 'Ᵽata smok mau.'

Go atao sikaret. Me nmarok, itapi tenen kin ata tae naftekin ipreg maroṁit mau.
Ilakor pi sikaret, ilakor pi nai, me nrak pei ata sua mau. Me nrak pei ata su maroṁit mau.

Me mees ne, naliati iskei, kafo mas sol mersin,
mersin ni maroṁit. Ipiatlaken itu, atu panpan malen anrogo iwelkia ato pam,
kaimer pan wesi iskei. Amingi kaimer tu.
Sprei, rutraem nrik wou kin me amalki.
Nlaken sprei ipi tenen kupilo ᵽulᵽog. Kefei pak paket. Me tetenrak apak talṁat pa me ametᵽakro ito.

Malen ipaakor ki wou talṁat, ipi malwan apato talṁat to.

There is no man who can beat me drinking.
When I open a bottle, I stand it up in my mouth and I throw it away.
I drink kava, but I'm telling you about alcohol in those days.
In those days there wasn't a man who could beat me. I drank and I smoked, two packets a day.
But when I drank, three packets. But in 1977 the doctor said, 'Don't smoke anymore'.
And I gave up cigarettes. But my breathing, I don't know why I have got asthma.
It could be cigarettes, it could be alcohol, but before I never had asthma. But that time I hadn't caught asthma.
But today I have to take medecine,
asthma medecine. I have some, and when I feel I am starting to pump,
I go and take it, I drink it down.

They tried to get me to use spray, but I didn't want to.
Because this spray you take when you wake in the morning. It goes in your pocket. But sometimes I go to the garden but I forget it is there.
Then it comes on me at the garden, it is the time I am at the garden.

Dokta ipo nrik wou ki sprei. Ipo tao ki.
Amai atu tiawi neu ki. Tiawi neu iskei ipato sanpe. Kalon. Harry Kalon. Atuaki.

The doctor told me to use a spray. He gave it to me.
I came and gave it to my father. My father who stays over there. Harry Kalon. I gave it to him.

Ale kalo Meibel imai, ga. Anrik Meibel ki, 'Apiatlak sprei inru, me amal to iuski.
Nlaken kafak talm̃at tenrak, ametp̃akro me apato talm̃at tu me ipaakor ki wou go amat talm̃at.'

Then Mabel came. I said to Mabel. 'I've got two sprays, but I don't want to use them.
Because I go to the garden sometimes, I forget it and I am at the garden and I could have an asthma attack and die at the garden.'

Me taplet iwi. P̃ulp̃og asol taplet atae pak sap, sap ko sap apa.

But the tablets are good. I take one in the morning and I can go any place.

Malen aler mai kotfan welkia anrogo astat pam ale wan taplet.

When I come back in the afternoon, and I feel it start, I take a tablet.

Ipi nam̃olien neu nen atu wes tu mees.
This is text 040.

That is my life as I am today.

Kaloros Kaltaf †
A story of Kaloros's life

Kaloros's working life, in the hospital, as a carpenter and in the electricity generating plant.

Kineu atap skul tete naor mau askul vilej skul m̃as.

I didn't go to school somewhere else, I just went to the village school.

Go edukesen neu ito vilej skul
ñas, inom.
Pes nawesien neu. Nañolien neu
kineu atap taf pak nawesien tete
naor mau.
Me aweswes skot tiawi, natkon,
komiuniti.
Go alekor tiawi neu panpan
panpan tete rumat alekor- mer
lekor teptae,
nen kin rupi famle neu nen rupi
tiawi. Alekor wer panpan rumat.

Temlaap alekor natañol msak,
nasuñ namsaki, taos hospitel.
Askoti to hospitel ntau itol, ale
weswes skot sista, nes,

Eñrom ni hospitel (NT) Panpan?
(KK) PMH (NT) ntau ipi? (KK)
Ntau itol
(NT) Ntau itol, ntau, naintin..
(KK) 1949
50, 60, sori, 1950, 1959,
1960, 1961. Malnen kin ntas itutki
naur
kineu ato hospitel, go alekor
nañer msak, malnen kin Uma
ipregsaki hospitel.

Go ato mufki nañer msak eñrom
pregi rupak sef naor nen kin ipi
naor nañolien.
Go nawesien kaaru selwan
atñalu hospitel.
Anrookot mai pak natkon. Aler
mai pak natkon. (Ga iminki
nafsan inru a?)

My education was just at the
village school.
Started my work. In my life, I
didn't go somewhere else to
work.
And I worked with old people,
the village, the community.
I looked after my old people
until some died, I kept looking
after the others,
those who were my family who
were old. I looked after them
until they died.
I looked after many sick people,
in the clinic, like a hospital.
I was there, at the hospital for
three years, I worked with the
sisters and nurses.

In the hospitel (NT) Until? (KK)
PMH (NT) How many years?
(KK) Three years.
(NT) Three years, nineteen...?
(KK) 1949.
1950, 1960, sorry, 1959.
1960, 1961. When the sea
flooded the island
I was at the hospital, and I
looked after the sick, when
Uma was damaging the
hospital.
I moved the sick people inside,
made them go to a safe place.

And my next job when I left the
hospital.
I crossed back to the village. I
came back to the village. (That
means the same thing twice,
eh?).

Aler mai pak natkon ato mal sees, ale aweswes na elektrik.

Ato lekor enjin, malnen kin p̃og aliat.
Ato ntau nain. (NT) Ilfot (K) a.a, Efat.
Ale ntau nain inom apiatlak namsaki sees sup̃ ni masut.
Sernale teflan rupregi kas itop em̃rom ni nam̃olik.
Go atao go tete nawesien mten nen ipreg emaloput neu ita kerkerai mau ipregi atao nawesien.
Me nawesien pei neu nen kin ipi taos nafrengnrogon nen kin p̃otae nawesien ipi PMH kapentri.
Aweswes skot tete kapenta nen ruto Australia mai. Gawankia esuan asrafwes kia.
Ipiatlak nagi kapenta nen askotir ipiatlak Lori,

a.a., Lex, go David, a, Buckingham ko fei ametp̃akro.
Go ipiatlak temlaap imer visit wou atlag pei na ruipa esan, a.a.

Mr. Waily, nen rapreg skul nen nen ito natkon. Kin ito malfane.

Kineu askoti, go esuan kineu apiatlak tete namroan ni nawesien wes.
Nen atae preg apreg nasum̃ neu,

I came back to the village, I stayed there a while, then I worked for the electricity company.
I looked after the the generator night and day.
I was there for nine years.

After nine years I got sick because of the diesel.
All that made too much gas inside my body.
I left and some heavy work that weakened me made me leave the job.

But my first work, my attempt at another job was at the hospital as a carpenter.

I worked with some carpenters who had come from Australia.
That's where I made a mistake.
There was one carpenter when I was with them, he was called Laurie,

Lex, and David, a, Buckingham and who else, I forget.
And the last one came back to visit me the first month after they left here.

Mr.Waily, who made the school that is in the village. That is there today.
I was with him, that's how I learned about working.

So that I know how to make my own house,

tae preg mtakseu. Na mtakseu ipi nafsan ni kastom, kapenta, mtakseu.
Go selwan atae preg tene, inrok go apo pak nawesien ni elektrik.

Selwan atkos inom, amai, namsaki ipi nlaken ato esuñ.

Ato esuñ me ato lekor nafet tiawi, tiawi laap nen kin rupi tiawi neu alekor wer,

aweluer. (NT) Ag kuweswes talm̃at? (KK) Talm̃at.
Go nafte kin rumurin na kafregi agar pregi.
This is text 045.

know how to be a carpenter. 'Mtakseu' is the custom name for a carpenter.
And when I could do this, I went back to work at the electricity company.
While I finished there, I came back, because I got sick and had to stay home.
I was at home and looked after all the old people, many old people who were my old people, I looked after them.
I helped them. (NT) You worked in the garden? (KK) Garden...
And whatever they wanted me to do, I would do for them.

Waia Tenene †
Waia Tenene, a story of his life
Waia Tenene, the chief of Erakor in the 1990s and early 2000s telling a story of his life

Ore kineu, apaakor Erakor, naur ses, 1916.
A, 19, a, 37
ajoin a, British police, 1937
afinis, go,
join Amerika 1942 weswes skot Amerika armi.

Upan upa raru ni BP.

Umos masin gan ρ̃ur inru lρ̃eki kaaru Emos, ulρ̃eki kaaru Maniur, uler mai.
Ale upak namlas skot armi.

Yes, I was born on the small island of Erakor in 1916.
In 1937
I joined the British Police, and finished in 1937, and,
I joined the Americans and worked with the American army in 1942.
We were in a boat owned by BP (Burns Phelp).
We took two big machine guns and went around Moso and Maniuro, then came back.
Then we went into the bush with the army.

Upreg kam - kam maloput Efat,

upuet telefon waia pak Forari.
Go imai pak Efil.
1946 malnen kin nafkal inom,
1948 amer pak na Franis polis.
Ato Franis polis 1955, 56.

Go afines mai pak natkon Erakor.
Go api polis ni naot Charlie Kalmet.
Malnen 1959. Malnen nlag iwat utm̃alu naur sees mai pak Efat. 1959, 1960.
Malnen umai pak natkon faum Erakor, Efat.
Go Charlie ipregi api polis ga ni natkon.
1960 pi polis tkal 1967.

Amer 1967 api polis me 1968 api kaonsel ga.
68, 69, 70 go api naot aslat nawesien nig Charlie.
Aslat nawesien ga tkal 1998 mees.
Api naot ni Erakor.
This is text 060b.

We made camp in the middle of Efate,
we put up a telephone wire to Forari. And it came to Vila.
1946, then the war finished.
1948 I joined the French police.
I was in the French police until 1955, 1956.
And I finished and came back to Erakor village.
And I was Chief Charlie Kalmet's policeman.
In 1959, the cyclone hit the small island, and we came back to Efate, 1959, 1960.
Then we came to the new village, Erakor, on Efate.
And Charlie made me his policeman in the village.
1960 I was a policeman until 1967.
In 1967 I was a policeman, but in 1968 I was on the chief's council.
1968, 69, 70 and I was the chief, I got Charlie's job.
I got his job until today 1998.

I am the chief of Erakor

Tim Kalmet
Timteo Kalmet, a story about his life

Tim Kalmet's description of events in his life, including his kidnap in the Phillipines.

Kineu nagiek Timteo Kalmet.

My name is Timteo Kalmet.

Api teesa ni Charley Kalmet go Pali.
Apaakor 1954, no.25 February.

Api naflak nawi,
rusosoki mleo, naflak mleo.
Mleo miel nlaken ipiatlak mleo inru, mleo tar go mleo miel.
Go api naflak mleo.
Go kineu apak skul 1961 naur sees.
Apaakor 1954, me apo stat skul 1961.
(NT) Ag kupaakor naur sees?

(TK) Naur sees.
Kin askul malpei, upei skul vilej skul malpei kin kindi.

Kindergarten ntau iskei ko inru m̃as,
tene, ipi 1958, 59,
go Wabaiat kin ipi tija nigmam, go Kaltap̃au.
Ale English, [a]. Inom, malnen skul ni Esnaar,
rupregi istat. Go upak Franis skul,
komam ulaap kin upak Franis skul, go astat 1961 kin askul Esnaar.
Pan tkal 1963 go apas pak skul, Ecole
Communal ni Port Vila.
Ato 1964 pan tkal 1967.
1968 go astat lycée, go ato lycée 1967 pan tkal 1973,
so skul neu itap, itap top mau.
Atap pak tete iunivesiti mau.

My parents are Charley Kalmet and Pali.
I was born on February 25th, 1954.
My clan is the yam,
they call it mleo, the mleo clan.
Red mleo because there are two mleo, the white and the red one.
And I am of the mleo clan.
I went to school on the small island.
I was born in 1954, and I'd start school in 1961.
(NT) You were born on the small island?

(TK) The small island.
That's where I went to school first, we went to the village school, first to kindy.
I was at kindergarten for just a year or two,
that was 1958 and 59,
and Wabaiat was our teacher, and Kaltap̃au.
English, eh? Finish, then the school at Esnaar,
was started. And we went to French school,
and many of us went to the French school, and I started at Esnaar in 1961.
Until 1963 and I went to the school, Ecole
Communal in Port Vila.
I was there from 1964 until 1967.
I started at the lycée in 1968 until 1973,
my school life was not too long.
I didn't go to any university.

Me lycée askul fom wan, tu, tri.

Ale fom tri go apak ata kontiniu
kin mau, me apak komesel
school,
ipi teknikal skul pak
nanre ni komes nanre ni
taiping, akaonting go
sekreterial wok.
Ale anom skul,
apo ta fines ki skul neu mau
nlaken ntau mlaap nen itu go
apak Nume reki nen kin rukmas
namtak.
Namet kineu isa, rukmas slatlua
ito ptin.
Go namet kineu isa, 1963,
waia ni sulok isup̃ti.
Me malne runa ruksentki kineu
kafak Nume ko Australia
reki nen rukfreg tenmatun me
mama imal.
Mama neu imal, itli na inrom
kineu go itli na kafei to.

Go ato pan namtak kipe to taar
pan pan istat ptin,
ipreg nñauk kito ptin ser mal.
1972, namba tortin December

go apak hospitel Nume.
Doctor ijek ki kineu sa me apak
hospitel Nume reki nen
rukslatlua.
Ruslatlu tenen rupus met psir
ne,
me ata ta jenjkin mau tkal
mees,
nlaken ruta nrik kineu ki gas

I was at the lycée for form one,
two, three.
After form three I went to
commercial school,

it was a technical school
to learn commerce, typing,
accounting and secretarial work.

I finished school,
I didn't finish school
because the last year I went to
Noumea for them to cut out my
eye.
My eye was bad, they had to cut
it out because it hurt.
My eye was bad, 1963
an umbrella wire pierced it.
Then they wanted to send me to
Noumea or Australia
so that they could do something,
but my mother didn't want it.
My mother didn't want it, she
said she loved me and she said I
should stay first.
And I stayed until my eye was
going white and started to hurt,
and gave me headaches all the
time. In 1972, on the 13th
December
I went to hospital in Noumea.
The doctor checked me here, but
I went to hospital in Noumea so
that they could take it out.
They took it out and put in this
false eye,
but I haven't changed it until
today,
because they didn't tell me when

kin kafo jenj kin mau.
Go malfane wik nentu namba 26
October go amer pak Nume nen
rukleka,
nlaken kipe to muf ito pak elag
kipe to sees.
Go ga wankia.
Me 1964 pak 73 kin askul lycée.
Malen atli na apak Nume, 1972,

apan 72 me aler 73 March.

Mer ler mai na kaskul. Me kaipe
tapi intreski skul mau.

Me ipi ntau mlaap neu ni
komesel nen utae sat na natus
neu ni teknikel skul.
Me kaipe ta mro wi kin na kafak
skul mau. Atli na amur
kaweswes.
Go apan weswes. Go kaipan
weswes. Aweswes radio
telekomiunikesen,
stat 1973, 22 March 1973.
Ale apo risaen mal ntau ilakor
pi ato 1973.
22 March uto panpan 1979.
Go utransfe mai pak Et stesen,
satelait, satelait, Et stesen pei
nen rusosoki Hebritel,
nen kin 1980 go rupo sosoki
Vanitel,
mees ipi Telecom.
So malen utransfe mai pak
Hebritel,
go ato eṁrom, telegrafik rum
go ato preg teleks, telegrafic,
telefon,

to change it.
And now, next week, on the 26th
October I will go to Noumea for
them to look at it,
because it has moved, it has
moved up a little.
That's it.
1964 to 1973 I was at high school.
When I'm talking about I went to
Noumea, 1972,
I went in 1972 and came back in
March 1973.
Came back to go to school. But I
wasn't interested in school
anymore.
It was my last year at commercial
when I got my papers at the
technical school.
I didn't want to go to school. I
said I wanted to work.

And I went to work. I worked in
radio telecommunications

from 1973, 22 March 1973.
Then I resigned maybe it was
1973.
From the 22 March until 1979.
And we transferred to the first
satellite Earth station
that was called Hebritel,
that in 1980 would be Vanitel,

today it is Telecom.
Then we transferred to Hebritel,

and I was in the telegraphic
room, doing telex, telegraph,
telephone,

me rupaṁori na awi nanre ni akaonting, nanre ni akaonting, go, administresen.

Go rupregi apak em̃rom, akaonting go administresen go aweswes esan pan tkal 1981, go arisaen.

A risaen nlaken amur kames miusik.

Nlaken, a, malen kin 1963 sori 1961, kin astat intres ki miusik kin astat tkal miusik. Nlaken malen kin 1961 kin astat tkal miusik, gita me yukeleli.

Gita me yuk, yukeleli. Even ipo piatlak akodien iskei ito esum̃. Kano ni Aneityum, Tanna iskei, ga imai to esum̃ nigmam to mal pei me ipitlak akodien iskei, Sori, ga ipiatlak banjo me akodien ne ga ipi teni gka neu kaaru, gka Tom, Tom Kalmet, brata ni gka neu, gka Charlie. Ale ato ato mes ki akodien ne. Plak gita mana, me runrogo na ames wi, p̃otae lag seserik. Go stat miusik karie neu istat bild up esa. Go 1981, malnen arisaen Vanitel apan mes. Apan weswes as resevesen maneje, Hotel Le Lagon. Me kineu astat 1976 kin astat mes Hotel Le Lagon, me malpei kotkot ames naor laap. Me awelkin ato tae ki miusik

and they found that I had accounting and administration skills.

And they took me in to accounting and administration and I worked there until 1981, when I resigned.

I resigned because I wanted to play music.

Because then, 1963 sorry, 1961, I started being˙ interested in music and started playing music. Because then, 1961, I started playing music, guitar and ukelele.

Guitar and ukelele. There was even an accordion at home. A man from Aneityum, from the south, he came and stayed at our home and he had an accordion. Sorry, he had a banjo but the accordion belonged to my other uncle Tom, Tom Kalmet, my father's brother, Charlie. So I played this accordion. With the guitar and so on, and they heard that I played well, and sang a little.

And my music career built up from then.

And in 1981, then I resigned from Vanitel I went to play.

I went to be the reservation manager at the Hotel Le Lagon.

In 1976 I started at the Hotel Le Lagon, but in those days I played at lots of places.

I knew my music and its work,

neu skot nawesien ga,
aweswes Le Lagon aliat me p̃og
go ames elag.
Taos 1968 ames nait klab
rusosoki Tahitinui.
Inom 1973 ames Le Pandanus
restoran,
inom 1976 go apak Le Lagon.

Ale ato Le Lagon to ato mes esa.

Me ato weswes radio.
Mai pak Vanitel mana, 1981, go
arisaen Vanitel.
Apan weswes Le Lagon as
resevesen maneje.
Me astil mentein ki nameswen
neu, miusik pefomans,
pan tkal 1977, 1977 go
Intercontinental Hotel.
Ipuetlu kineu sanie nlaken
rumur asistan sels maneje, gar,
hotel gar.
Apan weswes skotir, go mal skei
mau ne
go ruproposki kineu ki mane
nen imer pak elag nanre ni
miusik.
Go atao Le Lagon miusik go
nawesien me ajoin
Intercontinental.
Go apato sanpen to pram.
Pan tkal 1982 kin apato Hotel Le
Lagon,
pan tkal 1982 m̃as go atao.

Apato Intercontinental pan tkal
1984.
Orait 1984 aweswes skot Sound

I worked at Le Lagon in the day
and at night I played up above.
Like, in 1968 I played at the night
club called Tahitinui.
Finished in 1973, I played at the
Pandanus restaurant,
it finished in 1976 and I went
back to Le Lagon.

Then I was at Le Lagon, I played
there.
I worked at the radio.
I came to Vanitel then I resigned
in 1981.
I worked at Le Lagon as a
reservation manager.
But I kept up my playing, music
performance,
until 1977, 1977 it was the
Intercontinental Hotel.
He took me there beccause they
wanted an assistant sales
manager at their hotel.
I went to work with them, and at
the same time
they offered me more money
than I got for the music.

And I left the music at Le Lagon
and the work and I joined the
Intercontinental.
And I was there for quite a while.
I stayed at Le Lagon until 1982,

I stayed at Le Lagon until 1982,
then I left.
I stayed at the Intercontinental
until 1984.
In 1984 I worked at the Sound

Centre.
Rupuet kineu sanpen, ne rumur na kaweswes skotir.
Go apan asinia selsman.
Go malne go apo to demonstret ki sernale ni nameswen, taos piano, gita, elektronik sernale.
Pan go, ipiatlak group ni Papua New Guinea, West Papua iskei rumai pak sa, nagier Black Brothers,
rumai 1984 go 85.
Go rupuet kineu ames skotir.
Ana ames skotir go ipiatlak janis nen, rusent ki kineu apak Papua New Guinea.

Apan rikod ki kaset neu inru.
Papua New Guinea inom,
aler mai, go ames skot Black Brothers BESA klab kin mees ipi Club Vanuatu.

Go ipi BESA klab malpei ipi, British ex-Servicemen's Association.
Ale ames esan pan go ipiatlak tete p̃og kineu askei mes, taos wan man band.
Me tete p̃og ames skotir, taos, grup
pan. Go manejmen ni Besa klab rutli na iwi na rukstop ki Black Brother
me rukemploi ki kineu ful taem.
Gar nawesien gar. Nlaken ruleka na ijip.
Go kineu askei me miusik ipiatlak veraeti,

Centre.
They took me there to work with them.
I was a senior salesman.
And I demonstrated how to use all the instruments, like piano, guitar and electronic things.
Until there was a group from PNG, West Papua who came here, called Black Brothers,

they came in 1984 and 85.
They got me to play with them.
As soon as I played with them and there was this chance, and they sent me to Papua New Guinea.
I recorded my two cassettes.
After Papua New Guinea,
I came back and played with the Black Brothers at the BESA club which today it is called Club Vanuatu.
Before it was called the BESA club, British ex-Servicemen's Association.
So I played there and some nights I was solo, like a one-man-band.
Some nights I played with the group.
And the management of the Besa club said it would stop with the Black Brothers
and employ me full time.
That's their work. Because they saw it was cheap.
And on my own I could play a variety of music,

nlaken alagki Bislama, Franis, English, go tete Spanish.
Ipregi go Black Brothers runom,

me kineu ato me ipo piatlak tete dispiut seserik. Black Brothers runrogtesa.
Runrogtesa go rupregi ruto mai lek manejmen ni BESA klab.

Pan go kineu atao.
Malen atao go Intercontinental Hotel rumer puet kineu.
Runa rupuet kineu, 85 pan tkal 87.
Okay, ato 87, me Fairstar, ipiatlak p̃og iskei ipitlak imatur p̃og iskei nuof.
Ale, nlaken ipitlak malne ilakor pi, ilakor pi Maj ko, ia, ore Maj ko Epril. Me ipitlak nlagwat iskei, go Fairstar imai, imatur p̃og, imtak ki nlagwat, go imatur p̃og.
Me ipitlak anaonsmen ni saeklon, nlagwat iskei.
Go Fairstar imai, imatur p̃og, imtak ki nlagwat, go imatur p̃og.
P̃og krus daerekta go tete nam̃er nen rulekor raru na, Fairstar.
rumai min hotel, rumai sak to me ruto min hotel.
Ruto nrog miusik, pan go runrogo iwi na, krus daerekta ga imai me ipaosi ki kineu, 'Me kumur p̃amai mes Fairstar?' Go ana, 'O yes.'

because I sing in Bislama, French, English and some Spanish.
So the Black Brothers were finished,
and I stayed, but they felt bad about it and we had a dispute. The Black Brothers felt bad.
They felt bad and they went to see the management of the BESA Club.
Until I left.
When I left, the Intercontinental Hotel took me back.
They kept me from 1985 until 1987.
In 1987 the Fairstar was here overnight, they stayed at the wharf overnight.
It might have been March or April. There was a cyclone and the Fairstar stayed overnight, it was scared of the cyclone and it stayed overnight.

A cyclone was announced.

And the Fairstar came and stayed overnight, it was scared of the cyclone so it stayed overnight.
That night the cruise director and some of the crew of the Fairstar.
came to drink at the hotel.

They heard the music, they liked it and the cruise director came and asked for me,
'Do you want to come and play of the Fairstar?' And I said, 'Oh yes.'

Ana, 'Iwi me akam kofaos ki
boss neu ni san.'
Go gar rupo paos ki boss neu ki.
Boss nen malne ipi jenral
maneje, Oriliano Viniati.
Ipi kano ni Italy. Rupaoskin go
Mr. Viniati itli na,
'O itae neet mes, me kemer mai.

Keta pato Fairstar to mau,
kemer mai.'
Runa, 'Ore, kefreg krus kenru,
okay.'
Go 1987 ne, apreg krus inru,
krus 16 go af ni 17 ale rumai
rumer lp̃eki kineu.
Go mal ne welkia ipregi
repiutesen neu taos miusisen.
Ga imer pak elag tol nawesien
nen atae pregi taos em̃rom
administresen.
Go promosen neu welkia apak
naurur apak naur ni Vanuatu.
Apan lag ipitlak Pentecost,
Esanr, Emlakul, Epi, Tanna go
tete naur seserik nen ruto ni
Efat.
Me 1987 go nametp̃agon ni krus
neu na aler mai aweswes malses
Intercontinental.
Ale komam Mary rapak Filipin.

Mtulep neu Mary ga iweswes
Asian Development Bank.
Go mal ne ga ipitlak nsaiseiwen
ga ni sanpen.
Me headquarters ni Asian
Development Bank ito Filipins.

I said, 'Good, but you should talk
to my boss here.'
They asked my boss about it.
My boss then was the general
manager, Oriliano Viniati.
He is Italian. They asked him and
Mr. Viniati said,
'He can go to you but he has to
come back.
He can't stay on the Fairstar, he
has to come back.'
They said, 'Okay he will do two
cruises.'
And in 1987 I took two cruises,
cruise 16 and half of 17 and they
put me back here.
And that was how I built my
reputation as a musician.
And it grew to more than I could
do as I was inside the
administration.
To promote myself I went around
the islands of Vanuatu.
I went to sing to Pentecost,
Santo, Malakula, Epi, Tanna and
some islands around Efate.

And in 1987 at the end of my
cruise, I came back for a small
while to the Intercontinental.
So Mary and I went to the
Philippines.
My wife, Mary, works at the
Asian Development Bank.
At that time she had a meeting
over there.
And the headquarters of the
Asian Development Bank was in
the Philippines.

Me mal ne apiatlak asel wi iskei, ga apiatlak fren wi iskei ga ipi, ga ga ipi nana alternate executive manager ni Asian Development Bank.
Ito mai pak esan reki nen kin iset up ki Asian Development Bank ni sa.
Ga ipi teni Papua New Guinea. Nagien John Natera.
John imai me ipi fren wi neu.
Go itae na mtulep neu iweswes Asian Development Bank.
Go itae na mtulep neu kefo pak Filipin nametp̃ag June ni 1987.

Go ineu pakot pases. Ineu pakot tiket ni plen, me komam mtulep ranru pa.
Rana rapan go mtulep ga ito pak semina ga.
Ale kineu ato pak kos ni nalag.
Amur na kafreg na nalek kemer nrus wi.
Go ato pak kos sees neu, Yamaha Yupango ni Manila.
Ale go ruto runrik kineu ki na, 'Kuta nid nen p̃alearn ki nalem mau.' Nlaken rupregi alag nalag itol.
Nalag iwelkia ihaf klasikel, 'Don't cry for me Argentina.'
Go tekaaru ipi 'I just called to say I love you', go rok an rol iskei.
Rujajki nalek me rupam̃ori na alag leg ki mal.
Go apuet nmarok wi. Go aiuski diafram neu wi.

At that time I had a good friend, I had a good friend, he was the alternate executive manager of the Asian Development Bank.

He used to come here to set up the Asian Development Bank here.

He was from Papua New Guinea. His name was John Natera.
John was a good friend of mine.
He knew that my wife worked for the Asian Development Bank.
And he knew my wife would go to the Philippines at the end of June 1987.
He paid for my ticket and me and my wife both went.

We went and my wife went to her seminar.
And I went to a singing course.
I wanted to make my singing voice better.
And I went to a short course at Yamaha Yupango in Manila.
And they said to me, 'You don't need to improve your voice.' Because they made me sing three songs.
A song that was half classical, 'Don't cry for me Argentina.'
And the other was, 'I just called to say I love you', and a rock and roll one.
They judged my voice and they found that I sing in time.
And I had good breath control, And I used my diaphragm well.

Go vokal kods neu iwi.
Ale rutli na itap nid nen.
Ale me ato pan totan skot
nañer nen ruto pan lenki
piano.
Go ato lek teflan ruto plei, me,
ato pnakon, wel ki nlaken
ato leker ñas ruto mes. Me ato
leker me welkia amur katae
teflan rumes.
Go iwelkia ato kopikir.
Malen kin welkia ato pai ñas.

Inom, go ñeltig nen rakfe ler.

Me kineu askei pak sto,
komam mal ilaap ga komam
rato nru pak sto.
Me malne, aliat toknak iskei,
me askei pak sto aliat.
Pan go rukidnap ki kineu sto.
Rukidnap ki kineu me rumsag
kineu pak,
rutao na Coca Cola me ipitlak
sliping pil eñrom.
Me amatur eñrom loto, me
rupan rutau kineu natkon iskei,
rusoso ki Pulakan, eñae, eñae.
Mary ito Hotel, iler pak Hotel
pa, me ito pan 6 klok kotfan, go

ileka ata pan mau ipanik go
ipreg inkwaeri pan pan pañori
na apuel.
Apuel sto rulek kineu pag skot
nañer ne,

go inom san, rumer ta lek kineu
mau.

And my vocal chords were good.
So they said that I didn't need it.
So I went and sat with people
learning the piano.

I watched how they play and I
copied it, well, because
I just watched them as they
played. I watched them so that I
could learn how they play.
And that is how I copied them.
As I was just filled up (my
knowledge).
Finish, and we were about to
come back.
I went to the shop alone,
we had been to the shop together
many times.
But that time, Saturday, I went to
the shop alone in the daytime.
They kidnapped me in the store.
They kidnapped me and they
carried me to-,
they gave me Coca Cola with a
sleeping pill in it.
I slept in the car and they took
me to this village,
called Pulakan, a long way.
Mary was at the hotel, she went
back to the hotel, but it was
nearly six in the evening, and
she saw I wasn't back, she
panicked and made inquiries and
found I was missing.
I wasn't at the shop, but they saw
me climb into a car with this
man,
and that's all, they didn't see me
again.

Eniwei, welkia rupo pam̃or kineu,
p̃og wan klok p̃og.
Eleven klok p̃og kin rupam̃or kineu me wan klok kin
loto imai po mai mai mai po mos kineu, nlaken em̃ae.
Ale apo mai olwei pak hospitel pan rudren ki nrak welkia glukos a.
Me dokta ina, 'Ku laki a, nlaken kum̃ol.'
(NT) Me rupnak tenamrun?
(TK) Rupnak mane, go kompiuta softwe neu plak su ni teesa,
go su neu nen aslatir,
waj, sanglas,
me am̃ol, go aler mai me gawankia.
Ana ataf hospitel leg mai pak eroplen.
Rapa plen trau ler.

Amer mai tkal Intercontinental go amer mes esan.
Ames pan tkal 1991, go anom.
Ana anom Intercontinental go 1991 pan tkal 1993
ato esum̃ to nlaken apakot tete sernale nig nkas,
me ato weswes ki seserik ki nkas.
Me atu p̃al tu ata weswes mau.
1993 go Mary ina, 'E ilakor wi p̃afan weswes tete ofis, nlaken

kupiatlak tetenamrun nranre ni ofis, na kutae weswes ofis me

Anyway, they found me,

at one o'clock in the morning.
At 11 pm they found me, but at one am
the car came to get me, it was a long way.
OK, I went to the hospital and they drained my blood because of glucose.
The doctor said, 'You are lucky because you are alive.'
(NT) Did they steal something?
(TK) They took money and my computer software and kids' shoes
and my shoes that I had bought, watch, sunglasses,
but I was alive and I got back, that's it.
I left the hospital and went straight to the plane.
We went to the plane and returned.

I went to play at the Intercontinental.
I played until 1991 and I finished.
I finished at he Intercontinental and 1991 to 1993
I stayed home because I bought everything to do with wood,
I worked a little with wood.

I did nothing, I didn't work
In 1993 and Mary said, 'It would be good if you worked in an office since
you have good office skills, you know how to work in an office

kuipe to miusik teetwei mai, me
malfane p̃atraem.'

Go alel nawesien, astat amer
stat Hotel Le Lagon me alel
nawesien.
Apaoski nawesien pan pan apan
tkal taon me san ata paoski
nawesien mau,
gar rupios mai.
Go rutelefon, Jif Jastis ni kot
inrogo na ato lel nawesien.

Go itelefon pak Mary me ipaos
kin na, 'Kutae nrik maarik gaag
ki na kemai. Amur katraus
skoti.'
Apan traus skoti ana, 'Ore apes
ki English, Franis.'
Ipo traem kineu, test ki kineu.
Kompiuta itraem kompiuta, me
nlaken kineu ateetwei teetwei
mai ga apiatlak kompiuta mai
nlaken ato mur sernale ni
elektronik.
Go ipam̃ori na ntaewen neu
nanre ni kompiuta iwi.
Go apo taep naenti wod per
minet.
Go kalkulet fast, nanre ni
kalkuleting masin go akaonting.

Go ina, 'O, gawankia, ag kin
amur ag, me p̃afo tae stat gas?'
Go ana, 'Ito akam.' Okay,
rurikrut, rupreg advetismen
ga me ipo inteviu ki tete nakon
me itili na, 'Akano promis me
p̃afo traem.'

you've played music for a long
time, but try working in an
office.'
I looked for work, I started at Le
Lagon and I looked for work.

I asked for work all over the
town but a place I hadn't asked
called for me,
they called for me.
They telephoned, the Chief
Justice heard I was looking for
work.
He rang Mary and said, 'You tell
your husband to come. I want to
talk to him.'

I went to talk with him and told
him I speak English and French.
He tried me, he tested me.
He tried my computer skills, but
as I had a computer years ago he
saw that I liked electronic things.

He saw that I knew about
computers.
And I could type ninety words
per minute.
And calculate fast, on a
calculating machine and in
accounting.
And he said, 'When can you
start?'
And I said, 'It's up to you.' They
recruited, they advertised
They interviewed some others
and he said, 'I can't promise, but
we'll see.'

Kofo traem komam ulakor pi siks, me kineu awin wes go apo pa.

Go aweswes kot stat 1993, pan tkal 1996, go arisaen.

Arisaen nlaken amur kamer pak

Chamber of Commerce.

Amro kin iwi nlaken amur kamer rediskava ki komesel ntaewen neu ni nanre ni, na, komes, a?

Go bisnes. Komam upat, komam upat kin upan inteviu, upan inteviu.

Ale amer win wes. Go ga wankia pan tkal mees ato Chamber of Commerce, taos arisej, tred and invesmen, go infomesen ofisa.

Go asemsem nlaken aweswes naor ilaap go apitlak ntaewen neu iwelkia imer top nanre ni sernale fserser, nlaken ata fneski skul neu mau,

me aweswes panpan akraksok tete ntawen kin atik kin malpei. Nlaken nawesien atkalir welkia rupi nawesien p̃afp̃of.

Ale mal ilaap kafo mas pan saisei skot tete natañ̃ol nen gar rupi ekspets mana.

Nafet nawesien ne, go mal ilaap asat janis nen kin, apaoskir kin nen rutijki kineu ki tenmatun.

So gar rupitlak teori naor nen ruplaksok kineu welkia ato saisei skotir mana.

There were about six of us but I won and I got the job.

I worked at the court from 1993 until 1996 then I resigned.

I resigned because I wanted to go to

the Chamber of Commerce.

I thought it was good because I could rediscover my commercial training.

And business. There were four of us who did the interview.

And I got the job. Until today I work at the Chamber of Commerce as a researcher, trade and investment and information officer.

And I am happy because I work in lots of places I am learning lots of new things because I didn't finish school,

but I worked and learned as I went.

Because the work that I deal with is important.

Many times I meet with experts.

Many times I take the chance and ask them to teach me things.

They had theory that they taught me when I met with them.

Go ruto tau ntaen nen kin, mees
asemsem, nlaken apitlaken.
Go ato Chamber of Commerce
tkal malfane.
This is text 063.

They give me some skills. Today I
am happy because I have them.
And I am at the Chamber of
Commerce until today.

William Wayane †
William Wayane, a story of his life
William Wayane talking about his life, from his birth on Erromango
where his father was a missionary to schooling on Erakor
Island, and eventually his role as town secretary.

Histri neu malen kin api teesa
mai tkal mees.

My history, from when I was a
child until today.

Papa neu ga ipi evangelist iskei
teetwei, go ito siwer ur naurur
preg nawesien tap.

My father was an evangelist
then, and he went around the
islands to do religious work.

Ipi nlaken kineu apo paakor
naur nig Erromango,

That is why I was born on
Erromango island,

malen papa neu ipato weswes ur
Emlakul.

before my father was working
on Malakula.

Nafioson ipan nag keler mai pak
naur Erakor.

The call went out for him to
come back to Erakor island.

Go malnen imai tkal naur Erakor

And when he got to Erakor
Island

go rumer soso nen kefak naur
nig saot Erromango

they then called him to go to
south Erromango

ipreg papa go mama go p̃aluk
iskei, nagien kin Ashael.

it made him and my mother and
my brother, Ashael.

Go ga kin ipi taklep neu. Ruitol
tm̃alu reki naur nig saot
Erromango.

He is the first born in our family.
The three of them left for south
Erromango.

Go 1950 kin rutao naur Erakor
pareki Erromango.

And in 1950 they left Erakor
island for Erromango.

Go rupato ntau iskei nom, go
kineu apo paakor

And they stayed on the island
and I was born in

1951, 8 November, naur nig
Erromango.

1951, 8 November, the island of
Erromango.

Go uler 1952 kin uler mai pak

And we came back in 1952 we

naur Erakor.
Go kaipes pak skul naur sees,

1958 tkal 1959.
Go amer pan skul Bahai.
Go 1959 go nlag p̃ur iskei iwat
naur Erakor,
go nlag nen rusoso ki Kristof.

Go ipregsaki sernale laap
go ipregi maarik naot ipregi
unrookot mai naur p̃ur.
Go amer ler mai skul natkon pan
tkal 1967.
Go apan skul Iririki Distrik Skul.

Go apato skul ntau inru.
Malen atao skul, go apan weswes
British Office,
atlag ralim iskei atmat iskei. Mer
tao British Office kaimai tu esum̃
tu.
Pan pan nafioson imai 1971 nen
rukfan weswes Nume,
go kaipan pus nagiek.
Go kaitm̃alu pak Kaldoni, pan
patu ntau inru. Inom.
Go amer ler mai 1973, April.
Amai tu malses mer pan weswes
UNELCO mal sees, imer nom.

Kaitu p̃al tu pan, kaipreg tete
sup̃ kerkerai Hotel Lagon,

kaipak nasum̃ malik ntau iskei
go atlag itol.
Malnen ataf nasum̃ malik, mer
mai, mer pan weswes Post Office
ntau fiftin.

came back to Erakor island.
And I started at school on the
small island,
1958 to 1959.
And I went back to Bahai school.
In 1959 the cyclone hit Erakor
island,
the cyclone was called
Christophe.
It damaged many things
and it made the chief take us
across to the big island.
And I went back to school until
1967.
And I went to Iririki District
School.
I was at school for two years.
When I left school I went to
work at the British Office,
for eleven months. Then I left
the British Office then I came
home.
Until the call came in 1971 that
they go to work in Noumea,
and I put in my name.
I left for New Caledonia for two
years. Finished.
I came back in April 1973.
I came for a short time, then
went to work for UNELCO for a
short time, then finished.
I hung around until I was
involved in smashing up the
Hotel Lagon,
and went to gaol for a year and
three months.
When I left the gaol I went to
work for the Post Office for
fifteen years.

Rumer preglu kineu nawesien	They came and took my work from me
go kaimai tu p̃al tu ntau ilim inom.	and I came back to doing nothing for five years.
Go kaipreg natus neu pak provins reki nen kamai pi sekreteri go rumer trok wes.	I took my papers to the province about being the secretary and they agreed to it.
Go apo mai pes nawesien neu atlag ni June 1998.	And I started work in June 1998.
Go ipi tesees wan inom esan.	And it is where this small story ends.

This is text 067.

Daisy Wayane
Daisy Wayane, a story of her life

Daisy Wayane's work history, from school on Eraniao (Erakor Island) and the cyclone that moved everyone back to the mainland, through various jobs, to being secretary of the UMP in local government.

Askul naur sees, ata tae apitlak ntau ipi skul mau apitlak ntau ipi siks.	I went to school on the small island, I don't know how many years I went to school, I was six years old.
Go wik ilakor skei ko inru. Ale nlag iwat, ale umai pak naur esa. Ale askul esa, 1964 go apak Ep̃agtwei.	And one or two weeks. Then the cyclone came to the island. I went to school here, in 1964 I went to Ep̃agtwei.
I.D.S. tkal 1968.	I.D.S. until 1968.
Ale kaipe mai to esum̃.	I went and stayed at home.
(NT) To esum̃ to, me ag kuweswes 1968?	(NT) At home, but did you work in 1968?
(DW) 68, 69, sixty nine go apan	(DW) 68,69, then I started

stat weswes Hotel Lagon.
(NT) Kutap weswes haoskel
mau?
(DW) Aweswes haoskel tetemal,
me apei weswes Hotel Lagon,
69,70,71,72, go apan weswes
Nume, apan pi haoskel Nume.

1973 go amer ler mai
(NT) Me iku kin kupan pak
Nume?
(DW) Itik ato weswes hotel ale
ipitlak masta iskei, natamol iskei
imai tli na imur tewewes sanpe.
Ale apan ga weswes.

Ale aweswes tkal 73 go amur
kamai go amer ler mai, pak esa.

(NT) Me ag kuskul franis? Itik.

(DW) Itik me apan go apo
kraksok franis.
(NT) Go ipi nawesien mailum ni
Hotel Lagon, ko nawesien p̃ur?
(DW) Aweswes ne taos na,
malpei nen apan stat weswes,
aweswes londri.
A weswes londri atlag ilakor
inru, ale amai pi wetres. Tkal
1972
(NT) Me ipi nawesien wi?
(DW) Ore ipi nawesien wi.
Nlaken malpei franis man kin
ion ki Hotel Lagon, ga ipaakot
wi.
(NT) Me mees?
(DW) Mees nawesien itop mane

working at the Hotel Lagon.
(NT) Did you work as a
housegirl?
(DW) I worked as a housegirl
sometimes and I first worked at
the Hotel Lagon, 69, 70, 71, 72,
and I went to work in Noumea, I
went to work as a housegirl in
Noumea.
1973 I came back.
(NT) But why did you go to
Noumea?
(DW) No, I was working at the
hotel and there was a white
man, a man came and said that
he wanted to work there. So I
worked for him.
So I worked until 73 and I
wanted to come back and I came
back here.
(NT) But did you go to French
school? No.
(DW) No but I went and I learned
French.
(NT) Was it easy work at the
Hotel Lagon or was it hard?
(DW) I worked there like, that
time that I started work, I
worked in the laundry.
I worked in the laundry for
about two months then I went
on to be a waitress. Until 1972.
(NT) But was it good work?
(DW) Yes, it was good work.
Because before, the Frenchman
who owned the Hotel Lagon paid
well.
(NT) And today?
(DW) (laughs) Today there's too

isees.
(NT) Kuweswes Nume, kumer ler Hotel Lagon?

(DW) Ore, amai mer pan weswes Hotel Lagon.
Itik ana Nume mai, amai to esa.
Ale apan weswes restoran iskei, Pandanus.

Pandanus restoran, aweswes wes mal sees, ale
amer ler pan mai pak esuñ, ale kafo me ler pak Lagon. Mer ler pan weswes Hotel Lagon

Amer pan pi wetres. Amer pan, pak Hotel Lagon 1974, tkal 75.

Ore amai, amer weswes Hotel Lagon tkal 1975, ale apitlak teesa nen tu. Timothy.
Ale aweswes pan atkali kin 74, 75, apan na aslati ale amai to esuñ . Ato lekor wes esuñ
Aweswes Pandanus mal sees, ale nlaken manijmen knen itawi mau. Go iṗon, ale amer ler pak Hotel Lagon pa.

Ale aweswes tkal 1975, ale amai to esuñ to pan, ale amer pan ni Maxim Carlot pi haoskel, esuñ ga.
Ntau iskei ale amer pak, e ato ni Maxim Carlot weswes.
Sista neu iskei imai, itili na, natañol iskei imer mur haoskel franis man, Tasrik. Ale amer

much work and the pay is low!
(NT) You worked in Noumea and you came back to the Hotel Lagon?

(DW) Yes, I came back to work at the Hotel Lagon.
No, when I wanted to come back from Noumea, I came back here.
Okay, I went to work at a restaurant, the Pandanus.
Pandanus restaurant, I worked there for a small time, then I came back to the house, then I went back to the Lagon.
Returned to work at the Hotel Lagon.
I went back to being a waitress. I went back to the Hotel Lagon from 1974 to 1975.
Okay, I went back to the Hotel Lagon until 1975, then I had this child. Timothy.
I worked until 1974, 75, I went and had him, so I came home. I looked after him at home.
I worked at the Pandanus for a little time because the management there was not very good. It closed, so I went back to Le Lagon.
Then I worked until 1975, then back home, and then I went back to work as a housegirl at Maxime Carlot's house.
One year, then I went back, to Maxime Carlot's to work.
My sister came and said that a French man wanted a housegirl in Tassiriki. Ok, I went and

pan, aweswes ntau itol.
Apan ni natañol nen weswes ntau itol, tkal 1980. Ale ru, uindependent. Ale, franis man ruler, go amer mai to esuñ.
Mer mai to esuñ to pan ale, amer pan weswes e, restoran iskei, Bamboo Royal,
mer weswes ntau itol, ale amer ler mai to esuñ.
Ale amer ler pak na Hotel Lagon, 1991, tkal 1994.
91 pak 1994. Amer ler pak esuñ nlaken ato weswes me ipitlak eleksen ni politik.
Ale kineu atu leg kineu api memba, na ilekted memba.
Ni nanre ni politik ni U.M.P.
Ale komam utu leg, ale kineu api, amai pi na, Daniel ipi presiden, vaes jeaman kineu api vaes ga.
Ale raweswes ntau ipat.
Ale rudisolf ki lokal kafman, go taos kaonsel kipe tik go ipi malwan, idisolf.
Ale amer ler pan, paoski nawesien naur sees go apo weswes tkal mees.
(NT) Nawesien ni kaonsel ipi nawesien nen rupakot?
(DW) Tik sakrifais! Ore, utmom welu komam nawesien, nafte ipaakor komiuniti, komam utu leg. Ale uweswes.
Go api, taosi welkia kineu api vaes jeaman ni eria kaonsel, go apitkaskei pi reprasentatif ni

worked for three years.
I went and worked for that man for three years, until 1980 we got independence. Then, the French left and I came back home again.
I went back home, then I went to work at this restaurant, the Bamboo Royal,
for three years, then I went home again.
Then I went back to the Hotel Lagon, 1991 to 1994.
91 to 94. I went back home because I was working then there was an election.
And I stood and I was elected a member.
On the UMP side of politics.
So we stood, and Daniel [Daisy's brother] was president and I was vice-chairman.

We worked for four years.
Then they dissolved local government and as the council was dissolved.
So I came back, asked for work at the small island and I worked until today.
(NT) Was the council job paid?

(DW) No, sacrifice! We helped each other, whatever came out of the community, we supported it. So we worked.
And I was vice chairman of the area council and I was also the women's representative

nafet nmatu
pak nsaiseiwen, ur na nort Efate   to meetings, like in North Efate.
mana tefla.
This is text 084.

Kaloros Kaltaf †
Plantation days

Kaloros Kaltaf talking about working on plantations and some of the
sharp practices employed by the plantation owners.

Ipitlak nanre ni Franis, tete [discussing planters] There are
nanre ni Inglis. Me nanre ni those on the French side, some
Inglis rutap laap perkati mau. from the English. But there were
not too many English.

Teni Franis kin runrus laap There were many French ones.
perkati. Go tenen kin atae And those whose names I know,
nagier, ipi Mister Marinas, there's Mister Marinas,
Mister Ena nanre ni Franis. Mister Ena, on the French side.
Mister Harris nanre ni Inglis. Mister Harris on the English
side.

Mister Aru, franis, nanre ni Mister Aru, French, on the
Franis French side.
Tiker, nanre ni Inglis Tiker, English.
Go Platimiere, nanre ni Franis And Platimiere, French.
Mister Jacques Nichols nanre ni Mister Jacques Nichols on the
Franis French side.
Mister Frouin, ga me ipo pi Mister Frouin, he would have
nanre ni Franis. been on the French side.
Ohlen, Mister Ohlen, nanre ni Ohlen, Mister Ohlen, one of the
Franis nafet planter ki. French planters.
(NT) Go ruweswes esua? (NT) And where did they work?
(KK) Gar kin ruweswes ur nanre (KK) They worked along, some
ni, tete rustat Takape. Ruweswes started at Takabe. They worked
tefla nanre ni, ato til nagien like, at the place, I said its name,
nanre nen, pak Undine Bay. then to Undine Bay.
Toklos nanre nen pak Paonagisu Facing that side, to around
mana, pak Paofatu. Tete ruto Paonangisu, to Paufatu. Some

Emel. Mister Watt.
Nanre ni haf kast,
ipitlak Emi Laurent Ga me ipi
haf kast iskei, nen kin ga me ...
(NT) Ag kuweswes naroi?
(KK) Ruen- gar rupitlak na naroi
gar nen ruweswes wes.
(NT) Me ag. (KK) Kineu?
Kineu atap weswes wes mau, me
tete nen kin ito- ruto emeltig
kin aweswes.
Mal sees, kineu apreg tete
nawesien, ni na konstraksen.
Kontrak.
Me rekin kaweswes plantesen,
kineu ata weswes plantesen
mau. Itik.
(NT) Me ipiatlak tete natamol ni
Erakor nen ruto weswes?
(KK) Ipitlak tete nen kin rupi
taosi kin stokmen go kauboy
nen kin ruweswes, ipitlak tete.
Go tete nen kin ruweswes nanre
ni kopra, me ruta laap mau. Me
ipitlak namer ni Tanna.
Tete namer ni Emlakul naur ur
nen kin ruto. Me komam ni Efat
tepur rutap weswes. Tenrfaal
mas kin ruweswes.
(NT) Nlaken iku? (KK) Nlaken,
wel, rutap murin weswes skot,
namer taar, nlaken tete,
i, sup ni nafsan. Rutap tae pes wi
mau go ipregi rukano pak
nawesien.

Me atae na telaap ruweswes. Me
ruweswes mal sees ale ruler mai.

were at Mele. Mister Watt.
As for the half castes,
there was Emi Laurent. He was a
half caste, he ...
(NT) Did you work the ground?
(KK) They had ground that they
worked.
(NT) But you? (KK) Me?
I didn't work it, but some but
some similar things I did work
at.
For a small time I did some
construction work. Contract.

But as for me working on the
plantations, I didn't work on
plantations at all. No.
(NT) But were there some Erakor
people who worked?
(KK) There are some who were
like stockmen or cowboys who
workmen, there were some.
And some who worked copra,
but they weren't many. There
were some Tannese.
Some Malakulans were there.
But us, from Efate mostly didn't
work. Only a few worked.

(NT) Why? (KK) Because they
didn't want to work with white
people, because of some
issues with the language. They
didn't know how to speak well
and that meant that they
couldn't go to work.
But I know that many worked.
But they worked for a short time
then they came back.

Tete ito pan ileka na imur mane
sees, vatu sees, imer pa. Nlaken
kin teetwei, mane isees.

Upaakot kilo kopra, wan vatu
kilo.
Me ilegki teetwei. Kupaakot pis
nkal sees nen me kutae paaktofi
ki wan vatu.
Teetwei iwi, pret kupaaktofi,
wan vatu.
Go, sernale fserser, me ruta pi
mane p̃ur mau. Ilegki malnen
kin.
Ntaewen isees, a? Go nanre nen
ipitlak, na,

Franis kampani ga kin iweswes
nanre ne, Teouma.
San toklos nanre nen pak Ertap,
pak Eton mana teflan pa. Ipitlak
deGronz ito elag.

Go Franis misnari, nen kin rugar
me ruto Belvi, elag sanie.
Montmartre.
(NT) Malnen if wel kuweswes if
wel ipitlak naat nen ruweswes
kumatur esa, rumatur sanpe?
(KK) Rumatur na, naor nawesien
tete rumatur naor nawesien,
atlag inru, itol, ale ruler.

(NT) Go, nam̃olien ni naroi, ipi
nafte? Olsem, taem yu stap long
ples ia, laef i olsem wanem?
(KK) Ikerkerai pe kumurin na
p̃afitlak mane sees,
kuleka isa, me p̃afo weswes.

Some would go when they
needed a little money. Because,
in those days, there wasn't much
money.
We would sell a kilo of copra,
one vatu a kilo.
It was right for that time. You
buy a small piece of cloth, but
you buy it for one vatu.
Back then it was good. You could
buy bread for one vatu.
All different things, but they
weren't big money. It was right
for that time.
Knowledge was low eh? And
from that point of view there
was
a French company which
worked over at Teouma.
That place facing Eratap to
around Eton and further. There
was de Gronz (?), he was up
there.
And the French missionaries
who were at Bellevue, up there
at Montmartre.
(NT) Then, if you worked, did
you sleep there?

(KK) They would sleep at where
they worked, some would sleep
there for two months, three
months, then return.
(NT) And what was life in the
plantation like? When you were
there, what was it like?
(KK) It was hard, but if you
wanted to have a little money,
you see, it is bad, but you would

South Efate Stories

Kupa rekin pan kuwest mane sees kumai marmar. Kuleka na kumurin na p̃amer ler pa.
Mer ler pak nawesien ga. Ko naot ni planta isosok. Isos, 'Boy!' Imur na teweswes.
Tete rutmer mtaluer. Rupa pan weswes.
Me mane ipitkaskei. Go nam̃er ni plantesen ruweswes pitkaskei m̃as.

Rupreg praes gar. Tete isak isees m̃as, ipreg nrus mane ga inrus fakelag sees. Tenrak ipi wan haf peni, tefla, kilo.

Me, rutuer rukfam. Nafnag sees me rufam.
Go. Rupreg na rupregwiki na mal ne. Mal ne, mal nen kin ipi mal gar.
Rupregwiki natam̃ol ileg tlas nam̃olien nen kin rutkos.

(NT) Sup̃ ni masta?
(KK) No. Kefo pes keraikik tete nrak, tete nrak. Masta nen kin iwi, ipes kerkeraiki ag m̃as.
Me masta nen isa, tete nrak ifseiki stokwip.
(NT) Me malnen ita piatlak polis mau?
(KK) O polis ito me, ipi nawesien ni planta.
Tenrak ipregi usak hos kukop teem̃ol, taos kau mana. Kusraf tete, itaf tp̃er.

work.
You go to work, you waste some money and you come and rest. Then you want to go back again. Go back to his work. Or the planter boss calls you. He calls, 'Boy!' He wants some work. Some chose themselves. They went to work.
But the money was all the same. And the people on the plantation work just the same amount.
They would get their price. Some would raise it only a little, the money would be a little higher. Sometimes it would be half a penny a kilo.
But they gave them food. A little food, but they ate.
They tried to do well for that time. That was their time.

They were good to people, it was correct enough for their life as it was.
(NT) The way of the boss?
(KK) No. He would talk strongly to you sometimes. A good boss would only shout at you.
But a bad master, sometimes he would whip with a stockwhip.
(NT) But back then, weren't there any police?
(KK) Oh there were police, but this was the planter's work. Sometimes he would make you jump on a horse and chase animals, like cows. You miss

Inom. Ipes kerkraikik, tenrak isman̄ri ki stokwip me tenrak ipes kerkraikik mas.

(NT) Me itap krakpun tete naat?
(KK) Itik.
Amrokin tete mal kin. Mal sikskei mas tete nen ipreg israf nafietwen ga. Go ipregsaki boy. Me tewan ifisktofi boy ikano pregsaki. Me naskon kefo miel nlaken stokwip ikerkrai.

Me ita pi nrak laap mau.
(NT) Ipiatlak natam̄ol iskei nen ipi sup̄ ni naat nen? Sup̄ kerkerai?
(KK) Mista Ena. Ga kin. Me ga ipitlak skul wi a? Iskul wi me selwan kusraf itaos skul masta iskei ipo sm̄anri.

Ipeiki kin teflan kulekor kau kulekor hos, nanan, sipsip. Me selwan kuta satsoki mau kefo pes kerkerai ki, tenrak usraf, ism̄anrik.

Me nanre kaaru ipregwi kutae sernale.

Itilm̄ori ipitlak sup̄ kerkrai, me ipitlak ... iwelkia itu ag ntaewen, itu kineu ntaewen.

Go ru, rupreg boy rutae weswes nanre ni planta.

some, they go over the fence. That's it. He shouts at you, sometimes he whips you with a stockwhip, but sometimes he just shouts at you.
(NT) But he didn't kill anyone?
(KK) No.
I think sometimes. A few times only he would hurt one of the boys.
But some he would whip, the boy can't do anything about it. But his skin would be red, because the stockwhip was strong.
But it wasn't often.
(NT) Was there anyone who was like that? Particularly hard?

(KK) Mr Ena. He was one. He was well educated. He was well educated, but when you made a mistake he was like a school master, he would hit you.
He showed how to look after cows, horses, goats, sheep.
But if you didn't understand he would shout at you, sometimes you made a mistake and he would hit you.
But on the other hand he did good and you learned everything.
It is the truth, he was a hard man, but he had ... he gave you knowledge, he gave me knowledge.
And they took the boys who knew how to do plantation

Telaap ruletae go teflan kin ruwesweski tp̃er, go tete, tete rupiatlak, na ...
tete sup̃ nen kin gar me rumer tae pregi nen kin runrus ki ntan. Ruto puet ntan sees, a?
Tenen ipi sup̃ nen kin tete nam̃er, tete nam̃er ni planta ruweswes ki. Wel wan kin ilao ki pos tp̃er.
Taos yat blong buluk. Be nekis taem i jensem, a i muvem wan pas. Wan fut bakegen.
Blong putum pos. Mekem hem i stap siftem graon. Be hem i pulum i stret finis we, long tribunal i karem evri samting. Me malnen kin ina ke, kelaoki tp̃er foum.
Kefo preg boy rukmer preg natuer keskei. Wan fut, ale pos.

Nekis taem, namba tu, tri taem.

Ale ipregi inruskin ntan ga ito nrus top.
Ale sup̃ nen, ale tete nigmam rupam̃ori runrogtesa rupestaf naot ki.
(NT) Me naat nen, planta, rupreg ntan ... olsem wanem oli karem graun malpei?
(KK) Rupaaktofi. Me, imani sees m̃as.
(NT) Me maarik naot ko?
(KK) Rupaaktofi tu lan ona.
(NT) Kontrak? Ipi lis?
(KK) Itik. Teetwei kutae, tenen

work.
Many knew how to make a fence, and some had ...

a special way which they could move the land boundary. They pulled in ground.
This was a way that some of the planters worked. They would put in a fence post.

For example, the cattle yard. But next time they would change it, move it, one foot again.
To put the posts in. So he was extending his ground. He had put the fence in the right place, following the land tribunal.
But when he wanted to put in a new fence.
He would make the boys put their foot down. One foot, then the post.
Next time, second time, third time.
So he made his ground grow, it grew bigger.
Ok, that way of doing things, some of us found out and felt bad about it and told the chief.
(NT) But those men, the planters, how did they get the land in those days?
(KK) They bought it. But it was for very little money.
(NT) From the chief?
(KK) They paid the land owner.
(NT) Contract? Was it a lease?
(KK) No. Long ago, you know,

itik. Natam̃ol rusup̃neki serale.

Me rutrau, rutae famle ne, ale rumur ntan ga, rumur hektar tefla ne,
Orait tribunal iga pregi plak natam̃ol nen kin ipiatlak ntan.

Ipa. Ikano mtir, ko ikano preg nagien. Itkal....

Tete imtir nagien. Orait.
Ipaaktofi ki mani sees. Me tep̃ur ipa.
Kafman ranru. Tkanwan rupregi ki.
Paakot mani sees m̃as. Ale kafman itua ntan. Iga seveiki.

Me rutae selwan kin rupaoski hektar ifla pi, andred ko nafte, wan andred hektar ko nafte.

Me selwan kin rupaoski me, poinem long finga olsem ia. O, mo long andred hektar. Hemia nao.
Me ga itap tae mau nlaken ki ga itap skul mau

Welkia rumes nafet p̃arorwen toklos, kastom ona. Kano taar itae serale, mal ne.
Rumes na, ntaewen. Me ntaewen go nasup̃nekien ga rata pitkaskei mau. Ikerkerai.
Ntaewen itae pam nasup̃nekien.
This is text 087.

there wasn't such a thing.
People didn't know anything about it.
But they just, they knew this family, so if they wanted its land, if they wanted this hectare,
Alright, the tribunal would get them together with the person whose land it was.
It went. He couldn't write, he couldn't sign his name. He touched ...
Some could write their name.
Alright. He bought it for small money. But mostly it just went.
The two governments. That's how things went.
Pay small money. Then the government gave them ground.
It surveyed it for them.
They knew that when they asked for hectares, if it were a hundred or whatever, a hundred hectares.
But when they asked and, pointed with their fingers like this. Oh, more than a hundred hectares. Like that.
But he [the owner] didn't know because he hadn't had schooling.
They played the kastom owners for fools. The white man knew everything, back then.
They played with knowledge.
But knowledge and ignorance aren't equal. It's hard.
Knowledge can eat ignorance.

Jinane †
Jinane, her life and working at PMH

Jinane worked at the Paton Memorial Hospital and traveled around Efate helping with maternal health.

Ore, welkia kineu askul natkon Erakor.

Ok, well, I went to school in Erakor village.

Askul. Ore afaitau natkon Erakor pan ntau 1948.

I went to school. Ok I studied in Erakor village until 1948.

Go atm̃alu pak P.M.H. nen aweswes P.M.H. a.a.

Then I left for the P.M.H. (Paton Memorial Hospital), and I worked at the P.M.H.

Kineu api nes.

I am a nurse.

Aweswes ntau 1948, 49 me

I worked in 1948 and 1949, then

kaipe ler mai, kin go apo lak 1949, e 1950, a.a.

I came back, and I got married in 1949, or 1950.

Kaito esum̃ panpan, malen kin aweswes P.M.H., a.

I stayed at home until then I worked at the P.M.H.

Ipi mal ni tiawi, go ipi mal nen kin loto rutik, go ipi malnen ita- ita ta mram wi mau, a.a.

This was in the old people's time, when there were no cars, and it was a time that was not in the light (before Christianity).

Go welkia ipitlak sista go ipitlak Mis Kina.

And there was a sister and there was Miss Kina.

Mis Kina kin imai preg nalotwen iplaksok P.W. a.a.

Miss Kina brought Christianity and taught the P.W. (Presbyterian Women).

Go malfanen, iwelkia ito siwer ur ser natkon preg nalotwen go iwelkia ina kesiwer pak Efil.

And now, she would walk to each village to preach and she was going to Vila.

Go nes iskei kefo nrokosi, me kefo

And a nurse would cross over

pan nen keskelki teesa.

Ga kefo skelki teesa seserik me
Mis Kina kefo preg nasum̃tap.

Ita pi Mis Kina mau. Mis McRae,
Mis McRae.
Ale iwel ipak Em̃el nes iskei kefo
skoti pa, ga kefo preg nasum̃tap
me nes kefo skelki teesa.

Ko ifpak Ertap me ipo tefla.

Me, kineu kin, iwelkia, malen runa
rukfak Ertap, go ruto tli na kineu
kin kato pak Ertap.
Me selwan kin uto, upa loto nuof,
utotan Eluk,
san hotel p̃ur ito. Ale upo pa raru
nrookot mai pak Efat gakit ne.

Kin me, kafo to san po sol skel
panpanpanpanpan pak eslaor ni
Ertap.
Kin po tatue skel raru,

kin go kofo pa raru, pan,

go kafo skelki teesa.
Me iwelkia malen una kofak Ertap
go welkia ru-,
ruto mal slasol, nes.
Tete nes rumal slasol, runa kineu
kin kato.
Go apo to kerkrai me skel imten,
me kafo sati ur napu ne.

(to Ifira island) and would go
to weigh the children.
She would weigh the small
children, but Miss Kina would
give a church service.
It wasn't Miss Kina, it was Miss
McRae.
Ok, she would got to Mele and
a nurse would go with her, and
she would run the church and
the nurse would weigh the
children.
Or if it was to Eratap it would
be the same.
But as for me, when they
wanted to go to Eratap, they
would tell me to go to Eratap.
When we took the truck to the
wharf, we would stop at Eluk,
at the place where the hotel
(Le Lagon) is. Ok, we would
paddle a canoe and come back
to Efate.
And I would stay, would bring
the scales, until we went back
to the passage at Eratap.
And would load the scales into
a canoe,
and we would paddle the
canoe and go
and we would weigh children.
And when we wanted to go to
Eratap, and well,
they didn't want any nurse.
They didn't want some nurse,
they wanted me to come.
I had to be strong as the scales
were heavy, but I would take
them around this road.

Ruto san pak Ertap ipi em̃ae, ipram.
This is text 111.

Here to Eratap is far away, it is long.

Daisy Wayane
Daisy Wayane, A life story

Daisy Wayane's work history, from school on Eraniao (Erakor Island) and the cyclone that moved everyone back to the mainland, through various jobs, to being secretary of the UMP in local government.

Ore taosi kin iwelkia malpei welkia komam uskul pan, uskul su, ale umur na komas koweswes, ale kokerkrai lel nawesien.

Okay, so before, we would go to school until we finished then we wanted to work, so we tried hard to find work.

Me teesa ni mees ga itik. Iskul pan inom. Imai to esum̃ ileka ito kop namurien ga,

But a child today, he doesn't work. He goes to school. He comes back home, he does what he wants,

ita mroki nawesien mau. Ita mroki skul fi nen tmen me raiten raspent kin, ko raius kin

he doesn't think about work. He doesn't think about the school fees that his father and mother spent on him, that they used

reki fi ga, skul ga mana mau, itik. Nam̃olien ni mees iponp̃tae. Ruto p̃al to me ruleka na iwi. Ruta mur nawesien mau.

for his fees, for his school, no. Life today is different. They do nothing and they think it is good. They don't want to work.

(NT) Go nawesien ni nmatu mees, ita pitkaskei nawesien ni nanwei mau?
Nanwei ruto mes petog. Me nalelewen neu, nmatu ruto preg nawesien p̃ur.
(DW) Ore itilm̃ori.
Ito ntau laap, malpei nmalok itik, mal ni apap nigmam mana,

(NT) And women's work today, it's not the same as men's work?
Men play petanque. But from my perspective, women do all the hard work.
(DW) Yes, that's right.
Before, there wasn't kava, in our parents' time, they didn't

---

nmalok ruta ius ki nmalok teflan mau.

Go aleka na taos krup ni nanwei, talpuk ni nanwei ruweswes kerkrai. Me mees, welkia nmalok itop.

Nmalok itop go, nanwei nawesien gar itap sef wi mau, me nmatu nawesien gar isef, isef, isef olwei a?

Taosikin, taos ipi, taosi nawesien ni na nfanu, nmatu rutu leg ko nanre ni nasum̃tap P.W. mana. Nmatu rukerkrai weswes.

Go mees kuleka, nanwei laap ruto esum̃, nmatu mas rulel nawesien ruweswes reki nam̃olien ni famle. Ore.

(NT) Me iku kin, nlaken iku?

(DW) Gawanki, utatae nlaken kin. Ilakor pi namropirwen, namropirwen ko nasertep̃alwen.

Ruta mrokas reki na nam̃olien ni em̃rom mau.

Rupo kop namurien gar itop.

This is text 114.

use kava like they do today.

And the men used to work hard. But today, there is too much kava.

Too much kava, and men's work doesn't go well, but women's work goes on and on and on all the time.

Like, for work to do with the nation or the church or the P.W. (Presbyterian Women's Union). Women work hard.

And today, many men stay at home, it is only women who look for work and who work for their families. Yes.

(NT) Why is that?

(DW) Exactly, we don't know why. It might be that they don't like it, or they don't believe they should do it.

They don't think about life inside.

They follow their own minds too much.

Kaloros Kaltaf †
Kaloros on national independence

A description of the movement to Independence in 1980.

Taos komam sup̃ ni independen, ipiatlak krup ni Nasonal Pati,

ipiatlak krup ni UCNH.

As for us, the time of independence, there was the National Party group,

there was the UCNH group (Union des Communautés des

UCNH gar rapi Pati inru. Go kaaru ikenski independen, kaaru imur independen.

Me nafsan ranru mur independen.

Me namroan ni UCNH imurin na ifla pi ntau kemer lim go tukfo mai sat independen, me Nasonal Pati,

ga imurin na. (NT) Malfanen m̃as

(KK) Ga UCNH ga imurin na taos kafman ranru rakmer nrus defelopki.

Go rakmer tfag na nfanu kenrus pak elag. Go skul me keta nrus pa.

Me Nasonal Pati ga ina, 'Kipe tlasi. Kefi mees kefi mees.'

Tenen kin ipi kens. Me kineu ato UCNH me tete ruto Nasonal Pati komam telaap

Erakor. Me utap tli isa mau. Utli iwi,

tukta tao kafman ranru rakta tu kit edukesen keta lakor pa.

Me selwan tuknrogtor, rakmuti go akit tukano preg namrun.

Me nam̃er taar rupiatlak ntaewen nen kin iwi.

Rumurin na rukwelu sermal akit tumalkir, tukp̃asir rupa. Me gar ruslatsok akit tutau narur tau.

Rulekor ptaki kit.

Nouvelles Hebrides).

The UCNH was two Parties. One was against independence and one was for independence.

But their policy was for independence

But the UCNH wanted independence in maybe five years, but the National Party

wanted (NT) Right now.

(KK) The UCNH wanted the two governments to develop more.

And to build the country to make it come up. And schooling should also grow.

But the National Party said, 'It's enough. Let it be today, let it be today.' That is the one who is against us. But I was in the UCNH, and some were in the National Party.

Erakor. But we didn't say it was bad. We said it is good,

we leave the two governments to keep giving us education, that it should keep going.

But when we hurried, they were greedy and we couldn't do anything about it.

But the white people have good knowledge.

They always want to help us, but we don't want it, we chase them away, they go. But they would take us, they hold us in their hands.

They looked after us.

Namer taar rupiatlak na-
ntaewen nen iwi, go nmaeto
itikir. Rumur rukwelu ser naat.

Go ipi sup̃ wi nen kin, komam
me kolemsi go kotae.
Go namroan nen kin ito komam
tenakon nen uto Pati kaaru, uta
murin na kofregsaki kano taar
mau.
Nlaken akit nrakit ga iskei m̃as.

Me tekaaru rumurin na rukfreg
saki asler, namer taar rupreg
mistek. E, tete nakrakpelwen,
taos nakrakpelwen mistek.
Kupreg mistek sees rup̃asik,
dipot.

Tenen ipi sup̃ sa, tenen kin
komam nanre ni UCNH,
taos UMP uleka na itap wi mau.

Natam̃ol p̃atua mal go ga ipiatlak
educated wi.
P̃atua mal nen kin ga itae nriki ki
nafte kin ag kusraf wes.

Kurog wes taosi kurog kusraf, a,
kusraf napu kia.
Ga itae, kano taar itae tafnau ag,
nlaken ga ipiatlak education p̃ur
ito np̃aun.
Akit namer got tumroki na,
tuipe tae itop me itik.
Kupanpanpan kusursap̃ napu, yu
mestem rod, kusursap̃ napu.
Ale malfanen p̃afo ler. Naoia yu
mas kam bak.

White people have good
knowledge, and they don't get
angry. They want to help
everyone.
It is a good way that we can look
at and know.
And the thinking then, for us
who were in the other Party, we
didn't want to do harm to white
people.
Because our blood is just one
blood.
But the other one, they wanted
to harm their friends, white
people, they made a mistake.

If you made a small mistake they
would chase you out, deport
you.
That's a bad way, the way that
we in the UCNH
like, the UMP we saw that it
wasn't good.
If you give people time they can
have a good education.
You give some time so he can
tell you what you have done
wrong.
You are wrong there, you took
the wrong road.
He knows, the white man knows
how to teach you, because he
has lots of education in his head.
We black people we think that
we know alot, but it's not so.
You go on and on, but you miss
the road.
Ok, now you will go back.

Blong hem i advaesem yu bakegen yu luk? I nogud yumi hariap. Ita wi na tuktrapelpel mau.
Mailum siwer. Ore.

So he could advise you again, see? It's not good that we rush. It is not good that we hurry.

Go slowly. Yes.

This is text 119.

Kaloros Kaltaf †

Kaloros on working with the Americans in World War Two

Some of the older people worked with the Americans during the second world war, and they learned important things that served them well after the war finished.

(NT) Ore, mal ni nafkal ipiatlak natamol America ni Erakor?
(KK) Ipiatlak tete nen kin ruweswes skotir.
Go rulaap tepur ruipe mat.
Ruipe mat. Me tete sikskei kin ruto iskei kin Kalsarap. Iskei kia ipo mat. Tupo psi malfane sanie.

Gar nen ruweswes skotir.
Komam useserik, komam uto lemsir mas, me reki nen kin kofan weswes,
uta pregi tete nawesien mau. Gar kin rupreg nawesien, skot namer ne.
Go komam uto lek nafte kin gar ruto pregi,
me welkia namroan nigmam teesa, isees, usat tete me tete umetpakro.
Go ipregi ukano trau soksoki. Me tete naat rukraksok wi ki,

(NT) OK, and the time the Americans were in Erakor?
(KK) There were some people that worked with them.
And, many died.
They died. But some who are here, like Kalsarap. One who died. Who we would bury just now.
They were the ones who worked with them. We were small, we would just look at them, but as for if we went with them,
we didn't do any work. They were the ones who worked with those people.
And we would look at what they were doing,
but we were young and not very wise, we got some of the knowledge, but some we forgot. Which meant that we couldn't get it. But some people got it

rupuetsok wi ki natrauswen ne. Go amrokin na tesees nen kin atae tili. Me selwan kanrus pa, kafo sraf tete naor.

Go isakin kafo psir em̃rom ni kaset gakit. Ore.
This is text 120

well, they got hold of this story. And I think that this small story is all that I can tell. But if I go further I might make a wrong turn.
And it is bad if I lie in our cassette. Yes.

Notes

The translations of these texts have gone through a number of checking processes. Some of the texts have quite opaque meanings (for example p.4, p.48) and are difficult for speakers of South Efate to interpret, especially when decontextualised on paper.

The South Efate transcribers found some parts of the recordings difficult to understand, due to poor recordings including background noise, fast speech, or other factors. Even when the transcript appears to be accurate, or at least true to the recording, there are issues related to narrative styles and the embedding of narratives in context that make it difficult to translate. As Duranti notes, 'I found that even people in the same village would misinterpret utterances when removed from their immediate context and the fact of speaking the same language or living in the same community was no guarantee of the accuracy of transcription and interpretation.' (Duranti 1994: 31)

Personal names are written here as heard in the recording. They have not been checked against historical records and so may not be the correct spellings of the names. I would appreciate any advice from readers that could improve the manuscript.

Note that the texts are as faithful as possible to the transcript, with some repetitions, false starts and similar artefacts of oral speech included. However, some of the speakers had the opportunity to edit their contributions, and this has resulted in additions, deletions or changes to the transcript. These changes are indicated in the source documents but not in the current presentation.

I have not attempted to cleanse the texts of my presence (e.g., Thompson 1978: 179 advocates that interviewers not perform back-channel cues as they may be culturally inappropriate). Rather than pretend that I was not present during the recordings, I think it is important to acknowledge the 'dialogic, contextualized nature of all discourse, including interviews.' (Briggs 1986: 13)

Stories are, of course, 'strictly linked to the context of their utterance, that is to say, to the social and historical reality of which they are both a product and an expression.' (Bensa and Rivierre 1982: 11). The topics of these stories are those the speakers chose to tell in response to my request to record them. Some stories, linked to immediate issues around the contested chiefly line or the sale of customary land, for example, have not been included here as they were thought to be too controversial by Erakor people I consulted.

Some of the themes presented here are similar to those recorded in other parts of the Pacific, for example the story of the octopus and the rat (p.116) and the story of the same name in Staudt (n.d. story 7); and the hermit crab and the barracuda story (p.63 & 98) is similar to the story in that same collection titled 'Bernard Hermit and the Snipe' (ibid story 17). The story of the angel from Erromango (p.110) has resonance with a similar story from Futuna told in Keller and Kuatonga (2007).

Terms
Commonly used terms that may not always be translated include:

Apu	grandfather, also a generic term for ancestors
Ati	grandmother
kleva	Bislama term for a healer or sorcerer
kulru	healer, 'kleva' in Bislama
lilip	a small and hairy being who causes mischief, in particular eating unattended food (same as *sputan*)
maarik	literally 'mister', but used as a term of respect for a male *natopu* or spirit of place
mtulep	literally 'misses', but used as a term of respect for a female *natopu* or spirit of place
munwei	healer or sorcerer
naaten, naat	an idol that has magical properties
nafit	'slave', someone who has to do the bidding of someone else, usually as a punishment for a wrongdoing
nakamal	Bislama term for a meeting house, now commonly used as the name for a place at which kava is sold and drunk
natopu	a spirit belonging to a particular place
ntwam, or *mutwam*	a local devil
sputan	a small and hairy being who causes mischief, in particular eating unattended food (same as *lilip*)
Tata	an address term for 'father'

tuluk   food made by grating cassava, mixed with coconut milk, wrapped around meat in leaf packets around 15cm long and cooked in an earth oven.

Technical notes

All of the texts presented here form part of a larger set of 120 stories that have been transcribed and translated. Many of them also have interlinear glosses. All texts and the original media are archived with the Pacific and Regional Archive for Digital Sources in Endangered Cultures (PARADISEC) (http://paradisec.org.au). The Toolbox file of texts is stored here: http://paradisec.org.au/repository/NT8/TEXT. An interlinear version is also located there and can be obtained on request from the author.

The interlinear versions of texts given here will be of use to linguists whose interested in reanalysing South Efate. I hope that my grammatical anlaysis will provide a coherent stepping stone on which further work can be built.

The recordings

The recordings from which these stories are transcribed were made on a variety of media and with several different recorders. Initially cassette tapes were recorded on a mono audio-cassette recorder, sometime using a built-in microphone, and sometimes an external microphone. Subsequently I used a Sony Professional Walkman with an external mic. More recently I used a Marantz PMD670 flashram recorder with a Rode NT-4 microphone. All analog recordings were digitised by Corin Bone at the University of Sydney in 1999 and then accessioned into the Pacific and Regional Archive for Digital Sources in Endangered Cultures (PARADISEC).

Note on orthography

The spelling system or orthography used in this volume largely conforms to that in use for South Efate since the earliest missionaries wrote the language. In my grammar I treated vowel length as a phenomenon associated with stress, so that words like *tesa* were written with one 'e' rather than two because that was the stressed syllable, and because speakers typically pronounce this word as *tsa*, dropping the 'e' altogether. In workshops in Erakor village in 2005 and 2006 it became clear that speakers wanted vowel length indicated so that, for example, *tesa* would be written *teesa*. This change has been made in the current volume and in the dictionary of South Efate.

References

Bensa, Alban and Jean Claude Rivierre.1982. *Les chemins de l'alliance / l'organisation sociale et ses representations en Nouvelle-Caledonie (region de Touho - aire linguistique cemuhi).* Paris: Centre National de la Recherche Scientifique, Secretariat d'Etat aux Departements et Territoires d'Outre-Mer.

Briggs, Charles L. 1986. *Learning how to ask: A sociolinguistic appraisal of the role of the interview in social science research.* Cambridge: Cambridge University Press.

Duranti, Alessandro. 1994. *From Grammar to Politics: Linguistic Anthropology in a Western Samoan Village.* Berkeley and Los Angeles: University of California Press.

Keller, Janet Dixon and Takaronga Kuatonga. 2007. *Nokonofo Kitea : we keep on living this way : myths and music of West Futuna.* Vanuatu / Belair, S.Aust. : Crawford House.

Rivierre, Jean-Claude. 1996. 'Mythistoire et archéologie dans le Centre-Vanuatu. L'histoire de Matanauretong (Tongoa).' In Michèle Julien, Michel and Catherine Orliac, Bertrand Gérard, Anne Lavondès, Henri Lavondès and Claude Robineau (eds) *Mémoire de Pierre, mémoire d'homme: tradition et archéologie en Océanie.* Paris: Publications de la Sorbonne, pp. 431-463.

Staudt, Jan-Claude. n.d. *Legends of New Caledonia.* [no publication details].

Thieberger, Nicholas. 2006. *A Grammar of South Efate: An Oceanic Language of Vanuatu.* Oceanic Linguistics Special Publication, No. 33. Honolulu: University of Hawai'i Press.

Thompson, Paul. 1978 *The voice of the past: oral history.* New York: OUP.

www.ingramcontent.com/pod-product-compliance
Lightning Source LLC
Chambersburg PA
CBHW051507170626
46811CB00002B/689